Discovering The God Imagination

Reconstructing A Whole New Christianity

by

Jonathan Brink

Dedication

To the One who overcomes.

What People Are Saying

In Discovering the God Imagination, Brink asks the hard questions about sin and atonement with not only humility, but also with candor, honesty. forthrightness, and clarity. You may not agree with all his answers and conclusions, but we can all agree about the immediacy of the issues he raises. Certainly we all will know ourselves to be have been made richer by his work. -- **Phyllis Tickle**

Jonathan Brink has given us a gift, a Gospel gift. He calls upon us to allow the story of God, the activity of God, the present reality of God to shape new questions of faith and life. Jonathan reminds us that faithfulness is not in starting with the answers, but in starting with God. In this well written and honest book he walks us back into the story of God and what we discover is both revolutionary and at the same time obvious. This walk is one that not all will want to take, but all who take it will be glad they did. -- **Doug Pagitt**

Table of Contents

Introduction

We can't solve problems by using the same kind of thinking we used when we created them. - Albert Einstein

What would compel someone to try and reframe the Christian faith? I've asked myself that question many, many times.

I grew up in the Evangelical tradition. I cannot and will not ignore the tremendous education, value, and history it has given me. I once counted over 2,500 hours of formal and semi-formal Christian education between the age of 8 and 20. I am deeply grateful for the people who transcended the institutional limitations and revealed the face of Jesus to me. I cannot ignore the influence my own upbringing had on my search and this manuscript.

But like any tradition, there were fundamental questions that remained unsolved, issues that were left hidden, and a subtle dissonance that pervaded a few very important things I had grown up with. I had questions nobody knew how to answer, and not because they were ignoring them, but because there were simply no immediate answers available.

I also grew up with a mom who loved working with and connecting with the heart of people. At the core of her work as a counselor, she was fond of asking one question: what is the root problem? She was known for listening intently with empathy, but at some point she would cut to the chase and call people out. The symptom, or problem, the person described was always an indicator of something deeper, and she had an amazing capacity to root it out.

This question always stuck with me. It was literally ingrained in me from a very young age. I was taught to look for the deeper question, the underlying idea, or the root problem. And while this question served me well in business, I didn't understand the real cost of this question until I reached my late thirties, when I could no longer ignore the underlying dissonance in my own faith.

In order to be honest with myself, I took the risk to begin looking for answers. I began with the idea that although most of what I had been taught was basically true, there was likely a better way of understanding it. My desire was to find a better story - not just the Christian story but also the human story underlying the work of Jesus. All I did was open myself to the possibility of seeing things differently. This process meant questioning some of the deepest and most cherished beliefs I had been taught for most of my life.

The underlying assumption I made from the beginning was simple. If grace were true, I knew it meant I could explore the edges. If Jesus were truly God he could handle my fears, my issues, my questions, and my doubts. I chose to take a risk, which could possibly kill my faith or make it stronger.

For more than a decade, I surrounded myself with people who were asking the same questions, taking the same risks, and pondering the same possibilities I was. There were many days that often felt like I was jumping off a cliff into oblivion. But at the same time, I never felt more alive than when I discovered the courage to question everything; not for the sake of being a jerk but because I was discovering some amazing possibilities.

I say possibility because I recognize I could be wrong. This approach to Christianity could and likely does contain flaws. It should be seen as a conversation to enter into, add to, and build upon. I am a human being wrestling with a broken body. I am bent towards getting it wrong. I welcome constructive criticism for the sake of discovering a better story.

What surprised me most was discovering although we have theories about the nature of justice and reconciliation, specifically what is happening on the cross between God and humanity, scholars and theologians admit there are deeply inherent problems with these theories. Both the Garden and the cross are in many ways a mystery. For more than 1,700 years, scholars and theologians have primarily settled on two primary "atonement" theories that explored the nature of justice and reconciliation. These theories are of central importance because they are our basis for understanding the Gospel. My own tradition taught the "penal substitutionary atonement" theory, which postulates a grand narrative of God's demand for justice, which is appeased at the cross.

I get why people accept these theories. We violently defend them not just because we think they are true, but they are also all we have. It is virtually impossible to abandon something for nothing, even for a while. And while I am presenting a new approach to understanding Christianity, specifically the nature of suffering, justice, reconciliation, I am not naïve to suggest I am the first to discover this idea, or that it is original. I can only suggest those in the early church understood the basic nature of it because Jesus was there to explain it.

But somewhere over time, the basic nature of reconciliation became a mystery. The human story became muddled and great minds simply came up with possibilities for understanding it. These possibilities become traditions and before we were even born they were handed down to us, likely before we were even capable of making effective judgments to their validity and meaning. In other words, we read the human story through the lens of a historical interpretation. We typically begin with the notion they are valid because of who handed them to us, even when our next-door neighbor doesn't share them. We are right and they are wrong.

To question the validity of these interpretations, especially when they are deeply held traditions, is often tantamount to social suicide. For the very people who accept them are the ones who have given them to us. The traditions then become self-reinforcing simply because they are already there. The systems we inherit are automatically accepted because they are older than we are and given to us by people we see as authority.

But what we often fail to do is question the fundamental assumptions of these conclusions, even when the traditions fail to deeply resonate in culture. We fail to ask how these interpretations are shaped and even bent by the very problem they are attempting to understand and solve? As Einstein suggested, we can't solve the problems using the same means that created them.

What if our understanding of the problem is actually shaped by the problem itself? Much like a scientific experiment, we lose our capacity for objectivity because we are part of the problem we are attempting to understand and solve. The tradition becomes a safer option because so many people believe it, even when the objective evidence begins to reveal something just isn't quite adding up.

My hope is not to destroy or tear down the traditions I love but to inform them. Any tradition worth keeping is worth fighting for. But to fight for something we have to have an intrinsic mobilizing story. Questioning the assumptions opens us to the possibility of rediscovering the better story, which renews them.

Confronting the reality I could no longer believe what I had grown up with, or any of the theories presented, was the hardest leap I ever made. But it was worth it to me to take the risk. It was worth looking for and discovering a better story, which would inform my own faith in a restorative way. I am grateful for the friends who stood by me, who were willing to question and wrestle with me, and wait patiently for possibilities to emerge.

The book you are reading is the product of that journey. My goal is to reframe our understanding of Christianity in order to understand and present the Gospel. To accomplish this goal, we need to understand the nature of suffering, justice and reconciliation in the human story presented to us in Scripture. It is an attempt to coherently present the root problem and how God solved and continues to solve it. In no way am I attempting to present an encapsulation of truth. That is impossible and I have no desire to try. I don't really think we're looking for all of truth. I think we're just looking for the truth that really matters.

What I found was incredibly liberating and not from God but to God. Getting to the root problem was like food for the soul. For the first time I could understand my own brokenness without an oppressive sense of guilt. I could see how God was working to restore me, and how I could participate. I was not a bystander in the process, but a major accomplice in what God was already doing in the restoration of the world.

This book is about simplifying our understanding of the root problem so we can become aware of it and overcome it. It's about exploring what captivates us and imprisons us, luring us into complacency and contempt for the soul. It's about finding meaning in the human story and coming to a place of peace once and for all.

This book will explore not just what we think, but also how we think. Once we understand how we think, we can begin to understand and even address our historical assumptions. We can begin to engage our own imagination with a critical eye. If we are not conscious of how we think, we are then subject to thoughts largely determined for us.

The book will also suggest our imagination is deeply informed by the Spirit. Most of our work is simply surrendering to the God imagination intrinsic to humanity. We just have to remove the covering keeping us from seeing it, engaging it and living it out. With the God imagination we can begin to actually live the Way of Jesus, which is so simple even a child can do it. In fact a child is better prepared to do it than an adult.

This is a book for those who can't do religion very well. It is not for everyone. For some, the traditions of religion do work really well. And by religion, I mean the invented, organizational structures we use to cope with our own guilt and appease our projections of God. For some, religion provides meaning, stability and guidance. In essence, it works for some people. The problem is it didn't work for me.

We live in an age of unprecedented permission to explore. We live in the forefront of history, always treading new ground, but completely removed from most of what happened. Our lives represent a thin slice of the entire picture. One of the advantages of living at the forefront of history, especially in the information age, is the capacity to listen to the story and look for informed and fresh perspectives.

We can no longer ignore what doesn't work. The evidence of obsolescence, especially within the traditional structures cannot be overlooked. We cannot assume what has worked in the past will simply work in the future. The world is calling our bluff. We can no longer ignore the historic opportunity to take a hard look at our assumptions about the Christian faith, and offer the world a better story, one of true reconciliation and hope.

Much Love

Jonathan

Chapter 1 – The Act of Discovering

"Love is something eternal; the aspect may change, but not the essence." -
Vincent Van Gogh

Discovering The Gospel

What is the Gospel?

As strange as this question may seem we've entered into a historical period that questions our basic conclusions about The Gospel. The Gospel assumes there is a problem and there is a solution. It's framed largely by two events: the Garden and the cross. It explores the nature of suffering, justice and reconciliation. It's informed by a long story of people interacting with God. But what is the inherent nature of the Gospel? What actually happened in the Garden of Eden? In order to follow Jesus, it would seem obvious that we would want to know exactly what Jesus is doing on the cross, what problem he is solving, and what it means to humanity. Yet there is no clear, historical agreement regarding our basic understanding of the Gospel. Scholars and theologians have been wrestling with this tension within the Christian tradition for roughly 1,700 years.

We know the Gospel is a story of reconciliation. Something is broken. To reconcile is to bring something back into agreement, or harmony. It is to restore something back to wholeness. But if we don't understand what is being reconciled, how can we effectively participate?

And as much as the solution may seem obvious – humanity is reconciled to God – at the same time it is hidden. We don't quite understand how. To understand a solution we have to know what problem it is solving. We have theories, but each of these theories suggests a different understanding of the problem. Each creates as many problems as it attempts to solve. And if we get our understanding of the problem wrong, it would seem obvious that our understanding of the solutions would be skewed as well.

This mystery of what is actually happening on the cross is called the "Paschal Mystery". The Paschal Mystery suggests we don't really know the exact nature of the cross. It is the acknowledgement from scholars and theologians that although we can choose to settle on a specific theory, each has enough problems and paradoxes to prevent a distinct certainty about the nature of the Gospel. Each theory has enough evidence to suggest it but not in a way that is significant enough to resolve it.

This book suggests a provocative possibility: much of our historical understanding of the problem is wrong. The basic assumptions we make about what is happening in the Garden of Eden are skewed by the very nature of the problem. We locate the problem in the wrong place and end up trying to resolve a problem, which doesn't actually exist. We cover the root problem and spend most of our energies solving the secondary problems it creates. The process of how we get it wrong is based on a very simple construct, yet the consequences are devastating. It leads to a human condition of needless pain, suffering and death.

But before we point fingers or suggest blame, most of the historical theories are the natural extension of the root problem. They are the natural conclusions we should expect if we misunderstand what is happening in the story. Once we understand the root problem, especially how it plays out neurologically, we can begin to see how to effectively address it.

My primary objective was to ask, "What is the root problem?" What problem is God really solving in the human story? When everything is uncovered, what is the embedded captivating story that creates human suffering? The assumption is that God is also attempting to solve the root problem. What is the nature of justice from God's perspective? What is the nature of reconciliation? Exploring and determining each allows us to participate with God in God's mission to restore everything.

The story reveals the root problem as the human capacity to "realize" an alternative or false reality to God's original perspective, a lie if you will. It is an event that takes place locally in the mind. The primary realization being distorted is the judgment of the self, and eventually every relationship we encounter. This idea is simplified in the single question of the Tree of Knowledge, which asks, "Are we good or evil?" The story strongly suggests it is the only question that matters in the human story. Everything else is secondary because everything hinges on this one question. In essence, humanity loses God's perspective in the most fundamental question of all, our fundamental human value, which we call dignity.

The lie then distorts our understanding of both the root problem and God's response. It casts our judgment back onto God and produces the perception of separation, what is commonly called the "chasm". This lie captivates humanity and produces a subjective context for judging the value of everything in creation, resulting in both a relational and physical death.

To explore the root problem, I have simply gone back to the original story that informs my own faith, the Bible. I have carefully walked through the story, listening deeply to the evidence directly therein, and drawn a conclusion about what is happening.

I chose the Bible primarily because it is a highly regarded historical document. I chose it because the story informs my imagination. It resonates unlike any other story I have ever read. It provides a remarkably simple understanding of the origin of pain, suffering, and evil that most religious systems don't seem to provide for me. It deeply informs how we already live. It reveals patterns so obvious that once we see them, they become almost humorous.

The Bible also provides an insightful possibility for how we transcend pain, suffering, evil and even death. Transcendence rests in becoming aware of the nature of the problem. Once we understand it, it changes the nature of the problem. It is no longer a mystery. It is no longer hidden. It is something to be solved. It reframes the story in a way that invites us into the Way of Jesus, which is love. It intrinsically mobilizes us to overcome by surrendering to and embracing the God imagination already present.

Solving the problem begins with a change of mind, with engaging the God imagination, with seeing the world from God's perspective. It begins with discovering what is already and has always been true. Once we understand what the problem is, we can begin to see how everything God is doing in the story is actually for our good. Transformation resides not in changing the world but in how we see the world. Participating with God in changing the mind becomes the path.

~~

Discovering the Problem

Some time ago, I was privy to an experience which completely altered the course of my faith. It jarred my original understanding of the problem in such a way that it compelled me to begin asking a very different question about what is really happening in the human body. It compelled me to look deeper than what I was used to, and eventually required me to question everything.

I was invited by my mom to provide mentorship to a group of men at a rehab home for men with addictions to alcohol and drugs. Every Wednesday I would meet with three or four men in the early hours of the morning for an hour each. My role was to engage them in conversation and hopefully explore some of the deeper issues behind the addictions. There were ample surface level details about their problems, but with time and trust, we would work to get to the root issues that were creating the problems. As a former addict myself, I was intimately versed in this world. Hopefully I could provide some kind of hope, stability and even healing.

Most of our conversations explored their stories, which always included their stories of self-destruction, crimes and their judgments about them. No matter how much punishment the state or even loved ones had doled out, it was nothing compared to the personal hell they would rain down on themselves.

Within the facility was a guy named "Bob". Bob was a living paradox. He had done everything he was instructed to do in order to become a Christian. He had said the Sinner's Prayer, spent time serving the poor and helpless, and constantly studied the Bible. The program required him to rise at 5:30 AM six days a week and spend 2-3 hours in study and prayer, spending the rest of the day in work.

Yet despite almost 16 months of hard work he was still the pure embodiment of internal rage. Bob unconsciously projected a deep-seated anger to those around him. He was the textbook definition of the walking wounded. He wore all of his emotion on his sleeve and reminded us of it. In spite of buying into the process of healing, Bob was still suffering deeply.

Bob presented somewhat of a paradox for those at the house. If salvation produced a change in action, the evidence was suggesting he wasn't "saved". Yet, he had done virtually everything the program instructed him to do. In spite of this doubt, Bob expressed a remarkable courage and tenacity. Something in him just wouldn't quit. In spite of his obvious lack of transformation, he was resilient enough to continue searching. It was this "won't quit" attitude that allowed people to stick with him. He was willing to try virtually anything.

The first time I saw him I couldn't help notice his massive furrowed brow. It crinkled into a natural frown, the way someone looks when they are really, really mad. The muscles just above his nose had literally grown to accommodate his mood and were permanently formed, creating deep wrinkles in which he could hide things.

Because of the trust my mom had developed with the men, I was granted a tremendous amount of authority to begin with, and Bob was no exception. Part of my work included using a form of guided prayer that would hopefully expose some of the deeper issues embedded in their lives. I asked Bob to close his eyes and simply imagine himself in a box.

He chuckled in disgust at the request, "That's not hard to do."

"Are you angry?" I asked.

"Yes," he said, the creases deepening in his forehead another half inch.

"Can you think of what you are angry about?" He didn't answer at first but eventually nodded. "In front of you is a door. It will take you to the moments of your life that God wants to heal you from. When you are ready, turn the handle and walk through the door."

Bob sat for a couple of minutes in silence and then finally responded. Immediately his face contorted into a childlike fear, revealing that he was experiencing a moment of tremendous pain. He tried not to cry, but his lip quivered and wouldn't stop. "Where are you?" I asked.

"I'm in my driveway," he said.

"What color is the pavement?" I asked, hoping to stir his memory of the situation.

"Grey with skid marks from my bike."

"How old are you?"

"I'm six," he said again, forcing back the tears. He was not going to cry if he could help it.

"What's happening?"

"My mom is leaving," he said, crumbling under the weight of the emotion. He let out a bark that seemed to come through his nose, like the sound of someone laughing with his mouth closed. At first I thought he was sneezing, but then his shoulders crunched up and his face revealed the depth of his pain. Tears began to flow. I could see he was recounting various conversations he had carried on with himself over the years, rationalizations as to why she had left.

"Where's she going?" I asked.

"She's leaving us for good," he said. His face reverted back to anger that had gripped him for so many years. He body tensed up. It seemed to be his only posture for dealing with the pain.

"What are you saying to her?"

"I keep asking her why she's leaving but she just keeps saying, 'I have to go,'" he said.

"Now I want you to do something. I want you to look around and find Jesus."

There was a long silence as he turned his head in several different directions. Then he stopped, transfixed on a point. "I see him," he said, for the first time revealing a shred of hope, but completely unable to understand how to process the experience. I didn't say anything for a while because I didn't sense any questions arising at the moment. It didn't seem to matter to Bob. He seemed to be stunned by the presence of Jesus in what was his darkest moment.

Then the question just seemed to come out, "Ask Jesus why she's leaving."

"Jesus, why is she leaving?" he asked. The fear emerged once again. In his mind, it was just as likely that Jesus would tell him it was his fault, as anything else. My heart began to race, hoping for the best but in a subtle way preparing for the worst. And then the levee broke.

Bob lost all composure and fell to the floor in the fetal position. He let out a loud wail followed by random gasps for breath. But instead of tears of pain, his face exposed a radical transformation to one of weeping and release. Even the creases in his forehead seemed to relax, revealing the face of a little boy who had been released from an oppressive prison. His body rested on the floor quietly weeping for at least five minutes. He wiped the tears from his face and eventually sat with a contemplative gaze.

"What did he say?" I finally asked.

"He said, 'She was hurting too much and she didn't know how to take care of me.'" He got up off the floor but it was as if I was speaking to a different person. A tremendous peace washed over Bob. "I always thought she didn't love me anymore," he said, crying, but at the same time aware of the new information. "But Jesus told me she did love me. She always did."

He opened his eyes and sat there for a couple more minutes just processing a lifetime built on a lie. He grabbed his face as images of a lifetime of self-mutilation and destruction poured over him. "What have I done?" he said.

I knew Jesus' response was critical to this moment in Bob's life.

His face seemed to glow, his forehead relaxed. Something had fundamentally changed in Bob. He was now able to see the experience in a radically different light. The only remnants were the permanent lines formed in his skin. The impetus for his anger was gone.

As I drove home, I couldn't help but ask what just happened. The experience arrested my attention, and changed my interaction with these men. For the first time, I began taking a deeper look into the specific nature of what had occurred. I began listening intently to what exactly was happening at the point of transition from captivity to hope. As I began looking for the root problem, many of the men had similar experiences. When we discovered the root problem, change was not long and drawn out, but immense and instantaneous.

My own formal training and traditions left me somewhat conflicted. We have traditionally assumed that if someone had walked through the traditional steps it would "set them free." Jesus even said, "The truth will set you free." But my experiences with Bob and the men who followed didn't fall into that category. Getting to the truth first required removing the obstacle keeping each man from embracing it. In every case, the men had experienced some moment that produced enough evidence to question their own value as human beings. Each had believed the lie that they were "not worth it."

The encounter with Bob would compel me to begin asking, "What is the nature of the problem people are experiencing?" What is the root cause of human suffering at the deepest levels? How do we create the problem and how do we get out of it? Was there some moment in the human story that suggested an original problem? I knew my own traditions could shed some light on the question. Over the course of the next ten years, I would spend much of my life asking these types of questions.

What I did not realize at the time was that my encounter with Bob was a peek into the root problem. The events and subsequent emotions of Bob's life appeared to conspire against him, forcing him to create an understanding or "realization" of this problem – specifically, how he judged his own value as a person. Something had happened which appeared to invalidate him. At the core of his being was something telling him he was unlovable, and he bought it. In Bob's own mind he was worthless.

Although the judgment he had made about himself was untrue, Bob had created it and thus given it life. And because he had created it, it was true for him. Instead of finding out what was actually true, he held onto the lie, which captivated him. In a moment he constructed a covering, a protective shell of both "victim and perpetrator". It hid his true identity as a whole human being. The event made him the victim, but he also unknowingly perpetrated his own victimhood by holding onto the lie.

For much of Bob's life he took on both the victim and perpetrator roles. He nurtured the original lie because his own bias looked for evidence to support it. The destructive fruit of his life continued to reveal the underlying problem, so he punished himself hoping to change things. Instead, the shame produced a downward spiral of devastating proportions. The more he fought it, focusing on it with all of his being, the more he produced and saw evidence it was somehow true. It was self-reinforcing. No matter how hard he had tried to deal with the problem on his own, even appealing to religious traditions, nothing seemed to work. The experience captivated his thought process, or imagination, in an overwhelming way.

Reconciliation was only possible by addressing and removing the original construct creating the problem. But at the core of the problem was not an experience, or emotion, or circumstance causing Bob to suffer. The events, the emotions, and the specific circumstances of the event were all true. His mother left. It was painful. His life was inevitably changed. What captivated Bob was the incorrect judgment he made about himself regarding the event. What kept him from seeing it was the "covering" of victim and perpetrator.

Reconciliation was not about changing what was true (the events), but letting go of what was false (the judgment) in order to discover what had always been true (dignity). Jesus simply provided a deeper understanding of the moment, but that understanding provided Bob with the evidence he needed to shed his destructive judgment. Without an oppressive judgment he could see himself as something other than victim or perpetrator. And for the first time, he could see his own dignity. He could see the way Jesus looked at him, and he was good.

But to do that Bob had to return to the scene of the crime. Jesus became the clarifying image for Bob. He became the authority who brought truth into the situation. It was only when Bob accepted Jesus' authority to speak into his life, that he removed the covering and exposed the lie. Together we discovered the root problem. We had uncovered what I would later describe as the God imagination, a way of seeing the world through God's perspective.

~~

Discovering the Mystery

The question that would haunt me was, "Why is the root problem such a mystery?" Why had the obvious eluded Bob? The event with his mother was the most pivotal event of his life, yet it had taken twenty years for him to confront it. Instead of dealing with the root problem, Bob had spent most of his life focusing on, and dealing with, the destructive fruit it had produced.

It was a second experience almost seven years after my encounter with Bob that would provide an essential clue into the nature of the problem. I was in a coffee shop reading a great book, which put me in a decidedly reflective mood. After I'd been reading for about an hour, a woman with multiple sclerosis walked in the door. I recognized the curling of the hands and distorted walk, the twitching and the awkwardness of the disease. For reasons I couldn't explain, her presence created an immediate sense of discomfort. She smiled at me as she passed by and I didn't know what to do. I tried to pass off what felt like a disingenuous smile back. But it wasn't just me. I looked around and noticed she had the attention of the entire coffee house. Everyone was looking at her, noticing her for her MS, for her inability to function in a "normal" way.

As I watched the woman order her coffee, I imagined what she must have been thinking. Did she notice our stares? Did she feel our discomfort? Derek, the barista, put on his best face, but it was obvious that he was uncomfortable in dealing with her. He couldn't help raising his voice to her, as though her hearing had also gone. It hadn't. It was an awkward moment for him, as much as for those who were watching.

At the same time, I couldn't help notice her sense of grace in the moment. As she held her coffee, she moved with a sense of peace, even in the midst of her jagged walk. It seemed like she had come to terms with her own condition. She smiled at everyone as she passed by and finally sat down with her coffee. She was the only one in the room who seemed to be comfortable.

Yet the room was not. I was not. Something about the disease pressed on me like a heavy weight. It made me uncomfortable. It arrested the attention of the room. It was only when she sat down and the effects were less noticeable that things finally returned to a semblance of normalcy.

But the experience had jarred something in me. What was it about her that made everyone uncomfortable? The obvious fact was: she was different. She was entirely unable to blend into the crowd. She stood out because of her MS, which forced those around her to deal with something different. Yet I knew her mind functioned the same as the rest of ours. She had the capacity to be conscious of the stares, and yet she was gracious in her response.

As I sat with the experience, I began to ask what was really going on. Why was I having such a visceral experience? Why had my body literally turned hot? It was obvious to me the woman was a child of God. She was just as important and had just as much value as I did.

And then it hit me. In this woman was the possibility of my worst fears. Had God somehow forgotten her? In her was the tangible evidence that God had, perhaps, forgotten her. She was the exception, forced to wear her imperfections in public. The problem was that her problems reminded me of my problems. It exposed my deepest fears and wants. Her presence made me conscious of my own frailty and of the breach within my own heart. Her brokenness reflected something I didn't want to be seen or detected. Her "disease" made me conscious of my own "disease" with this life. Her presence forced the room to question who else might be the exception. We were all tangibly perturbed by the experience.

The deepest fears of my heart were being laid bare. I was reminded of my own inability to fully embrace love in the moment, and to love others. I knew God had called me to love, but in this awkward moment I felt bent in a completely different way. If Jesus were truly found in the "least of these" then I had become the Apostle Peter. I had denied the image of Jesus sitting in front of me. I felt visceral sense of shame at my own judgments.

As I sat with the emotion of the moment, I recognized a sense of shadow, pushing me to ignore it. The easiest thing for me to do was to become blind to the moment, to avoid the reality of it. My fears were easier forgotten. The shadow wanted me to run from the coffee house. It wanted me to rise up against the woman and tell her to go away. The experience with the woman produced a strange suffering. In that moment I was the one uncomfortable. I could not ignore the problem had occurred in me. I was the one making judgments. I would later wrestle with this moment as I was contemplating the nature of suffering, and see it for what it was. I would be reminded of the words of the renowned author and Oxford scholar C.S. Lewis, who once said:

> "God whispers to us in our pleasures, speaks in our conscience, but shouts
> in our pains; it is His megaphone to rouse a deaf world."

The woman with MS had given me a great gift. She had taught me in this one moment the dominant role of suffering in our lives. Suffering produces a deep awareness of the root problem. It calls out and reflects something in our own lives, something that demands a response. This root problem offers us choices: to hide, to demand it leave, or to confront. If we choose to confront it we can begin the long journey of transformation.

~~

Discovering the Question

What would it mean to confront the pain and suffering, to step back into it and face it head on? If these two encounters did anything, they called my bluff. I could no longer ignore the dissonance in my own soul. Much like Bob, I too had been questioning my own sense of value. Something in me seemed incomplete. I was bent towards questioning love as opposed to embracing it and holding onto it. The longing revealed the embedded judgments I had been making.

The truth is I was good at hiding it. I had learned to manage the pain and suffering well enough that people didn't know. At the same time, the more I began to admit it, the more I became aware of what was missing. By facing my pain and suffering, I was actually increasing it. By exposing my own reality, I was forcing myself to confront it or be consumed by it. Admitting I was actually searching for love revealed I didn't quite believe I had love. This in turn opened me to seeing what became one of the most important pieces of the puzzle: the original question.

In my work with the men, we had learned to consistently listen for the "scene of the crime." We rarely changed the reality of the event. Transformation came from changing the judgment of dignity in the event. In every case, the men were seeing the event as something that invalidated them as human beings. These memories exposed their worst fears and compelled them to hide. And when it was something they had done to themselves, it was infinitely worse.

The idea of the scene of the crime drew me back to the human story in Genesis 1-3. Some scholars had argued for something called "original sin", which suggested a single isolated event that happened, as opposed to something that happens. But the more I examined the evidence the more I found it failed to resonate. Something about it didn't add up. The alternative possibility that suggested nothing happened didn't seem to provide much relief either. There was just too much evidence present in history to suggest something did happen. I needed a better story.

As I expressed my fears openly, I found out I was not alone. Many like me were beginning to express doubt over the validity of our traditional theories of the story. I was engaging in dialogs with people who, like me, had come to the point that the old stories just didn't work anymore. Yet unless we offered an alternative, we were doing little more than complaining. Our doubts ultimately led us to a profound willingness to question, which opened us up to consider other possibilities. It was the doorway to seeing a better story.

As I explored Genesis 1, 2 and 3 over a period of three years a remarkable simplicity began to emerge. God creates a magical world of beauty and harmony. There is so little information – only a few simple, vital details. God establishes creation with an extraordinary sense of imagination, then embeds in the story this significant insight: over and over again God judges it as good. Then out of this same sense of imagination God shapes humanity and calls it very good. God's judgment becomes the key. Everything is good. There is no exception. This is the God imagination, a way of seeing the world from God's perspective.

Creation is a world of remarkable freedom. Humanity is given exceptional permission to "eat", or partake, of everything. But in the midst of this creation is also a single tree. The tree is identified as the Tree of Knowledge of Good and Evil. Everything is permissible, with the exception of this one tree. This tree essentially asks one single question. Are we good or evil? Seeing this question opened the floodgates to everything. Through it, we come to see the root problem God was attempting to solve in the Garden.

The tree prompted a confrontation with the nature of truth and reality. Could humanity do something to change God's perspective of what was true? Could humanity experience evil, even know evil – and thus become evil? Everything hinged on how we answered this one question, because the judgment of the self produced our understanding of reality.

Exploring Genesis happened to coincide with my own exploration into neuroscience, and how the brain operates and processes information. For the first time in history, scientists were beginning to understand how the brain constructs judgment and a sense of reality. Was it possible that the story would present a tale that was consistent with science?

As I examined the story, the answer was unequivocally yes. The entire scene of the crime rested on a single verse:

Then the eyes of both of them were opened, and they realized they were naked; so they sewed fig leaves together and made coverings for themselves. (Gen 3:7)

In other words, the story was presenting a problem happening inside the brain. Adam and Eve were already naked, but for some reason their judgment of its meaning had changed. Naked was still true but no longer good. The evidence that followed revealed that their judgment of its value had changed. They had gotten the one question wrong.

Everything hinged on the word, "realized", essentially a construction of a sense of reality. Realizing didn't mean it had to be true. They just had to agree it was true. This false realization created a sense of disorientation with the self that was devastating. Their sense of reality was suddenly different than the God imagination. They had in essence constructed and agreed to a lie. Worse, neuroscience was now revealing that once a lie is embedded it creates a bias towards information that reinforces it.

To my amazement, Scripture was locating the problem in a much different place than the traditions. Was it possible this was the root problem in humanity? Was Genesis suggesting the origin of pain and suffering? Was it possible, as human beings created in the image of God, we could construct a sense of judgment about the self that was counter to what was true? The story strongly suggested it was. The problem was in essence an ontological shift within the self about the nature of the self.

The hardest part was actually reconciling the simplicity of it all. Was our understanding and access to the kingdom of God really as simple as a single question? And if this were true, what would it mean to look at the rest of the story through this different lens? Would the story validate this idea? Would it transform our understanding of the rest of the story, especially the cross? Would it radically alter our understanding of the nature of sin, the religious systems and the law, the atonement, the work of Jesus, and especially the cross? Was it possible to redeem the very essence of the Christian faith, and ultimately what it means to be human?

As I examined the story I couldn't help but notice that my own historical theories didn't line up with the story. The evidence suggested something entirely different. Yet one of these theories had lasted for over 1,700 years, and my own tradition's theory had lasted for over 1,000 years. How was it possible for the obvious to go undetected? How was it possible for great minds to come to conclusions that seemed to skip right by what the story was presenting? The obvious answer was that it was not possible to see what was happening until I had stepped out of my own tradition.

If the evidence in the story does anything, it reveals the captivating nature of the judgments we make. We become prisoners of our own imagination. We create an alternative (some would say dualistic) world. When we believe something is true, we make it true in our world. And if this judgment is false it blinds us to what is actually true. The nature of the root problem is then like a covering that keeps us from seeing both the root problem creating the blindness, and the God imagination that informs us of what is actually true. And if we believe our judgments to be true, if we believe we are evil, then our existence can likely be described as hell.

Without a clear sense of the answer to this one question we feel the void. We don't want to be evil, yet we can't ignore the evidence that seems to suggest it's possible. Instead we live in between these judgments, hoping for the best but struggling with the worst. The only way to deal with our judgments is to run and hide – to ignore the root problem – which virtually everyone in the story does.

To fill it, we create alternative means of self-validation like pride, relationships and social comparison. We create laws to deal with social structures and the problem of murder. We invent oppressive systems of religion as a means to deal with the problem of guilt. But instead of ignoring human constructs, God uses them to speak directly to us. God consistently meets humanity in the midst of its brokenness. God uses what we create to reveal its oppressive nature in order to remove it. And all along, God waits patiently as we exhaust these possibilities.

The story slowly reveals the God imagination in relationship to the people of Israel. Love refuses to give up. The story also presents the clarifying image of Jesus. In Jesus we see the God imagination made real. We see the true image of humanity. We are designed to overcome, love, and suffer under the weight of terrible circumstances, and remain undefined by them. In Jesus we also see the true image of God's response to what happened in the Garden and throughout the story. When humanity is at its very worst, God remains whole.

And finally the story presents the atonement – how God is actually reconciling humanity to God. To understand the human story means confronting our traditional notions of what is happening on the cross, to ask, "Where is the problem located?" Once we answer this question, a new understanding of the atonement opens up. We are invited to discover the depth of what is happening, to shudder at the sheer magnitude of love it reveals, and embrace it with open arms. The story reveals God's central concern is not a punitive sense of justice for breaking a law, but an overriding concern for the consequence of death.

The entire story is God's methodical mission to restore humanity by producing evidence of love so profound it shatters the lie which consistently produces death. The cross is God's means of destroying the stranglehold of death which overshadows humanity, keeping it from seeing the God imagination. Restoration is something that happens locally in the mind and has more to do with how we see the world than anything else. God is restoring our image of the created order.

At the heart of this process is the extraordinary requirement of faith. Faith is taking the risk to discover the possibility that God is not like our projected images. God is whole, unchanging, fierce and unwavering. Repentance is letting go of false images to discover what is already true. It's stepping into the mystery for the sake of uncovering reality. In other words, the quickest way to change the world is to change how we see the world. It is an embrace of what has always been true.

In order to remove the lie, we must be willing to participate in this process. We must be open to the idea of a new imagination, a God imagination. It is seeing the world through God's eyes. It is finding the extraordinary image of God in each human being. It is seeing the brilliant image of God hidden under all the lies, the garbage, and the oppressive baggage. It's discovering the God image in ourselves, and in our neighbors, and in the world around us, in spite of the overwhelming evidence to the contrary.

~~

Discovering the Way

If we're honest, we're attracted to Jesus for selfish reasons. Something is seemingly irresolvable in our lives and no matter how hard we try to address the problem it just doesn't seem to work. We long for reconciliation to make sense of our own existence, but our religious and legal constructs leave us wanting. But we can't ignore Jesus said things like, "I have come that they may have life, and have it to the full." (John 10:10) We wrestle with the selfish notion of wanting what Jesus is trying to give us, which is life. It is so easy to just roll our eyes at this statement and wonder what in the world is he really saying. How is it possible?

The root problem essentially creates a problem of judgment. Everything in life becomes subjective and individual. Everything is relative. So we have to judge in order to figure it out. At the root level, we're trying to judge whether or not we're good or bad. We build a case to justify that we're good, but encounter mounds of evidence to suggest we're the "exception". If we get the judgment wrong, we encounter a profound level of relativity, which eventually produces pain, suffering and eventually death. This process extends to every relationship we can encounter.

The story suggests a remarkably simple transition to an objective life that became known as the Way of Jesus. The Way began with love as the defining judgment. Love is the judgment of good. It is any action that holds or restores someone's dignity towards wholeness. There are no evil people, just evil realizations about people. Discarding these realizations and discovering the God image in the world around us becomes the journey.

Love draws each of us into reconciliation with reality by discovering the image of God already present in each human being. It validates the soul by seeing it the way God sees it, as good. It invites each person out of oppression and into the journey toward restoration of one's own dignity and also the dignity of those around them.

Realizing this Way of Jesus is only possible by removing the covering that blinds us to reality. It requires stepping back into the scene of the crime and finding a way through. Only when we face death can we discover resurrection.

The brilliance of the Way is its simplicity. Even a child can do it. There is no exception to worry about. There is no subjectivity to manage. There is only good. And it's all good. Love addresses the question of "the exception". Is there something we can do to change God's perspective of us? Could humanity actually do something to permanently remove itself from the Kingdom of God? Jesus reveals that even when we attempt to kill the God image, the answer is no. There is, in essence, no exception. By removing any possibility of exception, we remove the possibility of being the exception.

Just because the Way is simple doesn't make it easy. The Way calls us into a radically different paradigm for life, one diametrically opposed to what we're used to. The Way puts us in direct conflict with our own biology, as well as the religious and political cultures we live in.

Where my experience with Bob helped me locate the problem, and my experience with the woman in the coffee house helped me begin to see the nature of the problem, solving the problem was ultimately about living into the Way. What would it mean to live an objective life, to see everything from God's perspective? What would it mean to love without exception?

I began to ask these questions on a trip to Seattle with my wife and three young children. As we passed the Starbucks in the waterfront district, a woman named Lenora walked up to us. She was obviously homeless and didn't have any shoes on. I was acutely aware of my natural reactions to protect my children from her. Something in me wanted to keep them from any harm, as if she was actually a threat. This instinct made me wonder how anyone would feel to be always seen as a threat. She was a modern day leper. As we began talking to her the crowd stared at us, wondering why we were giving her our time.

My instincts to run were momentarily quelled by the idea that standing in front of me was Jesus in the flesh. Instead of being limited to the superficial realities of her condition, I chose to look for the God image in her, to look past what I was used to judging her by. I tried to see her from God's perspective, as a child suffering under the weight of an oppressive judgment.

She tried to sell me a story that she needed money for a key deposit for the shelter. I knew it was most likely a well-scripted lie, but it didn't matter. I didn't really need a story. This was my moment to meet Lenora. Something in me just felt like $20 was the right answer. I don't know how to explain it other than I just went with my heart at the moment.

I looked into my wallet; all I had was a $100 bill. I turned around and saw a Starbucks, so I excused myself to go get some change. I bought a coffee and then went back to Lenora. I handed her a twenty, and then something inside of me said to give her the coffee too. So I asked her if she wanted the coffee. She smiled at me as though I had saved the world that day. Believe it or not, the coffee meant more to her than the money.

I asked her if she wanted cream or sugar and she did, so I took the coffee back to Starbucks and got her cream and Equal, four packets. I found out most coffee establishments in Seattle wouldn't allow the homeless in unless they're wearing shoes. Lenora wasn't. Her circumstance had excluded her from an institution well known for its sense of community.

While I was gone, Lenora talked with my children and was deeply gracious to them. She made my son laugh and complimented him on his Spiderman skills, which he loved. She complimented my girls, which made them smile. I returned and handed her the coffee just the way she liked it. I introduced her to my family and they all were gracious to her. Lenora really didn't know how to act. Our interaction was transformative. When I left she was beaming.

As I walked away with my family, Lenora held onto the coffee as though it were gold. It had become a symbol; she was still valuable in this world. It reminded her she was still important. She still mattered to someone. The staring eyes around us no longer held the power to judge.

Lenora awakened something in me. In giving her money, I was satisfying a present need in her. She may have been telling the truth about the key deposit. Or she may have been waiting for her next heroin dose. I'll never know. When I stopped and served her, got her coffee, went back for cream and sugar, she lit up. In serving her, I was satisfying a deeper need in her, the need for validation. It reminded her of her inherent worth – something she struggled to hold onto.

The exchange worked both ways. In this encounter we were *both* experiencing a restorative love. I was taking part in the discovery of her dignity as a child made in the image of God. When she looked into my eyes, she felt validated. And strangely I felt validated as well. I was discovering my restoration was intimately linked to restoring others. I was discovering my capacity to participate in restoring God's creation through my encounter with her. In just giving money and walking on, I would have missed why God had called me to this moment. I got to see the image of God in her. Love had given me the imagination of God.

For some the Way will be a radically different paradigm. It will seem, "too good to be true". Or it might cause fear and anger. I completely understand these feelings. Understanding the nature of God's perspective is a direct confrontation with the root problem. It will invite us to wrestle with the basic nature of what is true. For others, it will resonate at a level so deep it will awaken the heart. It will speak in a way many have called "salvation." It will release us from the oppressive weight of religion and open the door to freedom.

Chapter 2 – The God Imagination

"Give me a place to stand and with a lever I will move the whole world." -
Archimedes

Archimedes' Point

In the beginning...

The story begins where we need it to, doesn't it? It begins before time and memory, before there was any recollection of suffering. It begins before humanity could recall exactly the moment when everything went wrong. Before the pain, there was a brief moment of hope and possibility. Time has yet to speed up as we linger through the delectable moments of love and honor, ecstasy and delight. It has yet to stand still as we suffer through moments of courage and catastrophe, passion and pain. Its brevity is so painfully short because of its unlimited potential.

Of all the possibilities and stories of Creation, of all the things we can come up with to explain our origins, nothing has captured our imaginations and attention quite like the creation story in Genesis. Over half the world's population, encompassed in the Abrahamic faiths, uses it as a beginning point of reference. It loiters in our collective imaginations hinting at something so devastatingly true, the only way to live with it is often to sweep it under the rug and ignore it.

Genesis informs us even when we don't want it to. The details easily attract our attention as much as they repel our senses. Why, we ask, hoping to make sense of the story, knowing the tragedy as it plays out. Something went terribly wrong and it isn't supposed to be like this. Many people have wrestled with the story, hoping to make sense of it in a transformative way, and rightly so. If the story is true, then we want to know what it means.

We need to understand don't we? We need a story to fill in the missing pieces and explain why things just don't quite add up. Without a story informing our sense of humanity, we're left with a strange void—one meant to be filled by dignity, identity and purpose. We're left wondering what happened, the same way we feel after a punch to the gut by the shocking news of someone's tragic death. This void holds the potential energy to draw us back to the story.

What if embedded within the story was a hidden key to solving the mystery of the Gospel, an Archimedean point providing us with just the right frame of reference to completely shift our understanding of the rest of the story? And with this frame in place, the rest of the puzzle would begin to come together.

Archimedes, a Greek mathematical genius, believed there was a point outside of time and space in which we could be absolutely objective. And from this space we could move the world. The Archimedean point was essentially a space of objectivity. It was a point of view that allowed us to see everything for what it truly is.

Archimedes reminds us that as long as we are part of the story, we cannot be objective about the story. We can never remove our own interests enough to see outside ourselves. Werner Heisenberg clarified this in his uncertainty principle when he essentially stated the same thing - one couldn't be a participant in the process and at the same time be an observer. In order to see what is true we needed an objective frame of reference.

What if the first part of Genesis provides us with our Archimedean Point, the one space of objectivity in the story? As humans, we are limited in our ability to grasp a place of such objectivity. We can't control it or recreate it. We can only test it out by faith and experience it. Is it true? Does it hold up to scrutiny and produce life?

Genesis begins with a unique frame of reference. It is the one moment in the story we are not part of. For five days humanity is still a possibility but not yet a reality, more like a thought without a clear word to communicate it. For a brief moment, we see life exclusively from God's perspective, and we are reminded we are not the creator but the created. And even on the sixth day, as humanity enters the story, we see no commentary or reflection on our part. God doesn't ask our permission about the process, nor does God check in on how we feel.

This frame of reference is God's imagination revealed. It's God's perspective alone. This is the Kingdom of God. Heaven and earth are one. It is the image of reality in harmony with itself. It is a world of good and beauty, identity and purpose. It's a world of freedom and simplicity, with virtually no constraint. This image is then placed into humanity. It can't be altered or changed. It is true. And oh what a perspective it is!

Although we no longer stand before history, we do gain something from hindsight. We begin with the possibility of seeing the story from God's perspective again. We begin with the possibility of a fresh perspective that has always been there. We just have to look for it.

~~

Dignity

The God Imagination begins with, of all things, an artistic sense of poetry. There is a rhythm to the verses of the story which conveys a rich, creative experience. Poetry is interesting because it can communicate easily identifiable content on the surface, and hide a deeper message in plain sight. And unless we see the hidden message, we'll miss the full meaning of what is really going on.

The verses contain a distinct rhythm of creative act and response. God creates and then steps back to judge it. God creates light…and it is good. God creates the water and dry ground…and it is good. God creates vegetation…and it is good. God creates day and night…and it is good. God creates water creatures…and it is good. God creates land creatures…and it is good. God creates humanity… and it is very good.

It's very easy to see the content. Over and over again God distinctively creates and brings forth a world through the act of naming. God creates the light and separates it from the darkness. God creates the sea and land creatures and separates the kinds. Each element possesses its own distinct purpose. The act of distinguishing gives presence and recognition to the created order. But through this entire process, each time God stops and notices something – its value.

Content is obvious. Value is not. It's easy to sense the presence of something but harder to judge the value of it. No one argues whether there is light or darkness. We just see it. No one argues whether there are land or sea creatures, or water and dry land. They are obvious, even empirically provable. But when it comes to the value of each, it's not so easy, especially when it comes to the last part about us humans.

In fact, it's easy to just skip over the value part. It's easy to miss the hidden message. But what if the second part is the meaning of the story? What if the purpose of the poetry offers us a hidden key to the Kingdom, one unlocking the answer to the very question humanity will wrestle with throughout the entire story?

The God Imagination reveals God's divine judgment on creation. We need to know how God sees the situation. Value is the defining question of our existence. It is the central underlying question in all conflict, social interaction and human experience. It is the one question embedded in the tree in the Garden. And in this moment God renders the answer.

What is subtle but important about the judgment is the change occurring when humanity is included in the process. For five days God creates and it is good. But on the sixth day God creates humanity, and creation is not just good, but "very good". It's like God is giving us a little wink of the eye to say, "Remember that one."

The hidden message calls out the first and most important truth in the God Imagination. The dignity of creation, of our value, is established as true. From God's objective perspective everything is good. There is no exception. Humanity is even very good. This judgment is not based on what we've done, or something we have created, worked at, invented, won, or presented. It is not based on success or failure. It doesn't even include our opinion on the matter. It simply is because God declares it to be true.

~~

Identity

As we take in the poetry of the text, it is essential to call out a very important distinction in the creative process. The original elements of light, water and dry ground, vegetation, day and night, and living creatures are all reflections of God's creativity. Their beauty is reflected in everyday nature. But humanity is set apart for a very distinct honor.

Then God said, "Let us make man in our image, in our likeness..." (Gen 1:26)

Humanity's original identity is a reflection of God. God casts the God imagination onto humanity. In essence, we begin as children of God. Our inherent identity is one of nobility, royalty and honor. No other part of creation holds this distinction. Who we are can only be understood in relationship to God.

It is important to also call out this distinction of the God image reflected onto humanity. The word "man" is better translated as "Adam", which is a distinction of humanity. We need to know the God image is cast onto both man and woman. They are one. In other words, the God image in humanity is deeply understood in both man and woman. To lose one half is to miss the deeper reflection.

The God image calls out the second great truth of the God Imagination, which is identity. Before we are men or women, black or white, Jew or Gentile, Christian or Muslim, gay or straight, we are first human beings created in the image of God. Our original identity is a child of God who reflects the God image. We are noble, honorable, and whole and called very good.

As with dignity, our identity is not self-defined. We don't assume an identity because we believe it to be true. We realize our identity because God declared it to be true. It is the purest identity of humanity. Any attempt at distinction or further definition can only render a limited expression of what God has already created. It can only express a portion of the whole.

~~

Purpose

The God Imagination then offers our primary purpose. As God creates humanity, God also reveals a specific order: first our identity and then our purpose.

> *"Let us make man in our image, in our likeness, and let them rule over the fish of the sea and the birds of the air, over the livestock, over all the earth, and over all the creatures that move along the ground." (Gen 1:26)*

Purpose is derived from identity and not the other way around. In other words, all effective action is derived from a correct understanding of identity. Our purpose comes out of our design. We derive our call to rule from being made in the image of God.

The order means everything. If we limit or lose sight of the first part, it will naturally distort the second part. If we reverse the process, assuming our distorted actions reveal our identity, it contributes to a debilitating effect on humanity. We inform our understanding of our identity using the wrong means.

The original purpose is to rule. To rule meant "to exercise authority, dominion, or sovereignty," over the creatures God had created. Embedded within each human being is an instinctive purpose to oversee, make decisions, and exercise authority over the created order. Human beings are gifted with the prefrontal cortex, or the rational brain, which biologically supports the call to rule.

The original purpose also has relational boundaries. The call to rule didn't mean over each other. Humanity was not created to rule over other human beings. We were born into a very intentional freedom. And this freedom wasn't just from being ruled by the other. It was also from the responsibility of ruling over each other.

The God Imagination also provides us with the distinct little phrase, "over all the earth." At first glance this may appear as ruling over the dust and dirt. And it can be. But what if it's bigger than that? It's easy to forget that Adam is created from the earth, from the dust in the ground. Read this way, the story reveals our purpose is also to rule over the self. The God imagination empowers Adam to experience a sense of self-control. It calls humanity to rule over its own distinct kingdom, which exists in the self.

When we apply this to our own imagination we can begin to sense a very specific desire to engage this rule. At the center of our desire for reconciliation is to be at peace with our own heart, and with the world around us – to experience a sense of control over our impulses and desires. Instinctively we know we need to control our sense of desires and passions. We feel this need for control when we encounter our addictions and self-destructive habits. We long for control when we do things we don't want to do.

Understanding our purpose as the rule over self informs our daily life. It's personal in a way that most endeavors or activities cannot be. It gives us a constant, enduring sense of meaning. It provides us with a deep sense of significance that informs everything we do.

~~

Freedom

The God Imagination provides us intriguing clues as to the nature of God's rule, which the story calls Kingdom. Heaven, which is God's perspective, and earth, which is the created order, are in harmony with each other. God establishes what feels like an irresponsible level of freedom.

> And the LORD God commanded the man, "You are free to eat from any tree in the garden; (Gen 2:17a)

God designs the freedom to "eat" or consume anything in creation as a fundamental characteristic of the Kingdom. The assumption is that we're going to explore and imagine, try and seek out. God establishes a freedom that provides an intense level of permission. This idea would later be revisited in Paul's famous words, "Everything is permissible." Humanity begins with a framework that is empowering and permission-oriented.

But the story reveals not just by what is there, but also by what is NOT there. The story completely lacks an identifiable basis for human interaction, or what we would describe as moral law. In other words, there is no moral code of any kind. God spends no time defining or revealing complex systems, rules, list of laws, or even a handbook on what it means to live in the world. God originally omits certain things which we would naturally expect to be there because we know the story. It would seem prudent in hindsight for God to provide some basis for human interaction at this point. But God doesn't. The story contains no tangible or even illusory code of human conduct.

This glaring omission is easy to miss as part of the story. We're so used to seeing life through the basis of the law we skip right over that part and just assume it exists. But it doesn't. The Ten Commandments don't show up for another 2,500 years. The one command God eventually gives to the children of Adam is, "don't kill each other," which can almost seem a little irresponsible, given what follows.

It's easy to ask, "What do you mean God didn't provide the law?" The natural inclination is to immediately run to the First Command given to Adam and Eve.

> And the LORD God commanded the man…"but you must not eat from the tree of the knowledge of good and evil, for when you eat of it you will surely die." (Gen 2:17b)

The first commandment provides the context for understanding our freedom. Freedom is informed and governed by the judgment of good. God's command follows the original declaration of good for all humanity. Our actions are then first defined by an understanding of how each affects all of creation. The only way to corrupt the system is to lose site of the judgment.

If we're honest, it's either reckless on God's part or revealing of something deeper within the context of what is going on. What if God understands that the basis of all human interaction begins with harmony to this single judgment of value? The assumption we can draw from this is that the judgment of value provides the underlying basis for all human relationship and interactivity. If we see life from the God Imagination, as good, our actions are governed by this judgment. If we see God, the self, our neighbors, and even the world as good, we begin to hold it as valuable.

Jesus intimated this in the Great Commandment.

> *"'Love the Lord your God with all your heart and with all your soul and with all your mind and with all your strength.' The second is this: 'Love your neighbor as yourself.' There is no commandment greater than these."* (Mk 12:30-31)

As long as we remained in harmony with God's judgment of value, effective social interaction was assumed. As long as we held onto the truth of our dignity, life would remain in harmony. Love was the only defining ethic needed.

The opposite was also true. If we were not in harmony with God's judgment, if we lost sight of value, then our social interactions would suffer as a result. Technically, we didn't need a legal construct to tell us when something was wrong, because the fruit of our relationships would reveal it for us.

We see this in Jesus. His interaction with those around him was so intriguing, so beguiling, it was almost overwhelming. Jesus continually held onto to who He was because He remained in relationship with his Father. He never lost sight of the dignity of those around Him, even of His oppressor, because He always held onto the value of everything. He never lost sight of his purpose, because He understood his identity as a child of God.

The absence of law still seems reckless, doesn't it? If we assume at some point there would be failure, why not provide the law as sort of a safety net? Why not just add a dash of caution to the mix? What if this great omission is really evidence suggesting the original concept of grace as the operating structure of the Kingdom? The Apostle Paul clarifies that it existed before time.

> *"This grace was given us in Christ Jesus before the beginning of time, but it has now been revealed through the appearing of our Savior, Christ Jesus..." (2 Tim 1:9-10)*

What if God assumed, as human beings created in the image of God, we could overcome anything we do to each other? The problem wasn't the actions or the consequences but the underlying judgment we make about the actions or consequences. If we held onto the judgment of good, freedom would be governed by the need to preserve and support life. Even the proverbial "accident" would still be governed by the judgment of good. It would place the value of both parties above any consequence.

With this framework, it becomes possible to understand why God is capable of moving past consequence, even murder, so quickly. God never loses sight of the value of creation. Much of the story is God consistently transcending human error. Consequence doesn't define creation but it does affect it. Holding onto the judgment of value allows us to stay grounded in our true identity as human beings created in the image of God, called very good. It allows us to stay true to our purpose, which includes ruling over our emotions of the moment.

Grace is in many ways foreign to the human experience because it is counter to what we think of as the "normal" system of judgment. It rubs us the wrong way because we assume it means we're invalidating the effects of consequence. But it's not. It is clearly embedded in the fabric of creation. God consistently requires confession in order for grace to work. True justice is both truth and grace. Grace invites us to root our identity in the God imagination. But to do so we have to let the false realizations go. Grace requires transcending negative judgments of value.

Grace is a strange concept. We don't actually need it unless we have something to transcend. Much of the story is the unfolding of grace, which allows humanity to transcend the subjective judgments, so we can discover and hold onto what is true.

~~

The Great Omission

The God Imagination also provides what we could call a great omission. Humanity begins in a state of freedom from any kind of false judgment. In the second chapter God reveals the woman as a hidden part of humanity. The God image includes both man and woman. They turn and look at each other. They're naked and completely exposed. It would seem intuitive to call out what is there. We would expect something like, "The man and his wife fell in love," or even, "the man and woman saw it was good too." But it doesn't. The story calls out what is NOT there.

"The man and his wife were both naked, and they felt no shame." (Gen 2:25)

This observation is counterintuitive unless it has distinct meaning for humanity. Humanity begins without the judgment of the meaning of nakedness. In other words, nakedness was normal, but they weren't even aware of it because there was no need for judgment as part of human experience. In calling out the lack of judgment we can then contrast it with the later experience when humanity's perception of nakedness changes. It is important to call out something about shame. The story states they "felt" no shame. Shame is the body's physical response system to a false judgment. It is a physically tangible event happening in our body letting us know something is wrong inside of us. This allows us to effectively locate the problem.

We often assume shame indicates a problem outside of the self, when the problem is in fact occurring inside of the self. Shame is only possible with judgment of value. It is the invalidating judgment crushing us under the weight of its disapproval. It's the voice saying the exact opposite of truth. It says, "You are not really your Father's child. You are not really good. You're just kidding yourself. You are worthless and void of value." But all of these feelings of shame are only possible when we agree to the judgment being made.

Judgment of value is the wisdom of God, but actually defining value is a role reserved exclusively for God.   We can only judge as long as we begin with God's perspective. As long as we didn't lose sight of the God Imagination, our fundamental sense of value, humanity could always overcome slights, accidents, harm and even devastating circumstances.   As long as we remained inside the love of God, we could experience the consequences of an event without judging the persons involved in the event.

~~

Unchanging Truth

Subtly ingrained in the God Imagination are two questions which have to do with the nature of truth.   What is the nature of truth, and can it be changed? The value of God's perspective is that it provides a basis for something that doesn't change. The assumption we can make about it is that it's fixed and firm. Establishing what is true, much like math, provides a basis for understanding the rest of the story. If it can change, however, then God's original declarations hold no real value.

The first is, "what is the nature of truth?"   Is God's perspective objectively and eternally true? The story strongly suggests the answer is "yes". Dignity, identity, and purpose are true from God's perspective.   Freedom is true.   Good is true. They don't change. God's declarations are analogous to the rules of the game. We can ignore them, fight them, reject them, and hide them, but if we do, we suffer the consequences of doing so. Much of the human experience involves coming to terms with this.

Subjective circumstance, action, human opinions, social constructs, and even rejection cannot change what is inherently true.   The data of events may all be true – they actually happen – but they do not change the underlying constructs of value written into the fabric of creation. They can't change the intrinsic dignity, identity and purpose, which are truths.

We instinctively feel their validity when we break these constructs.   Justice is not possible without them. We can ignore, break, discard, or contemplate them, but they are true even if we don't want them to be.

If we choose to believe they are subjective and flexible we have no basis for understanding our own value. Everything becomes relative and subject to our own sense of judgment. We might choose to ignore them. But by invalidating them or making them relative, we become subject to the standards we agree to. So if value is relative, our own value is relative.

Much of our search for what is true is for the sake of understanding what affects us. We want to know what is true and objective. Much like math, God's perspective can be tested and experienced. It can be explored and tried. And those that have tried have not been left wanting.

The second question is then an extension of the first. "Can we do something to change what is true?" Can humanity permanently lose its inherent value? Is truth contingent on subjective circumstance, human action or even whim? Is God fickle and wanton, subject to mood swings, and prone to changing what is true? In essence, does God look like humanity after the Garden? Or is God firm and solid, unaffected by the anything humanity can invent or do?

What we're essentially asking is if there is an exception to the God Imagination. Much of the story is humanity exploring imaginative ways of embodying death as a means to explore and answer this question. How far can we go before God says, "You are no longer very good." We wrestle with the meaning of events because they ultimately loop back to the original question. An apple falls from a tree. A boy crashes his bike and scrapes his knee. A man murders his brother in cold blood. We rarely question the meaning of events until they produce suffering. When something negative happens it suggests the idea that God has somehow forgotten us. When someone harms us it forces us to question our value. When bad things happen to good people we wonder out loud what it all means. These fears are universal because they reveal the root problem.

These first two questions make up the logical paradox in the story. They lead to an intriguing problem residing in human imagination. We can't change what is true, but we can change our perception of what is true. We can lose sight of God's perspective by seeking the one thing reserved for God, the need to judge ourselves. And in that quest, we can become so captivated by our own judgments it we are kept from seeing what is true.

The only way to lose what is true is then to lose God's perspective, to lose the objective basis for judgment. When we attempt to judge we play God and lose our basis for what is true. We by definition become judge of the subject being judged. And all we have is our relative experience that resides as data. Our experience is then true but our basis for understanding it is not. The very thing we use to base truth on becomes relative, and we suffer the consequences.

~~

Time

To create a better distinction of the God Imagination, it is helpful to understand how truth resides in time. Something true is, was, and always will be true. Scientists often refer to this as natural law. Truth is written into the fabric of the universe. We wrestle with the nature of truth because we wonder if we can change the nature of it. And more importantly we wonder if we can change God's perception of us.

As human beings we approach time very differently than God does. We experience reality in something called "Chronos", which is a linear way of seeing reality. Chronos could be likened to watching a movie. As we watch the movie we are only watching a single frame at a time. We can only see one moment. We experience each moment and make meaning of it in reference to the previous moments.

We always live in the now, which we call the present. As we do, our brain processes information relative to learning events that occurred previous to the now, which we call the past. To make sense of the present requires constantly comparing our present perceptions to these previous learning events. We use time to create a categorical structure of those events and store them in our long-term memory. This structure gives us the awareness of past, present and future. We use the past to define patterns that suggest how the future will show up. But even as we progress through time, we are always only living in the now.

It can easily be suggested God then uses time in the beginning of the story because we need it. God uses time (the day) to help us understand the story. The suggested purpose of time is to create a reference point for humanity, especially to help us rest, celebrate, and coordinate but also for unity, rhythm and beat. We feel it in the sunrise and sunset, seasons and celebrations. It's extremely hard to imagine life without time because our brain uses it to create judgments about the world we live in. But some of our need for time also exists to measure our potential proximity to death. Time speeds up the older we get because we're focusing on the future as opposed to the present.

God's perspective of time is much different. God resides in something called "Kairos", which is a non-linear way of seeing reality. God exists outside of time because reality, or what is true, is not actually based in time. It's true regardless of time. God is, in essence, the true objective reference point. God even uses the distinction of "I Am" to reveal the idea that God is outside of reference. Kairos could be likened to experiencing each frame of a movie simultaneously. God already knows what happened, is happening and is going to happen but is not defined by what happens.

Awareness of what happens does not imply God makes everything happen. It simply means God is present with all things. It doesn't mean God chooses for us. It means God knows the path humanity is going to choose and God still chooses to create us. God knows the cost, the consequence, and the outcome and still makes it all possible. It doesn't infringe on God's sovereignty because embedded in God's sovereignty is the possibility of letting humanity choose.

Humanity experiences reality in Chronos, not Kairos. We make sense of it by referencing previous events. The event and even the root problem are true because both happened. We feel the effects of them. So when something happens, the events, the emotions, the circumstances, the data, and the consequences are revealed as true, in that they happen, but it doesn't change the underlying assumptions of what is true as established by God.

To effectively engage the story and the root problem God is solving, it is important to establish the world God creates. The God Imagination is a world filled with tremendous possibility and meaning, but also tremendous freedom and responsibility. It is also important to establish the dignity, identity, and purpose imparted in creation. Grace is present but not yet needed. There is no shame because there is no need for judgment. It is also important to establish the nature of truth and how it resides outside of time. This perspective, or the God Imagination, is the Archimedean Point for the story. It creates a basis for unity for understanding the root problem which God is solving in the story.

It can be a little disconcerting framing an entire story in such simple terms. But as we examine the story, these are the terms God provides. It really is that simple. To create a basis for unity it is important to begin with an objective viewpoint which in turn provides a framework for understanding the root problem.

Chapter 3 – Returning To the Scene of the Crime

"I believe in looking reality straight in the eye and denying it." - Garrison Keillor

The Traditions

Great stories always reveal a problem to overcome. And the human story has an epic one. Three chapters into Genesis we see humanity encountering an experience from which we are still recovering. The event is historically known as "The Fall" – as in a fall from grace. How does humanity lose sight of the God imagination? It's the pivotal point in the story where everything seems to change. Most theologians readily agree this is the moment where the problem first shows up. Understanding the story then requires understanding this moment.

Historically, the Fall has been seen from two vantage points. The first sees the event as the moment humanity sells itself into captivity to Satan. From this vantage point, reconciliation is God ransoming humanity from the clutches of Satan's captivity. The second sees the event as the moment in which humanity rebels against God's moral law. Reconciliation is consequently God satisfying a divine sense of justice for breaking the law.

The two main traditions see humanity as either captive to Satan, which requires a ransom payment in exchange for freedom, or humanity as captive to God's law, which requires payment to God for the sake of justice. Every major tradition essentially stems in some way from these two ideas.

The traditional approaches to the Fall leave us wondering sometimes why God even created humanity. We're the naïve victims unable to find freedom, or the wayward children unable to please the father. Or worse, we're the worms, unable to appease an angry God. We're so focused on what we've done to create shame we have no time to focus on God's pleasure.

To understand the nature of reconciliation means revisiting the assumptions that create these traditional theories. We have to revisit the scene of the crime and dig deeply into the root problem. In many ways, revisiting feels like sticking sharp pins under our fingernails. We don't need a reminder of what feels like a remarkably stupid event in human history. We read the historical accounts of what happened, the ones passed down for ages, and come to the conclusion. We get it. We're messed up.

But the burden of proof falls on our traditional conclusions of what happened. Traditions are based on assumptions we make about the story, and not the other way around. Our stories must then line up with what is revealed in Scripture. This means any element of tradition not matching Scripture must be discarded.

The problem with traditions is that they stick simply because they were around before us. When the traditions have been around for centuries, who are we to question something accepted by trusted authorities? They stick because in the absence of a better story it's virtually impossible to let go of what we're holding. We live with the contradictions and paradoxes because there just isn't something better to replace them with.

Traditions come with an unquestionable acceptance overpowering our senses. Even when something just doesn't seem right – like why God would create something requiring sacrifice of his own Son to appease his own sense of anger, or why would God be subject to Satan's power – it's just easier to stay with traditions than to question them. Furthermore, in a community often following along without question, it can sometimes feel like an "emperor with no clothes" moment. Everyone is secretly wondering who is going to throw out the obvious.

What if the problem lies not in our conclusions but in our assumptions? All traditions are, in essence, conclusions based upon a specific set of assumptions. And if we get the assumptions wrong, our conclusions will follow suit. They'll produce confusion and fear, debate and argument. They will refuse to reconcile. They won't resonate in helpful ways.

In spite of the conflict, we argue and debate for our conclusions, rather than rigorously criticize our assumptions. But wouldn't we do better by doing the opposite? It's easy to see why we don't begin with our assumptions. Assumptions are what we stand on. They are terra firma. To lose them can easily feel like pulling out the very rug we're standing on.

We can't ignore the nature of the problem. What if it actually leads us to a false assumption? What if the problem is the capacity for our assumptions to blind us to reality? And because we're personally involved, any sense of objectivity about it becomes virtually impossible to generate. We're the ones personally in the mix. We're the ones captive to evil in a way that is oppressive. We're the ones on trial, trying to make sense of our own guilt and manufacturing ways to get rid of it.

If our traditions are true, which ones are true? Can there be more than one when each contradicts the other? And if either one is true the scene of the crime begs so many questions.

First, the situation feels like a setup. Why is God absent the moment Adam and Eve encounter the serpent? If the serpent can actually hold humanity ransom, why didn't God warn them of the serpent? Why was the tree necessary in the first place? Something just doesn't feel right about the situation, given our traditional understanding of the problem. Why can't God get over something seemingly as silly as eating a piece of fruit?

Second, why would a loving God place humanity in a situation where the consequences were so catastrophic, knowing they would fail? If the primary problem is God's justice against a moral law, why would God place humanity at such risk, essentially trapping them into a state they would be unable to resist on their own?

Third, if humanity's actions separate them from God, how are those who walk with God capable of engaging relationship with Him, before any atonement system has ever been put in place? Does God make an exception for Cain, Abel, Noah, Abraham, Isaac, and Jacob at the expense of justice?

Fourth, why would God wait almost 2,500 years before revealing the Ten Commandments and the religious atonement system? Does God just not care to provide a means of restoration for those who come before Moses? In our traditional theories, the silence of God could seem more like abandonment than an act of a loving God.

Fifth, why would God allow a situation requiring the death of his own son to satisfy his own sense of anger and injustice? As strange as it sounds, we can't avoid the logical conclusion of our traditional story, one that essentially makes God a child killer. We can try and suggest Jesus did it voluntarily but it still means God required it.

Sixth, if God's true concern is our traditional notion of punitive justice, why does the cross seem to go to such great lengths to completely obliterate any notion of said justice? Why does God create a huge setup of Israel, the law, the religious system, exile, the Promised Land, a second captivity, and finally the cross, only to provide a response letting everyone off the hook?

None of these questions are new. Nor are they exhaustive. They are common historical responses to our traditional theories of the story. In an information age we can no longer avoid them, allowing the dissonance to reside just below the surface. We must face them, considering the possibility they are the natural outcomes of a story beginning with flawed assumptions.

What if there was a better story, one reconciling the apparent contradictions and paradoxes? Would you be interested? Would you be willing to look? And what if the only way to see it was to return to the scene of the crime? Would you go?

The truth is, we need a better story about what happened. We need better assumptions, ones that reconcile in a cognitive and logically discernible way. It has to work in a way that feels right and rings true. To return to the scene of the crime is to discover a better story first-hand. To return is to reexamine the evidence with fresh eyes. It is to discover how and why our traditions become skewed over time. Blaming someone doesn't solve the problem either. It's part of the problem.

Because we are personally involved, returning to the scene of the crime means setting aside our preconceived notions for a little while. It doesn't mean abandoning them. It means listening to a different story so we can objectively see a different possibility and then rationally weigh the evidence. It means coming to terms with the idea that our traditions have been tainted by the very problem itself.

~~

The Tree

The most complex and troubling part of the story is the actual presence of the Tree of Knowledge of Good and Evil. Our sense of fairness and awareness of what happened compels us to ask, "Why in the world did God include the tree?" What purpose does it ultimately serve? Our imaginations run wild when we consider what it would be like if Adam and Eve had never taken a bite.

> *In the middle of the garden were the tree of life and the tree of the knowledge of good and evil. (Gen 2:9)*

The location of the tree, if anything, actually draws our attention to it. God places it front and center. In some ways, the Tree feels like a sitcom moment when a parent points out the cookie jar and specifically tells a child, "Do NOT eat the cookie." Of course the kid is going to eat the cookie! It's not if he will, but when. And the next twenty minutes shows the kid trying to figure out how to hide the fact that he ate it.

What's intriguing about the tree is that the actual act of eating seems so benign. Humanity is just not supposed to eat a piece of fruit, which seems really strange, in and of itself. Why aren't we supposed to "eat?" Does the fruit somehow possess special powers of insight and magic? This is of course possible given that "the eyes of both of them were opened," but even so the powers don't seem to possess any immediate or productive qualities, given what follows.

The banality of eating and the lack of evidence to support any advantageous magical powers, suggest the real issue lies in the tension of boundaries. The tree suggests a very powerful and provocative question. What would it mean to perform some action outside of God's design? What would it mean to ignore the will of God and do something anyway? If love is God's judgment of good, could humanity separate itself from God's love? Was there a limit we could cross, a cliff we could fall over, or a one-way exit with no return? In other words, was God's love conditional?

The tree suggests a very provocative question. What if the tree actually is a setup? And not in the, "I'm ready to catch you in the act when you fail" kind of way, but in the "You need to get through this single question at some point" kind of way. What if the tree is the test designed to produce maturation, asking the only question that could pose a problem to humanity?

If we look at the tree in the context of the creation story, God has just spent his entire creative process declaring over and over, "It is good. It is good. It is good." And then God presents a tree essentially asking one question: Are you good or evil? God knows the answer. The declaration of value occurs before any tangible action on our part. It's not based on performance or attribute. Good and evil are not questions of activity, but of fundamental value. Humanity is good because God declares it to be.

But what if humanity does something contrary to God's will? Who needs to know the answer to that question? We do. We need to know the answer to the original question. We need to know if God's perspective is actually true. We need to know humanity's value is NOT defined by what we do or think or feel or construct, but instead by God's declarations. The only way to answer the question, to really discover the answer, is to engage it and wrestle with it in the conflict.

The Tree of Knowledge is then not just an exploration into the reality of evil or even rebellion, but a context for testing and proving the reality of God's love. The point of the test is not to discover we can fail, but to discover we can overcome failure. We need to know the way through death. We need to know it doesn't define us.

The tree actually suggests a seemingly reckless but courageous Father willing to throw His child into the deep end of the pool so she can learn how to swim. Isn't this just like the God we meet in the story? Isn't it just like God to throw us into the mix? God consistently relishes seeing us confront and *overcome* adversity. It's like God understands that deep within we have what it takes. We're God's children created with the God imagination. And if God really is our Father, it suggests a profound hopefulness for us, His children, to transcend the question, to come to terms with the reality of our own identity and dignity. In other words, God allows it to happen because God thinks we can succeed.

The test isn't designed to earn God's love or somehow obtain what God has already declared. The purpose of the test is to realize the nature of truth. Our realization of what is true doesn't make it true in a cosmic sense. It simply aligns our mental image to what is already true. It brings us into a deeper state of maturity with truth.

The tree is simply the symbol calling out the possibility of conflict. God's eventual command not to eat calls out the possibility of a potential space humanity doesn't have to enter, but will inevitably enter at some point. The tree provides the true essence of freedom, which is the possibility to ignore God's design. The tree then identifies the possibility for humanity, setting it right in the middle of the Garden. The prohibition signifies humanity doesn't have to enter into that space. It is the harder way. Humanity can continue on without this knowledge.

The act of eating signifies the consumption of an idea, which identifies where the problem is located. To eat is to consume the profound possibility that God may not love us, and everything that follows. To eat is to enter the dark spaces of possibility, question, and doubt. To eat is to wrestle with the one question, which changes everything.

The tree is a question of knowing what God knows, and knowing only comes from experience. Eating gets humanity to the question. Within the tree is a single defining question providing the basis for all human interaction and relationship. It is the only question that matters: Are we good or evil?

If we enter this space of knowing, we also encounter the debilitating effects of truth's polar opposite: the lie. Could humanity be separated from the love of God? Was there some condition in which humanity could lose the love of God? If so then the truth of God's perspective was not objective. If humanity could perform some act that changed truth, then truth was not true after all.

God places the question front and center to provide us with the means to understand it and face it so that we could *overcome* it. The tree is actually necessary because it is the only question for humanity that can affect anything, the question of value. Dignity is the center point, the true North, the ground floor. And although God's command not to eat is true, the presence of the tree reveals the reality; confronting it is inevitable.

The question isn't just individual. It's also communal. Answering the question at the individual level is salvation. To be righteous is to get the question right. Answering the question at the communal level is the Kingdom. It's to fundamentally transform the way we see not just ourselves, but the world around us. What would it mean to collectively reach a conclusion that God's love is, was, and always will be true? It would be the end of death.

Understanding this single point radically changes the story itself. If we understand the tree as something designed to reveal the truth – we are not defined by our own judgments – the tree becomes restorative. And we need it to be. We need a way of understanding the tree that doesn't make God look like a jerk in the process.

Unfortunately we always approach the story in hindsight. We approach the story with the same thinking that first caused the problem. We see the tree as an unfair, even tragic, moment in the past, one defining and eventually separating us from God. We create a false assumption about the story.

~~

The Command

We cannot ignore the reality that the Garden contains one single prohibitive commandment. The ramifications of this organizing structure are stunning. The entire system of human conduct rests on one prohibition. Where the Tree of Knowledge creates the means for the test, the command sets up context for the test.

The command is problematic because it is one the biggest pieces of evidence on which our traditions hang when creating an understanding of the problem. We assume the command is the establishment of God's divine law and thus unbreakable. If we do, we also assume that justice demands a punitive response. But is this what God is saying?

> And the LORD God commanded the man, "You are free to eat from any tree in the garden; but you must not eat from the tree of the knowledge of good and evil, for when you eat of it you will surely die."(Gen 2:16-17)

It's deeply important to notice God doesn't begin with "DE"manded. But it feels like a demand doesn't it? We read it as a moral structure. We project onto the story what our traditions have taught us without even realizing it. Given the circumstances and the impending consequences, you'd think God would offer a demand, but it doesn't say that.

The word is "commanded." And the difference is everything. Before we can understand the command, we first need to understand what a command is. A command is a unifying agreement of action. The prefix "co" reveals two parties are required. God presents the command, but humanity must also agree to it. The problem is the story never presents a verbal agreement to the command. Adam and Eve do verbally admit to the serpent the existence of the command, but they never verbally agree to follow it. Humanity never says, "Yes, God we agree to follow your command."

As strange as this may sound it is important to understanding what follows. God presents a command because the nature of God's kingdom is based on love. It recognizes the boundaries and responsibilities of the other. It recognizes the free will and choice we have over the self. It presupposes the individuality and distinct separateness of humanity in the Kingdom. The command is not invasive but instead hopeful.

A demand is different. The prefix of "de" does not require unity. It actually speaks of division or moving away from each other. A demand would mean the action is a requirement in the situation, which precludes choice, making it invasive. The statement "you must not" is not a demand, either because it is a condition of the command. Its meaning is still predicated on acceptance.

The command is then God's possibility. It recognizes the best possible option for humanity to take. But humanity doesn't have to take it. In this way the command shifts from invasive to invitational. It recognizes humanity's part in the picture. We can participate in God's possibility or we can try out our own. We are the "other" with a significant choice to make because the consequences affect humanity.

It's easy to see God as demanding isn't it? What if our understanding of the word, "commanded" is actually deeply shaped by our historical and even personal perception of it? We see the word command and think, "demand," because we would have made it a demand. We would have done everything possible to keep humanity from eating from the tree. But no matter how much we want it that way the Kingdom of God just doesn't work like that. Our projections reveal our naturally occurring fear about the scene of the crime.

If we're really honest, is it we who are making all of the demands in the story? We consistently demand God to show up when we want. Don't we?

They willfully put God to the test by demanding the food they craved. (Ps 78:18)

"But when that servant went out, he found one of his fellow servants who owed him a hundred denarii. He grabbed him and began to choke him.

'Pay back what you owe me!' he demanded." (Mt 18:28)

But with loud shouts they insistently demanded that he be crucified, and their shouts prevailed. (Lk 23:23)

Over and over again we make demands of God and each other. Demand is a control mechanism revealing a deeply embedded problem.

The second part of the command is also just as revealing. God's primary concern is NOT with breaking the command. God doesn't say, "If you break this I'm going to be furious." God doesn't say, "If you break this command, you will break breaking my perfect and Holy Law." God doesn't say, "If you break this command, I will rain down on you hellfire and brimstone." Once again, our traditions project these false assumptions onto the command, but these accusations simply don't exist.

What God does say is, "...for when you eat of it you will surely die." God's primary concern is not with breaking the command, which we assume creates an external, cosmic dissonance, but with the consequence of the act, which creates an internal, personal dissonance. Think about it for a minute. God's primary concern is for our welfare as human beings. If we really think about it, it's a deeply counterintuitive but whole move.

God is essentially saying, "If you trust me (the "co" part), you don't have to do this. Don't go this route. You really don't have to. But if you do, know you are going to experience something you've never known. You will experience suffering, and it's going to feel and even seem like death."

God's primary concern is not for some hidden, cosmic, moral system of law yet to be revealed. It is not for sin in the typical way we think of it. In fact, the word "sin" is never used in the entire scene of crime. God's concern is for humanity and the consequences of this one act.

And if we really think about it, what is fascinating about the command is in light of the evidence which follows; God is willing to take the risk. God is either loony, sadistic, or has something else in mind.

~~

Be Like God

It's curious how quickly the event actually happens. The story provides literally no detail of any activity before Adam and Eve are thrust into confrontation with the question. It's easy to wonder what compels humanity to take a bite. What need is manufactured that pushes them over the edge? Enter the serpent.

> *Now the serpent was more crafty than any of the wild animals the LORD God had made. (Gen 3:1a)*

The serpent is described as "crafty," a term describing a type of cleverness, or cunning. And if we look at the serpent's tactics, we see why.

> *He said to the woman, "Did God really say, 'You must not eat from any tree in the garden'?" (Gen 3:1b)*

The serpent is a messenger. It does very little other than simply pose questions. Its first question skews the data just a little, the distinction of "any," which creates a cognitive dissonance in the woman. The power is then not in the messenger, but in the message. All the serpent does is create a possibility for doubt through dialog. It can only influence humanity.

This is deeply important to understanding the nature of the problem. A lie, originally presented in the form of a question, in and of itself, is simply data. It has no power to captivate unless it is received. It needs someone to consume it. This is why God uses the concept of the fruit tree. The problem lies in the message, not in the messenger. The fruit is the recognition of consuming the message presented by the serpent.

And as we read the story we can begin to see her bite.

> *The woman said to the serpent, "We may eat fruit from the trees in the garden, but God did say, 'You must not eat fruit from the tree that is in the middle of the garden, and you must not touch it, or you will die.'"(Gen 3:2-3)*

Immediately we can sense the woman getting flustered. The data and emotions suggest where the problem is beginning to reveal itself.   The problem is occurring inside of her. She's wrestling with the reality of what she knows.

Her cognitive dissonance is revealed in how she adds to the data, which then creates an intriguing question. When does humanity actually get it wrong? The woman has already engaged a false sense of reality in order to make sense of it. She invents something neither God nor the serpent ever said. If there is an original sin in the historical sense, this is actually it. If the Garden is based upon perfection, this is the moment it gets thrown out the window. But something bristles against that possibility. It doesn't fit with our traditional assumptions of original sin because she hasn't broken the command yet.

At a deeper level, her brain is likely going haywire. Her amygdala, the portion of the brain responsible for immediate rash judgment and emotion, is thrust into overdrive as it confronts a new and strange possibility. The pre-frontal cortex, which is responsible for rational thought, is dealing with chemicals that could be potentially shutting it off. It's processing everything, trying to reference what it knows, but failing miserably.

This is a new situation, one which humanity has never before encountered. There is no data to reference in her long-term memory. This is her first EVER encounter with the nature of evil, which is something inherently untrue. It is logical to assume she has no basis for understanding it because she has no cognitive history with it.

At this point she is dealing strictly with data and emotions. She hasn't made a judgment yet of reality.

"You will not surely die," the serpent said to the woman. (Gen 3:4)

It's easy to read this in hindsight and know the serpent's intentions. We read the serpent as deceiving because we know the story. But Adam and Eve didn't have that perspective. The serpent has simply been present asking a question. And this is where we see the clever qualities of the serpent. What if the serpent is performing as a helpful friend? It is essentially saying, "Wait, didn't you get the memo? You've got it all wrong my friend. Let me tell you how this thing works." By creating doubt, the serpent has created a problem it can help solve. It creates a shared sense of connection. In this moment it is reasonable to assume the serpent is acting as a friend watching out for them. There's no obvious deviousness. The serpent's sense of craftiness is in its capacity to conceal its intentions, not flaunt them. From her perspective, it is much more likely the serpent is appealing to her goodwill.

So far the serpent has only asked questions, and the woman has developed a sense of dissonance with reality. But the questions are actually designed to set up and create a destructively cunning, false sense of need. The serpent then takes the connection to the next level to lure them.

> *"For God knows that when you eat of it your eyes will be opened, and you will be like God, knowing good and evil." (Gen 3:5)*

What is fascinating about the statement is the serpent calls out what is fundamentally true. They don't yet know good from evil. Only God does. They have never judged themselves. To "be like God" creates a false assumption of incompleteness. It stimulates a need to grasp for something already true. The serpent's statement essentially calls out a strange possibility. Is humanity incomplete if it doesn't yet know the answer? Is it fundamentally missing something central to what it means to be created in the image of God?

It is here we see the amazing cleverness of the serpent. By appealing to a natural sense of what is true about the existing situation, the serpent is able to create a false sense of need. The serpent calls out what is missing. To be like God is to know the answer to the question. The situation creates a quandary for Eve. Is humanity incomplete if it doesn't know this one thing? Does God's creation require the knowledge of good and evil in order to be whole? The space does exist but does that make us incomplete? The question demands an answer, doesn't it?

The serpent is essentially saying, "If you really want to be like God, then you actually need to do this." The need is by definition unnecessary because the judgment has already been made for them. They don't need to be like God in this way because good is not dependent on humanity's approval. They already are like God. Humanity has already been declared good. They have been designed in God's image.

And this becomes the compelling journey of the human story. They don't need to discover the knowledge of good and evil, but they choose to. To answer the question correctly is to align with the love of God. They didn't have to, but they chose to. While humanity does not have to engage it, answering the question reveals the evolution available to humanity. It reveals the central assumption the story eventually reveals. Good does not require perfect. It does not mean unchangeable. It reveals the room for humanity to evolve and grow.

The inherent problem in the journey is the possibility of getting the one question wrong. The Garden becomes the epic moment of tragedy, not because Adam and Eve are about to break God's moral law, but because they are about to get the question wrong. They are about to enter into the dark spaces of doubt, confusion and subjective judgment that lead to death. This is the captivating moment in the human story which changes everything.

It is important to recognize God is not physically present to humanity as they encounter the serpent. This lack of presence is significant because it suggests one of two things. It suggests abandonment, which is easy to feel in hindsight, or it suggests trust. God either doesn't care what happens, choosing to leave when temptation is upon us, or God really believes we can make it through whatever we will encounter.

In order for the false need to be realized Adam and Eve must agree to it. The choice resides exclusively with humanity, not in the serpent. The serpent can't force them to agree to it because the choice resides inside, in the mind. If we listen to this moment, we can feel the tension. Will they take a bite, sending them on and into the journey of the human soul, or will they reject the need and live in a state of trust with God?

We know the answer, don't we?

~~

Trick

The moment has come. The trap has been set and humanity is confronted with the Garden's only true question. Adam and Eve have the fruit in front of them. And they take a bite. Historically this moment is seen as humanity's rebellion against God. Is it really? If we examine the moment, there is virtually no evidence to support this claim.

> *"When the woman saw that the fruit of the tree was good for food and pleasing to the eye, and also desirable for gaining wisdom, she took some and ate it. She also gave some to her husband, who was with her, and he ate it." (Gen 3:7)*

First, the word rebellion is defined as, "open, organized, and armed resistance to one's government or ruler; resistance to or defiance to any authority, control, or tradition." In order for rebellion to be actualized here there would have needed to be a reasonable evidence of defiance predicated upon an agreement to the command. Yet no such agreement or intent is ever presented.

The lead-up to the moment actually suggests an entirely different story. To label the act as rebellion completely ignores the context and the content of the previous conversation, and Eve's own stated reasons.

The woman examines the fruit and recognizes its tangible value as food. Her initial reason is benign and contains no evidence of intentional rebellion. It's simply food. But her second reason also suggests rebellion is not the reason. The story states, "When the woman saw…(it was) desirable for gaining wisdom…" Her desire is to actually know what God knows. Wisdom is the knowledge of God's judgment. The problem is that with the knowledge of judgment comes the responsibility of judgment. To judge includes the possibility of getting it wrong. And God recognizes this.

Eve's second reason actually connects back to the conversation with the serpent. She has bought the serpent's idea that she needs to become like God in order to satisfy her desire for wisdom. But her choice is not realized in her being until she takes a bite. Eating is the evidence of her choice to seek out wisdom. Adam's silence further suggests evidence against rebellion. Her response is reasonable because it is not stark rebellion. He takes a bite right along with her because it reflects a good intent, even if it is based on deception.

A more appropriate understanding of intent is the exact opposite of rebellion. Her choice is rooted in her desire to become like her Creator. It is reasonable to assume her desire comes from a space of admiration for, and the desire to become like, God. God is the only parent she has ever known. In her eyes, she wants to become like the one who gave her life.

The problem is then more aptly labeled as a trick. Humanity is being deceived into seeking the knowledge of what it already has. Her reason is fueled by a deception. The act seems reasonable because it is, from her perspective, a desire to fully realize the God image in her own being. She doesn't actually need it, but she is now compelled to want it.

If humanity is truly rebelling against God, we would assume a continued response of obvious rebellion immediately following this moment, but no such response ever materializes. Humanity is not gripped by fear of condemnation. Instead, we see humanity suffering the consequences of being deceived.

It's easy to understand why we frame the story as rebellion though. Rebellion allows us to respond to the problem with a sense of self-righteous anger. It allows us to deflect responsibility for the problem believing, "We would never have done that." It allows us to play the victim, unable to respond in any way. It releases us from any responsibility to choose differently.

Shifting the story from pure rebellion to deception then radically alters our understanding of the story going forward. It allows us to see humanity as not purely evil, prone to rebellion and defiance to God. It is instead seeking after the knowledge of God but in an entirely captivating way.

~~

Realizing

The choice to seek out the knowledge of God presents a watershed moment in the human story. There can never be a moment of return to naivety. The knowledge of God requires judgment. And something definitely happens to our bodies. We feel it in our bones, don't we? But more importantly, the story reveals the change.

> *Then the eyes of both of them were opened, and they realized they were naked; so they sewed fig leaves together and made coverings for themselves. (Gen 3:7a)*

The story presents an ontological shift in the self about the self. It's local. The change is detailed in the curious phrase, "The eyes of both of them were opened..." There isn't anything else. The story doesn't reveal a cosmic change. The fabric of the cosmos is not ripped apart and God's moral law is not stepped on. There's also no contract of slavery to the serpent. It hasn't wrestled them to the ground and demanded payment from God.

Instead we read a physiological change inside the body. It's not really logical to assume it was an opening of the physical eyes, because Adam was asked to name the animals. It is reasonable then to suggest this is the birth of the ego, or the wounded self in search of validation. The ego is the twisted version of the self, struggling to survive in the midst of an incorrect judgment. Some might call it the mind's eye, the interesting image in our heads, which often seems to have a mind of its own. Some traditions call this the consciousness of the self. "Opened" seems to suggest this ability was previously there but unused or unavailable to us. We can only speculate, but their previous moment did not seem to require it. What if this is the birth of a neural pathway?

Consciousness reveals the capacity not only to be aware of the self but also to judge the self, to take on the role reserved exclusively for God. The phrase is, "And they realized they were naked." The statement immediately connects back to their previous observations. "The man and his wife were both naked, and they felt no shame."

They were already naked but initially they felt no shame. Something has changed in their awareness about their nakedness. Is it simply self-consciousness, as some would suggest? Or is it a shift in awareness of how they see what is already there? The original statement, "(they) were both naked, and they felt no shame," suggests it didn't originally seem to matter. But now it suddenly does. Humanity realizes something already true but their judgment of it changes.

Science is now discovering we have the ability to see a perceptual image even in the absence of visual input. We can imagine things we have never seen before. We experience this in our dreams all the time. Some suggest this ability lies in the thalamus because it processes all forms of perceptual data. A damaged thalamus can severely hinder perception. Others suggest the brain's electromagnetic field is actual consciousness because at the root of all matter is energy. And the point is not to lay claim to specifically where it is but that the story indicates it. The problem occurs inside the self, in the imagination.

The root problem, or the first moment when a problem arises, is then in the act of realizing, fueled by a false sense of need. Realizing means, "to make real; give reality to (a hope, fear, plan, etc.); to bring vividly to the mind." Realizing is essentially a process of bringing something into reality in our mind, or agreeing to a specific construct in our minds. Our imagination brings forth a world. The act of realizing, by definition, does not require something to be true. It just means we agree it is true.

The present reality at this moment is that they are "naked." The term means exactly what we think it means. Yet, the story claims they were already naked. Nothing has physically or cosmically changed about their outward appearance. Naked has always been true. But the acknowledgement of shame reveals their judgment about it has changed. They have constructed a reality that naked means something different than it really is.

The only question in the tree is one of value. They are naked but what is the value of that? Is it good or evil? Their shift in perception reveals their judgment on the matter. This is immediately supported by the act of "covering." If we connect it to the conversation with the serpent, it reveals the depth of what is going on. To "be like God" is a lie suggesting incompleteness, that something is missing. This initial lie fuels the need for judgment. But in order to become captive they have to judge their incompleteness as evil. The shift in thinking about the self is then an agreement to the original lie. It reveals the subjective judgment they've made about themselves. What has changed is their perception or judgment of reality.

What is remarkable about the moment is the root problem's universal nature. Humanity is wrestling with its own nakedness, an almost universal human concept. It exposes a problem of judgment, which every human being can and does wrestle with. It's not esoteric or singular to Adam's experience. It's not murder, which would exclude almost everyone. It's not specific to a certain culture or context. It's the primal fear of the idea that we are somehow incomplete, and thus invalid.

The root problem is then our capacity to create and agree to a false reality, or dichotomy. It is the capacity to construct an alternative, false reality to God's perspective, specifically in regards to our value as human beings. It places us in the category of evil. God has declared everything to be good, even very good. From God's perspective, humanity is "inside the circle" per se. Suddenly humanity has constructed a reality that sees itself as "outside the circle." They have, in essence, gotten the question wrong.

Humanity gives life to evil by constructing a realization that it is evil. They bring forth an alternative world in their minds, one that sees them as evil and thus shameful. Humanity does create the realization, but the realization is itself a false reality because it is counter to God's perspective. It is untrue. So the reality of evil is created by the agreement to, or realization of, evil. Humanity brings it into life when they accept it as true.

It is also deeply important to realize why God is not present in this moment. The story wants us to know this is NOT God's judgment. It is humanity's judgment. All of this happens before God ever arrives on the scene. The root problem is happening inside the mind.

The destructive capacity of the lie is not in the data, emotions or the circumstances. All are true. The destructive capacity resides in our agreement to an alternative false reality, or lie. Eating the fruit is the signal that Adam and Eve have accepted the agreement. By agreeing to it in their minds, humanity becomes the embodiment of evil. It becomes the host of the thought.

~~

Wrestling With Evil

Embedded within the Tree of Knowledge is one single question. Are we good or evil? Taking a bite forces humanity to wrestle with the nature of evil. And the question presupposes not one but two possibilities, a judgment of good, or a judgment of evil. Embedded in the tree is God's perspective. Good is still an option. But the question remains. Why did Adam and Eve get it wrong? Over and over God has given them the answer to the question. Over and over God has declared, "It is good." God even gives them the test with the answer on it. It's in the Tree. Their response reveals the captivating nature of the subjective judgment.

The answer is rooted in the original trick. To "be like God" requires us to judge our qualitative value, or dignity. Are we good or evil? So how do we judge what is good, or evil? How do we judge the quality of something? Judgment requires a basis for judgment. We need a reference point or objective basis to judge something on. Ultimately these are judgments reserved exclusively for God. But to judge means we must ascend to equality with God, to be an equal. And once we are in the space of equality with God a funny thing happens. We can no longer use God's declarations as an objective basis. To use them would mean recognizing God as the foundation, which defeats the purpose of trying to "be like God."

As humanity looks upon themselves, they are reminded of their need to "be like God," and judge, but they no longer have God's declarations as an objective basis for judgment of their own value. They become blind to it because of the "need" to know for themselves. Good was inherent to life before the fruit, there was no need to judge. But now they're on the other side of circumstance. Humanity has crossed the line into knowledge, which includes the experience of evil.

What they do have are three important pieces of evidence. They have evidence of eating from the tree, the fact they are still alive, and how they feel. The first piece of evidence is the fruit, which has been eaten. They have stepped outside of God's original design for life. The core sits half eaten and discarded on the ground. The second piece of evidence is the sudden reality of what the serpent said. They didn't immediately die. They are still physically alive. Did God lie? Is God then even trustworthy? The third piece of evidence is the initial overriding emotion regarding the event, which we will get to. Emotion is likely the most pressing piece of evidence because it is felt, so it cannot be ignored.

Even if they consider the echo of God's original declarations, which probably lingered in the air, what's the point? They're just words. They're just thoughts. What evidence do they have to suggest the judgment of good is the likely option, or that God's love is actually real? Adam and Eve's agreement with the original need renders them incomplete. The evidence is immediately compelling. How can they be "good" if they are incomplete? And if they are not good, that leaves one remaining answer: evil.

This is the cleverness of the trick. It creates an unsolvable paradox as long as we agree to it. We can try, but we will always fail because the framework is based on something fundamentally subjective or conditional. We instinctively feel the subjective nature of human judgment when someone judges us, especially in a negative sense. We reject the judgment because we know things the other person doesn't. The basis for judgment is different.

The root problem is based on the assumption of incompleteness, which leads to the judgment of evil. This is the core lie, that humanity is qualitatively evil. It is the second possibility embedded in the tree. They judge themselves based on the evidence and give life to something fundamentally untrue. And as long as humanity holds onto that judgment, it becomes captive to it. They don't even have to agree to evil as long as they lose the judgment of good. The doubt of good produces virtually the same outcome. The only way they can recover is to remember who they are. But how can they remember when their world is in a spin, when everything suggests otherwise?

It is reasonable to call this moment traumatic in the truest sense of the word. This is the first moment in the story when humanity is thrust upon the unknown in the most extreme of circumstances. They have no basis for understanding it. In the midst of trauma everything is affected. Studies show that during trauma time seems to slow down. Our vision can close down to a small hole. Our hearing can literally shut off. But it is the initial memory in trauma that is important because it creates the reference point. Like Bob's experience with his mother, the primary judgment overwhelms humanity. If we agree with the judgment we're then predisposed to look for evidence to support it. The only way to overcome that reference point is to discover evidence that overwhelms it. We need something stronger than the original reference point.

The root problem then projects outward. Humanity's ability to relate is always based on its relationship to what is true. When we are good, it is easy to see everything as good. But if this base is somehow taken away from us, our frame of reference becomes skewed. The judgment leads to a natural series of ontological questions in order to construct a sense of reality.

If I am evil, is God good?

If God is evil, can I be good?

If God is evil, is my neighbor good?

If my neighbor is evil, is the world good?

If the whole world is evil, what is the point?

Who can humanity possibly trust? The evidence of covering and hiding reveals the downward spiral of judgment. Humanity gets it wrong. Good was the original basis for judgment. To lose it means to steal away our ability to judge everything. Like the woman with MS, the "other" actually becomes a reminder of the problem.

The loss of judgment doesn't mean we can't or don't judge. It just means our ability to judge is severely hampered because we have no basis for objectivity in the questions that really matter. When we play God, everything becomes subjective, because we are ultimately fallible. Each person's judgment process becomes his or her own. What is true for one person isn't necessarily true for another. The effectiveness of the trick wasn't just in the agreement, but in the agreement's ability to steal away our base of judgment to produce the right answer.

The overriding fear is that we actually are evil. It's a paradoxical problem of debilitating proportions and is essentially unsolvable. If we are, we are. If we are not, we are not. We have absolutely no say in the matter if either one is true. We can give into the evil and live into nihilism. We can live in a state of blindness and pretend the problem doesn't exist. Or we can take the risk that it's untrue and attempt to transcend the problem. This is the journey of faith.

~~

Constructing Reality

The Garden presents the birth of duality. For humanity, there is now good AND evil. Humanity constructs a world outside of God's acceptance. This construction of reality happens in the mind. To really grasp the root problem it is helpful to understand how the mind and our imagination work to produce the problem which leads to suffering. To participate in the end of suffering we have to begin to understand how we create it in the first place.

In many ways our mind and imagination can be seen and experienced as a creative force. They construct a judgment of the world in which we live. This duality of good and evil only exists in our imagination, but we give it life and consequence with our actions. We construct it in our mind and project that reality onto the tangible world in which we live in. The problem creates dissonance in our bodies, which creates suffering. Suffering is a loud voice in the process. As neuroscience begins to reveal how the brain works, researchers are discovering the amazingly simple patterns which are once again so obvious as to be tragic.

The brain's natural capacity for constructing a realization, true or false, is essentially a process of reading data and emotion to create judgment, which we package as a story. The body sends signals to the brain through the spinal cord and up to the amygdala, where it initially processes information. The data is often called "gossip" because some of it is true but some of it is also conjecture. We learn to fill in missing pieces of data with what we think is there.

The amygdala is likely what we call the "heart" because it is often considered the irrational or emotional portion of the brain. It listens to the gossip and suggests an emotional reaction and judgment of the situation. We feel the effects of emotion in the body, especially in our chest around the physical heart.

This content is then sent to the prefrontal cortex, which is the rational part of the brain. It is important to comprehend that the data and judgments don't have to be true to be sent from the amygdala to the prefrontal cortex. Information can be true in the sense that it feels true because our bodies have produced an emotional response to it, or that the data suggests it is true. The body can then create a reverse engineered validation system, independent of what is actually true. We think it's true because of the gossip and emotional content attached to it.

The prefrontal cortex then re-examines the content using a rational judgment process. This process is called a learning event. Learning events don't happen instantaneously. They occur over time. If the prefrontal cortex validates the content, it stores the information as a pattern or story of how we think the world works. But when we revisit an event, or something remotely similar triggering the original memory, it is then pulled out of storage for reference. We reexamine the previous event in relationship to the new one using the new data. This process of reexamination is called "reconstitution."

The original stories are deepened or weakened. Both are possible. If the new data weakens the original reference story it fails to produce the same charge. But the story is deepened if the new data seems to support it. The memory is repackaged in chemicals, solidifying it and then storing it as a long-term memory. Long-term stored memories become fairly permanent and fixed. We create our worldview from these long-term memories.

During trauma, or hyper real situations, the amygdala can literally take over the body as a survival mechanism. Cortisol is released into the system, which speeds up sensory perception but turns off immune responses. This process can also literally turn off the rational part of the brain for a short period of time. The irrational brain goes into overdrive trying to create some kind of survival response, which we call the fight/flight impulse.

Unfortunately, the brain is predisposed to actually look for data to support the event. Using a process called "bias assimilation," the brain will actually search for data to reinforce the current story and potentially ignore what contradicts it. The most obvious piece of data supporting the judgment of evil is the lack of presence of God. God is not there. Could it be that God has abandoned them because they actually are evil?

It is also important to ask why the event at the tree possibly takes precedence over God's original declarations. In the first moment of judgment they have no reference point in their bodies for shame. They have no equilibrium to understand it is a signal pointing to the presence of a problem. The moment of judgment is likely similar to a car crash. It takes over their bodies. The emotions of the event are so overwhelming because they are the first tangible experiences in their bodies. Judgment produces a debilitating physical response of shame because they assume they ARE the problem.

It is important to assert once again what is happening in the Garden is an emotionally traumatic event. This is the first time humanity has ever experienced the captivating consequence of judgment. Given there is no previous learning event to reference; they are for all intents and purposes physically captivated by the experience because they have no basis for understanding reality. Their logical reasoning would be that of a child. But it is not just the timing of the story that suggests immaturity. The evidence of their response does as well.

~~

The Covering

The nature of their judgment is to hide what is true. It literally covers the God imagination in their minds. This process of covering continues as they project it outward into the physical reality in which they live. In order for evil to hide in plain sight, it needs to be protected.

The original judgment is an action which produces a reaction. Their very first reaction is to participate in their own oppression. They create a physical covering to hide the evidence of their nakedness, which is true. The covering is a projected extension of the root problem embedded within. It creates a physical veil of deception blinding humanity from the God imagination. Humanity can no longer see the true self.

So they sewed fig leaves together and made coverings for themselves. (Gen 3:7b)

Here we see the lie play out its amazing capacity for deception. The reaction reveals they are convinced something about them is wrong and needs covering. They partner with the lie to hide what is true. The lie is now embodied inside humanity. But because it is inside humanity, they cannot separate themselves from it. They are convinced they are evil.

The act of covering hides what is true. The covering keeps us from seeing God's perspective in the matter. It keeps us from engaging reality. It first keeps us from identifying the lie. It blinds us to the reality of its existence. It numbs our senses and dulls our existence.

Think about that for a second. Humanity participates in hiding what is true… from itself. Covering is then an act of self-deception perpetuated BY the self. This is part of the trick. In the act of covering the God image, we actually propel ourselves into the downward spiral. We hide ourselves from the very thing revealing the truth. But what happens when we cover the God imagination? We lose the capacity to inform ourselves about who we are. We lose our identity in the process. We lose any capacity to see our dignity or purpose.

The question is then, why do they take on the cover? Why cover something reflecting reality? What if the answer resides in the volatile cocktail of both good and evil? As human beings created in the image of God, they possess immense power and creativity. As history will eventually reveal, what makes us capable of such art and beauty is also what makes us capable of such horrific violence. Mixed together it becomes a paradox.

If humanity is created in the image of God, if it does have the God imagination, if it is truly divine, the God image must be covered to protect humanity from itself. If humanity is capable of evil, then it must be controlled. The lesser of two evils is to hide the God imagination to control its destructive capacity. We hide the reality of our own divinity as a protective mechanism for ourselves, and for the world around us.

The covering then provides us with a distraction. It allows us to focus on secondary problems because it distracts us from the root problem. We hold onto it as a coping mechanism so we can deal with the root problem. But once again as we do so, it continues to hold us in captivity.

~~

The Chasm

Everything hinges on our perception of the root problem. What happens to the self the moment we experience evil? The primary transgression in the Garden is the judgment of the self, which creates a captive state to a lie and blinds us to our inherent dignity. To protect ourselves we create a covering that outwardly hides the God reflection and blinds us from our identity. But the final act of hiding blinds us from our purpose, which is to rule over our own emotions.

> *Then the man and his wife heard the sound of the LORD God as he was walking in the garden in the cool of the day, and they hid from the LORD God among the trees of the garden. (Gen 3:8)*

The man and the woman run. The emotional content becomes overwhelming and instead of overcoming the event, instead of ruling over it, it rules over them. The flight reflex has taken over. The lie has completely distorted everything.

The oppression is fully embedded.

What compels humanity to hide is an important piece of data, one of the most defining questions in the story. What is God's response to human captivity? What does justice truly look like?

It is here that our imaginations run wild, don't they? The void in our collective conscience demands a response the moment we do something self-destructive. How will God respond when our actions affect God's creation? And because we are part of creation, because we are personally involved, we want to know how God feels about it. This is the overriding question. But if the God imagination is covered, how can we see God's response, which is defined by what is true?

Instead of rationally waiting for God to respond, we assume an answer. We construct a reality about God's response based on our own imagination.

And they hid from the LORD God among the trees of the garden. (Gen 3:8b)

Before God has even arrived on the scene they have assumed God's anger and wrath. The only reason to fear someone is if there is potential harm. But their hiding reveals their assumptions about their circumstance. The projection is largely informed by how they feel about what happened. Their identity, or how they see themselves, is now informed by the event instead of by God's declarations. Their dignity is informed by the limitations of their own constructed identity. Who could love them if they are the sum of their circumstances and consequences?

Instead of dealing with the root problem, which is the incorrect judgment of the self, or the secondary problem of the covering, or the tertiary problem of purpose, there is now a massive fourth problem. What is the nature of justice in a subjective perspective?

If we get this question wrong – and humanity does – it produces a perceptual consequence called the chasm. The chasm is the assumption of separation. As opposed to being fully informed by God, they now see themselves as apart from God. If humanity judges itself by its own standard, God can't love them.

Justice demands a verdict and they are guilty. Humanity assumes God is no longer pleased with them. They assume God's rejection by their hiding.

The chasm becomes virtually insurmountable for several very specific reasons. First, the only way to restore the problem is to descend from this imaginary space of equality, and to render judgment back to God. But how can they trust again when trusting has just burned them? To step down puts them at risk of a God who might be like them, like us, one who could kill us for what we've done. If God were in our place, we would probably do the same. Evil must be removed, right? It's just easier and safer to remain in hiding, to avoid the question. It's easier to suffer under the weight of not knowing rather than discover the possibility our imagination might just be right.

Second, our subjective sense of justice continues to captivate us regardless of our hiding. Our bodies have to know. This question of justice is a search for God's response. It is our quest for theology. The covering hides the God imagination, which is God's perspective. It hides our ability to understand God's response to our transgressions. It hides our understanding of true justice, which is based on God's original perspective.

But instead of simply surrendering in trust, we search for an irrefutable theology, or logic of God. We attempt to construct an image of what God looks like based upon our own logical reasoning. To test it, we project our image of God onto the world. And like a puzzle we carefully and not so carefully put the pieces together. And what we end up with is still a subjective understanding of God through the covering.

God's response of grace doesn't make sense. Grace is entirely illogical from a subjective perspective. If validation resides in action, we are guilty. Justice is punitive so it can control destructive action. To excuse guilt would appear to validate the same action against us. And we can't have that. We miss out on the idea that grace is the act of overcoming the subjective judgment and consequence by rooting ourselves in the God imagination, not the act of excusing it as though it doesn't matter.

Third, our hiding isn't just from God. If humanity is evil, where do we go to hide from ourselves? Where do we go to deal with our own judgments residing inside of us? Avoiding the judgments allows us to ignore the lie creating the problem. It allows us to play victim – or worse, perpetrator – to our own humanity. It's just easier, isn't it? Facing the consequences means facing the possibility we actually are evil, which is a dead end. God's own words, "...for when you eat of it you will surely die," have become true but not in the way they expected.

~~

The First Death

It is here we see the first definition of death: the concealment of the true self. Without the God imagination, which informs our understanding of our dignity, identity, and purpose, we are essentially dead. We have no meaning or reason for being. The dignity that once informed our hearts has now been hidden away by the evidence of our own making. A covering has concealed identity. Our own running has hidden our purpose.

Death was first about losing the ability to see the true self, the one informed by the God imagination. We judge and declare our own guilt before God has ever arrived on the scene of the crime. And in response, we cast our own image back onto God and assume a response of anger and wrath.

The act of hiding becomes an act of running from our true self, which is found back at the scene of the crime. To hide is to invalidate the self in such a way as to become both the victim and the perpetrator. Both identities are intrinsically intertwined. Once we choose the path of victim, to run and hide, we in turn perpetrate on the self. Once we become the perpetrator, to fight back and lash out, we victimize ourselves. Both responses deepen the problem instead of solving it.

Our neighbor, or the other, also becomes a problem. If the "other" is evil, then we must remove it because it reminds us of what we are. If the "other" is good, then we must remove it because it reminds us of what we are not.

This shadow of death will eventually extend even further. If this life is really all there is, then we're compelled to make the most of it. It this is all there is, then killing the other becomes pragmatic, even prudent. Evil becomes a necessity for survival. We must protect ourselves at all costs because there isn't another chance. The only way to survive is to actually embody evil in its fullest form, to kill the other. Once we agree to become evil, to engage a pragmatic nihilism, we validate the subjective standard judging us as evil, which approves of others killing us.

Every relationship becomes distorted because life is subjective. Our image of the true self is lost, our image of God is warped, and our image of the other is self-destructive. And so, our worldview is regressively lost.

Reconciling our understanding of existence becomes impossible unless we listen to the one clarion call we all have: pain and suffering. The only way to overcome death is to face it, to stare it in the face and say, "You don't define me." When we face the fear and discover the God imagination, we expose the reality: we actually are good. But to embrace that possibility we need someone who will show us the Way.

~~

Finding Jesus

This is the scene of the crime in all of its strange detail. This is THE pivotal moment in the human story. It is the moment when everything turns south. This is not just their story. It is the human story. It is our story. We feel it moment by moment in our judgments, conflicts, and the tension of our social interactions. It is the memory we can't repress because it is deeply embedded in our DNA.

But before we leave the scene of the crime, we need to do one last thing. We need to discover Jesus in the Garden. Like Bob, we need to step out of our boxes and discover that Jesus was always there. We just have to look for him. If the cross does anything, it informs us of the fact God has not abandoned us. In our deepest moment of tragedy, Jesus is present, standing by our side. We just have to look.

And when we do, we see not an angry, removed God watching over humanity, waiting to catch us. We see the face of the Father crying out for his children knowing this is the harder path to walk. It's going to hurt. It's going to get messy and ridiculously ugly. But it is the path ultimately revealing what is true.

Exploring the scene of the crime allows us to revisit what happened, to discover a fresh perspective to our previous assumptions, historical traditions and judgments. Our historical approaches to the story may still exist, but now we can begin considering the possibility of a new, potentially better story.

The point of exploring is not to excuse or ignore what happened, as if it doesn't matter. To simply consider this as a comedy of errors ignores the brutal consequences of what is happening. Humanity is responsible for the choices we make, and we suffer the consequences for it. To offer amnesty ignores the importance of calling out what is true. To consider this a tragedy ignores the profound possibility of reconciliation embedded with the story. To assume nothing happened, ignores the profound consequences evident in history. To demand punitive justice ignores the reality and presence of grace.

True justice requires both grace and truth. God's response is restorative, even when we don't think it should be. But because we are personally involved, because this is our story, we tend to get it wrong. We often forget grace has never left.

The point of exploring the origins of the problem is not to revel in it but to discover the nature of reconciliation, to understand what problems God is actually solving in the story. It is to begin the process of reconciling the evidence against our historical assumptions. But to get there we need a whole story. We need evidence that God really is whole. We need an imaginative hope that overcoming death is possible.

If we get this part of the story wrong, our conclusions are predicated on a false assumption. Our lens for understanding the conflict is blurry at best and we end up with different versions that simply won't reconcile. The problem literally blinds us to seeing God's response because we have written it for him in blood.

And because we are personally involved, letting go of our assumptions is really hard to do for three reasons. First, to question the historical assumptions means that good people we trusted potentially got it wrong. This is a very hard realization to reconcile. It is sometimes just easier to ignore the possibility than confront it. But history clearly reveals we've already charted that path. If we've engaged it before, we can do it again.

Second, reconciling our assumptions sometimes requires leaving old stories behind. It means digging up and reconstituting old reference points, even painful ones. It means starting over again and building new ones. But it also means we're finally answering the deeper questions in our souls, the ones haunting us when we sleep.

Third, reconciling our own assumptions means we just might have to engage our own restoration. It means we just might have to tear away the covering which blinds us to the God imagination. It means coming out of hiding to discover our worst fears aren't true. It means engaging the Way of Jesus as a means of discovering life. To discover the root problem and fail to act would be nothing short of a tragedy.

The presence of a problem is evident. The story consistently points to something happening. Understanding the problem is critical to understanding the story of justice and reconciliation. It allows us to begin building a better story about what is true, so that we can confront the lies that are untrue.

Chapter 4 – A Mystery to Solve

"When we remember we are all mad, the mysteries disappear and life stands explained." - Mark Twain

Concealment

The scene of the crime gives way to a very long story of reconciliation. But if we get the scene of the crime wrong, we're likely to construct theories that support the problem as opposed to solve it. We cannot ignore that our traditional theories have significant problems. What if these carefully constructed theories are actually natural extensions of the root problem?

To grasp how this is possible we have to understand the nature of the lie. A lie by design is something untrue attempting to become true. It can only do that through a host. It needs someone to agree to it. And when we do, we no longer see it for what it is – something untrue – so that we can reject it. We tuck it into our subconscious for the very reason that it is true for us. This agreement validates it as something to store away in our long-term memory. Our body then uses the data as a reference point for understanding reality in the future. We can't see the true nature of it unless we agree it is untrue.

Our bodies are naturally designed to detect the problem. The design compelling us to survive is also the design compelling us to live. Our bodies produce tension, fear, guilt, and even suffering to let us know something is wrong. If we assume we are the problem, as opposed to the lie being the problem, the root problem persists. We protect the embedded information as opposed to rooting it out.

The easiest way for the root problem to survive is for it to be projected onto somebody else. By nature we project by casting an image outward. The God image was cast onto us. We just continue the process. If we're concerned with other people's response to the problem, what better way to prolong it than to make it someone else's problem? The obvious candidates in the story are God, Satan, and our neighbor. Both traditional theories of the problem project the problem outward.

When we cast the problem outward it becomes drama. Drama is manufactured conflict. It allows us to play the victim. We manufacture emotional content, which produces sympathy from those around us. We focus on the fruit of the problem rather than on the root. Hiding is in essence drama. It's a manufactured scenario designed to deflect our attention from the real problem. If our focus is on a secondary problem, we're not going to have time or awareness to solve the root problem.

Drama gives us an alternative problem to solve. Instead of the problem being ours, it is now circumstances and other people that need to change. This usually includes complex scenarios and paradoxes, which are typically impossible to actually reconcile. We create impossible barriers in order to garner sympathy.

Both of our historical theories follow this same pattern. Ransom Theory projects it onto Satan. Penal Subsitutionary Atonement Theory projects it onto God. We become the unwitting victims with no way to escape captivity. We don't have to, nor can we really do anything to, solve the problem. It's someone else's problem.

The sad part is these theories are just good enough to keep us sedated but captive. We justify them as reasonable because they kind of make sense. Over time we even defend them because they are all we have. And if anyone disagrees with our stories, we call them a heretic, a rather ironic way for the lie to defend itself. Rather than listen to the questions of those who critique, which also invites us to check our assumptions, we dig in and defend ourselves, regardless of the validity of our assumptions. Alternatives stories have meaning because they work almost well enough. But what is possibility for one generation is tradition for the next. This is the history of religion.

The force of the theory lies in its myth and longevity. It's been around longer than us and has been already been debated for centuries. Great people have followed it, people we admire and trust. It provides meaning in the gathering and practice of ritual and story. The story informing the tradition eventually gets lost simply because, "This is the way we've always done it."

Once a professional class has been established to administer the practices of rituals in the tradition, the original story inevitably becomes dogma. Traditions become dogma when those who hold them fail to entertain Socratic questioning or inquiry, when there simply is no other possibility. The fear of questions actually reveals the underlying, ironic tension embedded within the traditions. Dogma stifles growth because those who are actually trying to engage it through questions are often ridiculed for their desire to root out the conflicts.

It is important to say that none of these defense mechanisms are inherently intentional. For the most part we are blind to the underlying mechanisms creating them. No one sets out to create a theory that doesn't work, or that perpetuates the problem. There is no value in pointing fingers or blaming someone. These only continue the problem. The next step is to confront the problem itself.

~~

The Paschal Mystery

The traditional theories of reconciliation are often called atonement theories. They are a means of understanding both the problem and the solution. Atonement simply means "at-one-ment". It is big word for describing reconciliation between God and humanity and how we cross or eliminate the chasm between the two. Each theory describes both the problem and the solution.

These atonement theories come out of the Christian tradition, but they actually originate from stories in the Jewish tradition. The Jewish people were tasked with telling and eventually writing down the human story. The Christian tradition recognizes the Jewish tradition because it provides the basis for understanding the human story and the origin of the problem.

The Christian tradition culminates at the cross. Something happened there that changed everything. The problem is, Jesus didn't spell it all out. Instead of drafting a neat document explaining it all, Jesus lets us wrestle with its meaning. His own followers were often dumbfounded as to his purpose. At his most pressing moment of death most of his followers abandoned him, because they misunderstood or didn't know what he was doing. After Jesus died, someone had to figure out what it all meant.

Much of Paul's letters to the surrounding ecclesia was an attempt to explore the meaning of what had happened. If we look at the two major pivot points in the story, the Fall and the cross, or the problem and the solution, we might think the answer will be clear. But it's not. By the second century, Greek scholars began to ask, "What is the problem the cross is solving?" And surprisingly, religious scholars have disagreed for more than 18 centuries. In a quest for a coherent theology, they grappled once again with the fundamental nature of reconciliation. The question then becomes: "What is the problem being solved in each theory?"

This problem later became known as the Paschal Mystery, Paschal meaning lamb, and described the mystery of the exact nature of the problem being solved on the Cross. How do we engage reconciliation if we're not even sure of the problem we are solving? How can we effectively participate with God if we don't know what exactly we're engaging? And secondly, what are the consequences of attempting to solve the wrong problem? The Way of Jesus could end up looking exactly like religion all over again.

The first major tradition was called the Classical Theory, later called the Ransom Theory. Much of the basis for Ransom Theory was credited to Irenæus and later Origen in the third century. The Ransom Theory was based on Jesus' own words.

For even the Son of Man did not come to be served, but to serve, and to give his life as a ransom for many. (Mk 10:45)

Ransom Theory essentially posited this: Adam and Eve sold themselves, and subsequently humanity, over to Satan at the Fall. This captivity required a payment from God for their release. God, being the smart one, essentially tricked the Devil into accepting Jesus' death on the cross as a form of payment, because even death could not hold Jesus in hell.

Ransom Theory located the problem in Satan's dominion over humanity for the sake of justice. Origen argued:

> *"The payment could not be [made] to God [be]cause God was not*
> *holding sinners in captivity for a ransom, so the payment had to be to the*
> *devil."*

The Ransom Theory was adopted by many of the early church fathers, including Augustine of Hippo, and was the dominant formal theory for over 800 years. It is still considered to be the dominant theory of the Eastern Orthodox Church.

Ransom Theory suffered from terrible inconsistencies. Many argue Origen's theory ascribed a ridiculous sense of power to an entity created by God. Zechariah 3 as well as the story of Job revealed Satan only had the power to accuse, tempt, or inflict harm, and then only at God's discretion. The theory was helped by a distorted sense of justice, which held God captive to an unknown cosmic contract. It also required God to act in a deceitful manner to win the release of humanity.

In the eleventh century, an Italian Benedictine monk named Anselm of Canterbury offered a second tradition known as the Substitution Theory, which later became the basis for John Calvin's Penal Substitutionary Atonement.

Anselm took the opposite approach, locating the problem in God. Anselm argued:

> *"(to sin is for man) not to render his due to God."*

Anselm contended that man's refusal to render his due (or will) unto God incurred a debt. In other words, when humanity broke the command, divine justice required retribution and punishment. God's sense of justice essentially trapped humanity in a debtor's state which we had no way of escaping. The death of Jesus was in essence a substitutionary payment for humanity's debt to satisfy God's sense of justice. But unlike Ransom, in Anselm's theory the payment was being made to God.

The noted theologian and lawyer John Calvin took it a step further by emphasizing the penalty aspect of the atonement. He argued that the only appropriate punishment for the crime was "eternal death". The Penal Substitutionary Atonement Theory eventually became the dominant theory of the Western church.

Although widely adopted, Anselm's and later Calvin's theories produced significant paradoxes as well. The most notable paradox was, "Why would a loving God create a world that would eventually require the death of his own Son?" Many scholars have questioned the use of violence as a means of redemption when God speaks so intently on desiring mercy.

In the fifteenth century, an Italian theologian named Faustus Socinus argued that Calvin's version was "irrational, incoherent, immoral and impossible." He argued four responses to Calvin's theory: Giving pardon does not square with taking satisfaction: there is nothing that conforms with justice about punishing the innocent and letting the guilty go free, the temporary death of one is not a substitute for the eternal death of many, and perfect substitutionary satisfaction would confer on its beneficiaries an unlimited permission to sin.

It should be acknowledged that there are several other historical theories of atonement. The two most notable are Gustaf Aulen's Christus Victor and Peter Abelard's Moral Exemplar. Christus Victor assumes Jesus is a ransom payment, but suggests the cross was a voluntary act on Jesus' part, as opposed to a demand of God. Moral Exemplar Theory avoids the problem altogether, suggesting the cross is a moral example to follow for humanity. Both are not widely held and contain many of the same problems and paradoxes of the previous two theories.

Every major theory casts the problem outward. It sees the problem as satisfaction to someone else. Humanity breaks the law and someone else requires justice. Someone else is getting paid off for our guilt. Ransom Theory pays off Satan. Substitution Theory pays off God.

What is interesting about these theories is how humanity essentially gets left out of the picture. We are the worm, the depraved, the hopeless, and the victims. We are the observer with virtually no part in the cosmic play. Everything is done for us. All we can do is stand back and acknowledge it happened.

And we wonder why nobody does anything. There is no intrinsic mobilizing story compelling us to take part in the process. We're supposed to be grateful, but the gratefulness we feel leaves us cold. Something feels manufactured – or worse, untrue. And without a better alternative, many who question the theories are left standing at a dead end.

~~

Locating The Problem

But what if there was another alternative? What if there was a different lens in which to see the problem? What if there was a third option in the atonement, one that reconciled with the story? And if we were willing to be honest, to really see where the problem resided, it would give us the intrinsic mobilizing story that would transform the way we see everything.

There are only four entities in the Garden: humanity, the serpent, God, and the command. Ransom Theory originally located the problem in Satan. Penal Substitutionary Atonement Theory located the problem in God, and some would add in the law. But no major theory locates the problem in humanity.

If we locate the problem in the serpent, we're ascribing power to an entity that only has the capacity to influence, or inflict consequence at the discretion of God. All the serpent does is tell a lie. The serpent is essentially the messenger. To locate the problem in the serpent is to make humanity the victim. Yet it is humanity who accepts the lie and agrees to it.

If we locate the problem in God, we're left with a strange image of a God demanding the death of his Son to satisfy his own anger. To locate the problem in God means something must have changed in God in regards to creation. Yet God has spent the entire creative process declaring his judgment on humanity's value. This value is not based on human effort, or subjective judgment. It's based on God's love. To suddenly change this opinion means God's love is subjective and conditional.

If we locate the problem in the command, it requires humanity to have agreed with the command, which it never does. If God imposes on Adam and Eve something that they haven't agreed to, how can God hold them accountable for breaking it? It also creates several moral paradoxes. If Jesus becomes the substitution, thus taking on the penalty, how is He able to transcend the penalty He has taken on? If God's justice requires atonement, why does God wait four thousand years to solve the problem? How can God interact with humanity and even declare Abram righteous by faith without atonement?

These theories create more problems because they cast the problem outward. They may be historical but they aren't compelling because they try to solve the wrong problem, one that doesn't even exist. So who is left? Who else is in the Garden?

We are!

The root problem in the story is located in us, as if this isn't obvious by now. We are captive to the lie because we have agreed to it. If we locate the problem in humanity, everything shifts. Everything changes. We can begin to describe the problem for what it is, a lie that captivates the human mind.

If we locate the problem in humanity, it liberates God from being deceptive or requiring violent responses. It liberates us from a victimization that allows us to sit on the sidelines, watching and waiting for God to respond. If we locate the problem in humanity it opens our eyes to the fact that we are the ones making the violent demands. We are the ones requiring proof. The cross becomes a means to prove what always has and always will be true – humanity is qualitatively good regardless of our subjective judgments.

Jesus even tells us this truth, locating the problem for us.

> *Blind Pharisee! First clean the inside of the cup and dish, and then the*
> *outside also will be clean. (Mt 23:26)*

Jesus first located the problem within humanity. He understood the problem was the subjective judgment embedded within us, convincing us we were evil. As long as we held onto the problem, we would embody it. We would continue to produce fruit, consistently reinforcing the distorted image we were holding onto. The lie comes from outside of us, but it can only affect us when we receive it, when we consume it by agreeing with it. The captivating force in the lie is not in the data but in our agreement with the lie.

Locating the problem allows us to begin separating ourselves from it. We are not the problem. The problem is the problem. Once we understand the problem is not us but the lie we are holding onto, we can begin to separate ourselves from it. We can see it for what it really is: something deceiving us. Some Eastern traditions would call this "awareness". It is seeing the problem as separate from our created humanity.

This posture of seeing the problem as the problem releases us from identifying ourselves with the problem. We no longer need to be victims of some unchangeable force, controlling us at will. We no longer have to wait for a passive God who doesn't seem to show up. We can begin to address it by participating with God in the restoration of all creation.

Most of Jesus' interactions with demons reveal this. The problem is something within humanity, but apart from humanity. A "demon" is simply an expressive manifestation of the lie embodied in the person. So when Jesus casts out the demons, He is essentially casting out the lies. And what is left is a human being, unhinged from the problem. The response is an immediate change because the impetus creating the problem has been removed.

~~

Satisfaction

Part of what keeps historical traditions alive is the truth of their fundamental ideas. Ransom Theory and the Penal Substitutionary Atonement Theory get some of it right. Someone is receiving a ransom. Someone is being satisfied. Someone is being paid off. Someone can't come to a sense of justice apart from a sacrifice. But the entity making the demand is not Satan or God.

It is us.

This is the beginning piece to reconciling the story. It is the missing piece of the puzzle. It is the key to unlocking the Kingdom of God in our midst. What is arguably shocking about the story, but not surprising from the perspective of love, is that God satisfies our demands. The cross becomes the fullest expression that love actually is true. Love wins by going as far as we demand. Love takes on our worst by revealing its best.

Satisfaction is our demand for tangible evidence of God's original declaration of "good". It's our requirement for God to provide the one piece of evidence that will shatter our preconceived judgment about our own humanity. It is the word "good" made flesh.

Atonement is about satisfying our own sense of guilt. God didn't need it. We did. It is satisfying our own distorted sense of justice, which demanded payment. The ransom is a payment to humanity. It is about releasing us from captivity to our own judgments. It is about providing the undeniable evidence that love is absolutely true.

Only with payment could we see that God's original declarations were true. We needed evidence. We needed something so inconceivable, so unmistakably loving, that it would shatter any argument we could make to the contrary. Much of the religious process, as we will explore, is humanity defining the means by which it would agree upon satisfaction.

Chapter 5 – The Fruit Of The Problem

"I need direction to perfection, no, no, no, no. Help me out." - Brandon Flowers

Orientation

All great stories have a problem to solve and ours is no exception. But before we explore how God is solving the problem, it is important to see how the problem manifests in humanity and how God initially responds to the problem. Once we separate ourselves from the problem, we can begin to see through an entirely different lens, one revealing God's restorative response.

The agreement to the lie produces an embedded captivating story within humanity. As long as we agree to the lie, we can't see its basic captivating nature, which also means we can't solve it. This poses an interesting problem for God to solve. How do you convince someone that something is untrue when they have convinced themselves it IS true? How do you help someone discover or "realize" a different reality? This is God's mission, to convince humanity of what is true in order to release it from the lie.

The story presents a completely counterintuitive response. It's as if God is either oblivious to the problem, doesn't care, or is unphased by what is happening. God's initial posture suggests the problem is not as big as we make it.

> *Then the man and his wife heard the sound of the LORD God as he was walking in the garden in the cool of the day... (Gen 3:8)*

Once again, we must confront our historical assumptions. If they are correct and the problem is in God, it would seem like God would rush in like an overwrought parent, furious at the imposition, and demand an answer. God is angry for what Adam and Eve have done, right? But God doesn't do that. God arrives on the scene almost strolling in.

We must confront also our historical assumptions about the basic nature of God. If God is God, then what happened as an event is already true before it happened. The event has already happened in kairos. God is already aware of what is going on and has planned for this. And it is here we can begin to see the story with a very different lens. From God's perspective, what has happened cannot change what is true. Circumstance or even judgments cannot change humanity's dignity, identity or purpose. From God's perspective, the event does not define humanity. But it does affect them. It does have consequences.

Once we see God's perspective, we can begin to see how God immediately transcends the circumstance. Grace is immediately present because the problem is not in God. God remains whole. God meets humanity in the midst of its fear and shame.

But the LORD God called to the man, "Where are you?" (Gen 3:9)

It is easy to assume this is a question of location, as though God can't see them. But that idea ignores the nature of God. God can see everything. What if, instead, the question is one of orientation, or of how they see themselves? The question actually calls out the problem in a very relational way. We see this in people when they are lost in thought, confused and distracted. We know something is going on inside. They are here, but they are really seeing themselves as somewhere else. Their orientation is off.

Orientation calls out the reality of the chasm which exists in their minds. They no longer see themselves as a welcome part of God's kingdom. They are outside of God's care, concern, and even grace. We see the evidence for this in the man's response.

He answered, "I heard you in the garden, and I was afraid because I was naked; so I hid." (Gen 3:10)

We do this, don't we? We instinctively place ourselves outside of God's

Kingdom. Our assumptions begin with incompleteness. We see the reality of human brokenness and assume God can't love us. We see the evidence in our own lives and judge ourselves ruthlessly. We create a chasm between God and us. And the problem drives us away from God, rather than towards God. But we can only discover what is true when we are in harmony with God.

Disorientation is the problem acted out. Humanity judges itself before God arrives on the scene, assumes God is angry, and hides in fear. God's very first response is to seek out the lost child so it can be found. God immediately crosses the chasm and comes to Adam and Eve. But who really needs to do the finding? We do. We need to find ourselves. It is humanity that needs to be discovered. The question actually reveals the deep love of God, which is to seek out the lost. God's first act is then restorative, and reveals the central nature of the mission of God.

God then begins the process of restoration, which always begins with confession. God immediately draws out the lie.

And he said, "Who told you that you were naked?" (Gen 3:11a)

The only reason humanity has for using "naked" as an excuse is if there is something wrong with being naked. Nothing has changed here. Humans have always been naked. But now their judgment about it has changed. They have become conscious of the self in a way that now reveals their judgment of the self. It's as if God is saying, "Who told you that you were incomplete?"

God draws the obvious connection.

"Have you eaten from the tree that I commanded you not to eat from?"
(Gen 3:11b)

It's so easy to read God's statement from a position of contempt, isn't it? We assume we would never make the same mistake. We judge because it is someone else. Yet God is not responding from contempt. This is God's creation. It is still good.

The question is actually drawing out a much-needed confession. It's calling out the facts. Why? Because the only way to begin releasing the lie is to acknowledge the data and to process the learning event again, to reconstitute it, seeing it from a rational perspective. If we pull the data out, we can begin seeing it from God's perspective. The underlying judgments are not true. God understands that the lie wants to hide. It wants to remain hidden inside of humanity. And confession begins the slow painful process of uncovering the lie.

True justice begins with confession, with calling out the evidence of what is true. It begins with discovering what is true so we can see the lie for what it really is. When we confess, we are actually engaging in our own restoration. To confess is to step out of the false identity of victim, and rediscover our own humanity, which is based on responsibility and rule of the self.

This is the value of seeing the problem from God's perspective. What happened is true. They ate the apple. They stepped outside of God's will and design. How they felt about it is true. They felt fear. But their judgment about their own value as a result is not true. They are still "very good" because they are not defined by something subjective. But unless they let go of their own judgment they cannot see that truth, and their lives will continue to manifest a different fruit.

Confession is hard because it confronts our deepest fears, which are being produced by the lie. It requires us to face the evidence once again. It calls out the terrifying possibility that the lie we hold may actually be true. We fear the possibility of rejection. We assume there actually is a dualism, that there is a bad category. Confession invites us to into this risk so we can discover what is true.

Once we transcend the lie, the fear ceases to hold power over us because we now hold the evidence of God's grace. Fear goes away because the judgment that created it has been countered by new evidence of what is true.

~~

The Blame Game

The confession also sheds light on the common construct the lie uses to survive, which is blame. It casts responsibility outward onto someone or something else. And as long as we participate in blame, we won't see the lie. We will embody it.

God asks Adam a simple question.

"Who told you that you were naked? Have you eaten from the tree that I commanded you not to eat from?"(Gen 3:11)

The man responds to the first question, but instead of giving a simple answer, he embellishes.

The man said, "The woman you put here with me—" (Gen 3:12a)

Notice how he says, "The woman YOU put here with me." (Emphasis mine) His focus is outward. You can just feel the contempt in the statement. "Well God, I just want to remind you that you put her here." His confession casts a shadow of blame. He doesn't have an excuse. But he's quick to cast responsibility outward.

He then deflects responsibility for the act by casting blame outward onto the woman.

"she gave me some fruit from the tree," (Gen 3:12b)

God didn't ask him who gave it to him. God asks the man a yes or no question.

We do this, don't we? We're quick to cast responsibility outward, as if those around us have made the choice for us. If only God hadn't put HER here, things would have been different. If things were different, then we wouldn't have made the same choice. And only after highlighting her part and God's part, does Adam own up to his part.

"And I ate it." (Gen 3:12c)

It's not the greatest confession in the world, but nonetheless it is true. The man ate the apple. And guess what. It doesn't define him.

Then God turns to the woman and draws out a response.

Then the LORD God said to the woman, "What is this you have done?"
The woman said, "The serpent deceived me, and I ate." (Gen 3:13)

She does the same thing the man does. She first reminds God the serpent deceived her before admitting her part. The answer to God's question comes in the second part.

It's not hard to imagine the sense of frustration and despair welling up inside each of them. We cannot ignore the intense fear and trauma present in this moment. There is no reference point in their minds for understanding how God will respond. There is no basis or previous learning event to hold onto. In the midst of the pain, the rational part of the brain shuts down and all they can feel is the need for self-preservation.

Instead of unity, the man and the woman see each as the "other". The root problem has created disorientation with everything around them. The "other" is now a visible reminder of the problem. The man and the woman, who had previously been one, are now truly divided.

Blame is a highly destructive act because it does two things. First, it casts the responsibility outward and onto someone or something else. It places emphasis on the one who influences rather than the one who makes the choice to act. As long as we cast responsibility outward, we can't see what is actually creating the problem. It keeps the problem alive. We become the perpetrator and the victim at the same time and we don't even know it.

Second, blame distorts our relationship with the other because the act of casting blame throws the responsibility for the choice onto someone else. It makes both parties the victim and the perpetrator. The sad part is, we are blind to what we are doing. Everyone but us can see that no one can make the choice for us. When someone casts blame onto us, we feel the weight of its responsibility. It seems foreign because it is not ours, and yet someone is forcing it on us.

Confession reorients us by placing responsibility back where it belongs, on us, so we can see it doesn't define us. It pushes us to into our true purpose, which is to rule over the self, our emotions, and destructive judgments.

Adam and Eve's interaction highlights what happens when we lose sight of our true identity. Death creates a void that has to be filled. And in the immediate moment the easiest thing to do is "identify" with the circumstance and emotion. We grasp onto something…anything that will help us figure out who we are so we can respond.

We become the victim and the perpetrator – the two predominant, false identities in the story. The victim "flights", using her judgments to build a protective closure that traps her inside. We learn to hide from God, our neighbors, and even ourselves. The perpetrator "fights," using his judgments to throw stones at anyone who is within earshot. He lashes out in self-defense, creating a repulsive effect.

From God's perspective, identity defines action. We reverse the process by finding our identity through our actions. The destructive fruit simply reveals who we think we are. The fruit then forces us to wonder if the judgment is true. Is our hiding and grasping simply a revelation of who we really are?

~~

The Curses

The next part of the story sheds light on our idea of God as angry and even vindictive. The dialog that follows is historically known as "the curses." It is the moment when God reveals what will happen to humanity. Some traditions grasp onto this moment as the point where God slams humanity. It's so easy to assume God is casting a curse on humanity. The lie wants us to believe this. But we'd be wrong. We use it to justify a furious God. Why else would God "curse" humanity?

The truth is, we almost always read the story through the covering. We see the story through a historical conclusion. We read the words through the lens of the very problem God is calling out.

The curses first acknowledge the present state of each party's perception of reality. God is identifying for each how they see themselves. If we assume God is cursing humanity, it reinforces the idea God is now against us. But if we see it for what it is – God calling out their present state – then we can begin to reshape our understanding of what the story is presenting.

God first responds to the serpent.

> So the LORD God said to the serpent, "Because you have done this, Cursed are you above all the livestock and all the wild animals! You will crawl on your belly and you will eat dust all the days of your life." (Gen 3:14)

It's so easy to read this and assume God is cursing the serpent. But it doesn't say that. God doesn't say, "I curse you." God says, "Cursed ARE you." And the difference is everything. It's easy to forget the serpent is a creation of God. The serpent is presented as a cognitive being, capable of rational thought, which suggests it too can be captivated. God's statement simply calls that out.

Contrary to some of our historical assumptions, the curses are actually God's way of helping us. It doesn't seem this way at first because we are part of the story. A curse is not a magic spell that someone casts onto someone else. A curse is the state of agreement to the lie. It is the brain's subjective experience of being captivated by something that is untrue. A cursed person is someone who believes something that is untrue. So to be "cursed" is to be captive to the lie.

When God calls out the curse, God is calling out humanity's captivity to the lie. The curses simply spell out the fruit of that captivity. The Jewish scholars understood this. Unbound from our particular historical perspectives, they saw God's statements as "observations" instead of curses. God is not cursing humanity. God is observing the curse that is already in them.

> To Adam he said…"Cursed is the ground because of you;" (Gen 3:17b)

In both instances God uses the word, "cursed". God is simply calling out the perception inside of them. God is drawing their attention to the judgments producing the curse. "…Because of you." We hear that and think Adam is the reason the ground is cursed. But once again, the problem is not that Adam is the reason, but that Adam thinks he is the reason.

~~

The Search For Validation

The second part of God's observations reveals the primary patterns humanity will use to search for validation. The covering creates a void of dignity, identity, and eventually purpose that must be filled. The search becomes destructive because any attempt to replace God's perspective will ultimately be limiting.

For the woman the search will reside primarily in relationships, and for the man it will reside primarily in work. These patterns have so long been entrenched in humanity that they have slipped into our subconscious. We have lived with them for so long we fail to see them anymore. Once we see them, they no longer remain hidden. God calls them out to produce awareness.

God begins with the woman. She will seek out her validation primarily in relationships.

> *"I will greatly increase your pains in childbearing; with pain you will give birth to children. Your desire will be for your husband, and he will rule over you." (Gen 3:16)*

She comes from Adam's rib, a symbolism suggesting her strength is her heart. She will be bent towards emotion and feelings, which are pivotal to relationships. The woman's search will reside primarily in the relationship to her children and her spouse.

It is deeply important to call out the order of relationships. God first calls out her relationship to her children, and then her relationship to her husband, but the order typically begins the other way around. In the curse, her children come before the husband. This suggests the woman's primary search for validation will be as a mother.

The second part reveals why. The word "desire" essentially means to seek something, which cannot be fulfilled. It's a lusting after something. She will first seek out her identity and dignity in her relationship with her husband, but he just won't be able to satisfy this in her. He can't. He's not God. And the man will recognize his power over the woman and use it to control her. He will rule over her. The primary relationship of man to woman will become distorted because he was never created to rule over her.

But her relationship with her children IS a relationship of power and control. She is in authority over them. She will seek out her validation in being a mother. It will become her primary means of purpose, identity, and ultimately, dignity.

There are two protective measures God instills in the woman. They are actually meant to help her confront the consequences of the curse. The first is a protective measure between her and the serpent.

> *"And I will put enmity between you and the woman, and between your*
> *offspring and hers; he will crush your head, and you will strike his heel."*
> *(Gen 3:15)*

God actually gives the woman and her offspring a sense of enmity, which is "a feeling or condition of hostility; hatred; ill will; animosity; antagonism." This protective mechanism is important, given the woman's bent towards emotion. It will give her an instinctive feeling against evil.

The second measure actually has to do with the woman's search for validation in the act of mothering. God increases her pain in childbearing. The distinction of childbearing is not limited exclusively to the moment of birth. It is the entire process of rearing the child. God gives her pain to remind her that her identity doesn't reside exclusively in the act of being a mother. The role will tempt her because this will be a means of power over someone. She will invest her life into the child for the sake of validation. She needs the protective mechanism to keep it from blinding her.

God then addresses the man. He will seek out his validation primarily in work.

> *"Cursed is the ground because of you; through painful toil you will eat of*
> *it all the days of your life." (Gen 3:17b)*

As he engages work, man will always be reminded that work is somehow distorted. His relationship to his original purpose will be tainted. Work will be hard because of Adam's perception of himself. The struggle will strip away all of his work-related energy because it just won't fill the void.

> *"It will produce thorns and thistles for you, and you will eat the plants of the field. By the sweat of your brow you will eat your food until you return to the ground..." (Gen 3:18-19)*

He will seek out his purpose, identity, and ultimately his dignity in his work. He will sweat and toil until he bleeds, just hoping someone will notice. People will ask him, "What do you do?" and snicker when the answer is something ordinary.

The thorns are his protective measure. As hard as he tries to achieve, it will never fulfill him, pricking his conscience and reminding him of his unfulfilled desire. The toil never ends, even to the point of death because it was never possible to satisfy the desire.

The observations are essentially dominant patterns in humanity. They are not mutually exclusive to each sex. Women can attempt to find their validation in work, and men can seek to find their validation in relationships. The search is primarily about filling the delusional void of dignity, identity and purpose. All three already exist in humanity. We just can't see them. So we search for something to take their place.

It's not hard to see the observations as part of the human social structure. Once we know what to look for they become easy to observe. When we look for them they are obvious. They help us see what is already happening. The harder part is beginning the long process of removing the agreements creating the desire in the first place.

~~

The Reverse Approach

The search for validation is ultimately about answering the question in the tree. Are we good or evil? To get there humanity actually reverses God's process of dignity, identity and purpose. Where God begins with the fundamental, which provides understanding and illumination of the specifics, we reverse the process by beginning with the specifics to find an answer to the fundamental.

The basic way we do this is to find our purpose (or meaning) through some action of value, which then creates an identity someone approves of, which will help us to see ourselves as good. Instead of beginning with God's perspectives, we construct our own. And it's easy to see the origins of this. God gives humanity the original task of naming the animals.

> *Now the LORD God had formed out of the ground all the beasts of the field and all the birds of the air. He brought them to the man to see what he would name them; and whatever the man called each living creature, that was its name. So the man gave names to all the livestock, the birds of the air and all the beasts of the field. (Gen 2:19-20)*

The reverse approach begins in language. In order to understand the woman next to him Adam names her based on what she does, which actually reveals the bent.

> *Adam named his wife Eve, because she would become the mother of all the living. (Gen 3:20)*

Her identity is now found in the act of mothering as opposed to within God's declarations.

At the base of realization is the thought that pops into our minds. In order to make sense of the images in our heads we give them sound. When we have no understanding of the feeling, we just let out a sound to make sense of it. The writers of the Bible often described these as groans. When two people agree on a name for the sound, we have words, which are shared constructs of identification. Language is predicated on agreeing a word means something. The actual sound has no meaning other than to create a connection to the shared agreement of the thought.

Words become sentences, paragraphs, pages, chapters, and eventually stories. Language, stories, and histories are our attempts to create tangible reference points of understanding to what is going on within us as well as our perceptions of the world.

The act of naming creates a social construct of agreement about what we say that thing is. The name is an identifier calling out the reference of the image in our heads, which creates a cognitive connection about something. The act of naming does not actually create a true identity. It simply gives it a reference point.

Without a sense of objective center, we toss and turn in our own thoughts attempting to judge reality, which creates feelings of disorientation. We tangibly experience this feeling of disorientation when we go to another country with a foreign language. We often call it culture shock. Our common reference points become moot. These feelings often hit us like bricks upside the head when we have no basis for understanding.

This act of naming is a direct reflection of the body's search for meaning through identifying. Naming in and of itself is a benign act. It gives tangible understanding to parts of our expression as human beings. It is part of the human experience. God even allows Adam to name the animals as part of the means of rule. Naming is not inherently destructive unless the name becomes the means of deriving identity and ultimately a sense of false dignity.

Much of our search for meaning then serves to engage the reverse process; to understand the self and our value as human beings. Our limiting identities give us meaning to understand our own void. The reverse process begins when we assume that name provides a fully informing identity. Anything humanity "realizes" as an alternative to God's original identity for humanity will always create a limiting image. In other words, any false identity we create will always have natural limitations keeping us from fully realizing who we are.

The basic identity we hold onto may even be true in the sense that we perform actions consistent with that image. But the image is limiting in that it is not the whole of who we are. A woman may be a mother but the role is not the fullest understanding of who she is. A worker may be good at something but it is never his whole identity.

These limiting identities are never capable of creating ultimate meaning, purpose, identity and value. The image of mother or worker is noble in and of itself, but as a primary identity it can only limit a person. Once the person fails to be a "good" mother or worker or exhausts one's capacity to succeed in the role, the identity ceases to be of value, and a new void is created. We feel the weight of these labels when they become dead weight under strain of use. Worse yet is when the label is thrust upon us - words that hold disgraceful meaning like criminal, adulterer, or even sinner – then we are crushed.

Where the search points to primary patterns, we can fill in any virtually any image or word to replace them with. We can use doctor, lawyer, teacher, priest, coach, athlete, mathematician, intellectual, fireman, soldier, warrior, beauty queen, prostitute, slave, poor, rich, heterosexual, homosexual, republican, democrat, husband, wife, son, daughter, politician, comedian, rock star, or actor. Each construct derives its meaning from an action, which creates an identity and ultimately a value judgment. The original action doesn't even have to be socially acceptable. It just has to produce enough value for the individual to win acclaim from an authoritative group the person selects.

As long as the person can maintain the valued action, the identity is maintained and approval is received. Once the action becomes obsolete, or the person can no longer perform the action, the identity begins to wither and fade away, and so does the approval. The only option late in life is to have created a legacy of goodwill that compensates enough for a lack of capacity to act.

The writer of Ecclesiastes aptly pointed to the search and its unwitting futility.

> I have seen all the things that are done under the sun; all of them are meaningless, a chasing after the wind. (Ec 1:14)

Anything we construct is like chasing after the wind. It's empty. There is nothing that can provide true meaning. And worse, we'll keep trying even when we know it doesn't work.

Some of the strongest identities come from belief systems, race, and nationality.

We identify with those who share broader similarities. We search for the right words to describe ourselves because behind each word is a meaning. And when we find our meaning in words, we limit ourselves to that meaning. We create the proverbial box which imprisons us within that meaning. The problem is not in the word but in the limitation the word produces. The "right" label cannot define us. It can only express a piece of who we are and what action we produce at times.

But even this is limiting. Before we are Christians, Jews, Hindus, Buddhists or Muslims…we are first human beings. Before we are black, brown, pink, or yellow, we are first human beings. Before we are heroes or losers, the best or the worst, we are first human beings. Before we are CEOs, senators, homemakers, or high school dropouts, we are first human beings. Before we are straight, bigots, racists, or LGBT, we are first human beings. Before we are natives, illegal immigrants, or naturalized citizens, we are first human beings. Before we are daughters or sons, mothers or fathers, granddaughters or grandsons, we are first human beings.

We also use labels to identify the "other". We categorize and stereotype in order to make a quick judgment. We identify something specific about that person and then compare them with the broad category. But when we use these labels to identify the person in order to derive value, we limit that person. Or worse, we categorize them in a way that perpetually invalidates and indignifies them.

The only definition that can truly inform us of our dignity, identity, and purpose is God's original declaration. We are "very good," human beings created in the image of God, called to rule over the self. We begin with God's declaration of good. We see God establish this definition for Jesus as he is being baptized.

> "And a voice from heaven said, "This is my Son, whom I love; with him I am well pleased." (Mt 3:17)

Jesus found his identity first in God. It worked because it was true.

> "Believe me when I say that I am in the Father and the Father is in me; or at least believe on the evidence of the miracles themselves." (Jn 14:11)

Everything else is an expression. But unless we're first grounded in God's perspective, the God imagination, anything else will always be a limitation.

~~

The Philosophers' Dilemma

The reverse process creates a strange problem. Once we derive our dignity and identity from our thoughts, are we actually deceiving ourselves of our own existence? Behind these false identities are just thoughts we accept as real. But what if they are untrue? What if even our stories, our events, our words, our thoughts, even our existence is just a fabrication of our imagination?

The Chinese philosopher Zhuang wrote about this possibility.

> *"Once upon a time, I, Chuang Chou, dreamt I was a butterfly, fluttering hither and thither, to all intents and purposes a butterfly. I was conscious only of my happiness as a butterfly, unaware that I was Chou. Soon I awaked, and there I was, veritably myself again. Now I do not know whether I was then a man dreaming I was a butterfly, or whether I am now a butterfly, dreaming I am a man. Between a man and a butterfly there is necessarily a distinction. The transition is called the transformation of material things." (Zhuangzi)*

At the core, we recognize the subjectivity of our own thoughts. Both Plato and Aristotle explored what it meant to think about this process of thinking, or the knowledge of knowledge. Similar to Adam's first move, Aristotle tried to solve this problem by finding the objective reality of our existence in the validity of our thoughts:

> *"But if life itself is good and pleasant...and if one who sees is conscious that he sees, one who hears that he hears, one who walks that he walks and similarly for all the other human activities there is a faculty that is conscious of their exercise, so that whenever we perceive, we are conscious that we perceive, and whenever we think, we are conscious that we think, and to be conscious that we are perceiving or thinking is to be conscious that we exist..." (Nicomachean Ethics, 1170a25 ff.)*

René Descartes effectively simplified Aristotle's idea when he said,

> *"I now seem to be able to lay it down as a general rule that whatever I perceive very clearly and distinctly is true." (Meditations on Third Philosophy)*

This idea was poetically captured in his simple statement, "I think, therefore I am." In other words, we derive an understanding of our existence through the act of thinking described in words.

Descartes understood the need for certainty in the knowledge of the human experience. He said,

> *"But I have convinced myself that there is absolutely nothing in the world, no sky, no earth, no minds, no bodies. Does it now follow that I too do not exist? No. If I convinced myself of something [or thought anything at all] then I certainly existed. But there is a deceiver of supreme power and cunning who is deliberately and constantly deceiving me. In that case I too undoubtedly exist, if he is deceiving me; and let him deceive me as much as he can, he will never bring it about that I am nothing so long as I think that I am something. So, after considering everything very thoroughly, I must finally conclude that the proposition, I am, I exist, is necessarily true whenever it is put forward by me or conceived in my mind." (AT VII 25; CSM II 16–17)*

Descartes understood the need we have to convince ourselves of what is true. Many of his arguments were spiritual in nature, arguing for the idea that God was not a deceiver. But his argument perpetuated the problem by centering his objective point inside the human perception.

> *"Archimedes used to demand just one firm and immovable point in order to shift the entire earth; so I too can hope for great things if I manage to find just one thing, however slight, that is certain and unshakable." (AT VII 24; CSM II 16)*

Descartes, as well as his critics, understood the limitations of his own ideas. Words or the thoughts creating the words are entirely subjective. Two people can have entirely different understandings of the word love, so who is "right"? Even if two people agree, is it still objective? The reference point was still subjective to the individual(s). At the core level, humanity is still faced with the problem of perception, and ultimately of terra firma.

Humberto Maturana and Francisco Varela brilliantly explore this tension in their book, ironically titled, *The Tree of Knowledge*. Maturana and Varela argue heavily against the notion of certainty, claiming our biological construct limits our ability to fully grasp it. They understand that "cognition", or what we think we see, is not necessarily a true representation of the world.

"All we can do is generate explanations, through language, that reveal the mechanism of bringing forth a world. By existing, we generate cognitive "blind spots" that can be cleared only through generating new blinds spots in another domain." (p242)

They suggest humanity lives on "the razor's edge" between knowing nothing (solipsism) and full knowing (objectivism).

"Our purpose is to find a via media: to understand the regularity of the world we are experiencing at every moment, but without any point of reference independent of ourselves that would give certainty to our descriptions and cognitive assertions." (p241)

Maturana and Varela then suggest love is the only social medium that works, because it recognizes human limitations and still validates the other, even in spite of the different constructs.

"(Love) is the biological foundation of social phenomena: without love, without acceptance of others, living beside us, there is no social process and, therefore, no humanness." (p246)

Much of our need to connect as human beings is then a need to understand our own humanity. We connect with others as a means to connect and understand ourselves. We develop relationships as a means to relate with ourselves. Interestingly, Jesus came with the same message. What if Jesus understood that loving God, and our neighbor as ourselves, is the only means to solving the problem?

~~

The Second Death

It is easy at this point to wonder if everything is just one big misunderstanding. The temptation is to dismiss what is happening in search of something more complex because it seems like the problem is so simple. The root problem is simple but the consequences that follow are not. We cannot ignore the catastrophic effects the choice produced.

Where the root problem is a false judgment about reality, it produces a downward spiral that leads to a perceptual or spiritual death. Humanity is blinded by the lie to the God imagination, and to its own dignity, identity and purpose. The first death distorted our perception of everything.

It is here that we return to the story in the Garden. God turns the conversation to one of the darker consequences of humanity's choice, the physical corruption of the body.

> *"Since from it you were taken; for dust you are and to dust you will return." (Gen 3:19b)*

This is the second definition of death, the one casting a remarkably long shadow on the human story. The root problem has physical effects as well. This consequence cannot be overstated. It is the stunning evidence that God was right. Something gets physiologically bent in the body. The lie physically corrupts in a way that results in a loss of physical life.

The lie creates a functional impurity in the human system that has devastating consequences. The situation could be likened to a jar full of pure water. If we add even the tiniest drop of ink, the water remains impure, even if we can't see it. Once the lie becomes part of the human system, it can no longer be removed from the physical system.

The Apostle Paul wrestles with this notion of the corruption of the body and its physical effects in his letter to the Romans.

"I do not understand what I do. For what I want to do I do not do, but what I hate I do. And if I do what I do not want to do, I agree that the law is good. As it is, it is no longer I myself who do it, but it is sin living in me. I know that nothing good lives in me, that is, in my sinful nature. For I have the desire to do what is good, but I cannot carry it out. For what I do is not the good I want to do; no, the evil I do not want to do—this I keep on doing. Now if I do what I do not want to do, it is no longer I who do it, but it is sin living in me that does it." (Rom 7:15-20)

Paul deeply understands the corruption occurring in the body. Paul even understands the problem as the problem, and that it resides within himself. Paul effectively separates himself from the problem and identifies it correctly as the physical corruption occurring inside of him. The body doesn't fundamentally change in value from good to bad. It is still good from a God's perspective. What changes is its capacity to operate effectively as a corrupted system.

Scholars have wrestled with this notion of "the spirit is good, and the body is bad". This idea leads to what scholars call Gnosticism. It is the belief that the physical corruption changes the qualitative value of the physical being. The soul remains inherently good but the body becomes evil. This idea led many in history to engage the "mortification of the flesh" a process of literally punishing the body with whips and chains in order to subdue it.

We cannot ignore this: the story does not reveal a change in the value of the physical being. It simply tells what functionally happens to the body. It is corrupted, but remains qualitatively good. If we assume it is qualitatively evil we end up with an irresolvable and strange conflict that spirit is good but matter is evil. Death becomes preferable for the sake of separating the self from what is evil.

~~

Exile

This physical corruption of the body is deeply important to understanding why God removes humanity from the Garden, which we'll call the exile. God physically removes humanity from the Garden. The exile is perhaps one of the easiest pieces in the story to interpret as the act of an angry God. But if we examine what actually happens, we can begin to see that God is actually protecting humanity by removing them.

God begins the process by doing something for them. God actually clothes them.

The LORD God made garments of skin for Adam and his wife and clothed them. (Gen 3:21)

There are two possibilities happening here. The first is that God actually gives humanity skin. The phrase never mentions "animal" skin. This idea of human skin is possible but would suggest an extension of the creative process, which has already ended. But the second option is the more likely possibility. Even though it doesn't specifically say "animal" skin, it's implied. God gives them garments of animal skin. If this is actually what is happening, it suggests the first sacrifice on the part of God. God sheds the blood of his creation in order to cover the shame of humanity. This is the first atonement. It is the first moment when God provides a means of restoration for humanity.

Throughout the story, God consistently acknowledges and then uses the human construct to reach humanity. And God's version is always better. Humanity creates something it thinks will solve the problem, and then God gives them something like it, only better. When humanity uses fig leafs, God uses skins. Where humanity begins to develop the law, God gives them the Ten Commandments. When humanity creates empires, God gives them a nation of priests. When humanity creates the religious system, God gives them the perfect atonement.

But in the first instance of atonement, we can begin to ask: Who needs the sacrifice? Who needs the covering? God doesn't need it. We do. God recognizes the immediate human need for the covering in order to deal with the shame. This continues the process of God meeting humanity right where it's at, through love.

God then makes a remarkably strange admission, calling out the change in humanity.

> *And the LORD God said, "The man has now become like one of us,*
> *knowing good and evil." (Gen 3:22a)*

Most commentaries avoid God's statement. But the fact is, humanity has become like God in some way. The distinction lies in the second part, "knowing good and evil." Like humanity, God is essentially admitting knowledge of both good and evil. This stunning admission provides the provocative possibility that knowledge of evil, which comes out of experience, does not fundamentally make something evil. Humanity experiences evil by its own realization, and thus becomes a host to evil, but it is not fundamentally changed by it.

It reinforces the idea that transformation begins with discovering reality as opposed to changing reality. The problem is not one of humanity becoming evil and then needing full cosmic transformation of some kind. The problem is one of humanity letting go of the captivating realization that the experience of evil doesn't make something evil. The tree always held two possibilities. And the only one that is correct is "good". The fullest realization of being like God is not in seeing oneself as evil, but as good even in the presence of evil. And this is only possible when we discover the God imagination.

If this is true it then opens a second possibility in the story. The cross is Jesus "becoming" sin, which the story and the Apostle Paul both claim. It gives us a deeper understanding of what Jesus is actually doing at the moment of his death. We can't ignore the fullest extent of what this means. By taking on sin, Jesus is taking on the nature of death itself, both perceptually and physically. But after three days, he triumphs over it. What it suggests is this same idea. Even in the experience of evil, we are not fundamentally changed by it.

The call to repentance is simply a change of mind, a realization from evil to good. The prophetic imagination always centered transformation in the mind. We knew it was true when our lives changed as a result of it. The only way we could approach God was to see ourselves from God's perspective, not because of what we had done, but because of who we are.

The physical corruption of the body also creates the possibility of a new problem, one of which God is aware. Still within the Garden is a second tree, the Tree of Life.

> He must not be allowed to reach out his hand and take also from the tree
> of life and eat, and live forever. (Gen 3:22b)

The traditions often tell us God banishes humanity from the Garden as a punishment. The assumption is that Adam and Eve are removed from the Garden because of what they did, as if God as taking away the Garden simply because they don't deserve it anymore. But the evidence for God's reason suggests something entirely different. The prime concern resides in the phrase, "live forever."

God is not punishing humanity. A punishment is a controlled consequence revealing the painful effects of specific action, but under protective circumstances. The purpose of punishment is to reveal the consequences of an action without long-term effects. If this were a punishment for what had happened, we would expect God's reason to indicate so. But it doesn't. The reason for banishment has to do with the consequences of eating from the tree. Punishment is simply not what is happening here.

A more logical conclusion is that God is protecting humanity from the consequences of what would happen should they eat from the tree. If the body has been corrupted, then eating from the tree of life would create an unsolvable paradox. Humanity would live forever trapped inside a broken body. It would be stuck with no way of escaping the physical corruption of the body.

So God removes them from the Garden and places a protection around it so they can't enter back into it.

> So the LORD God banished him from the Garden of Eden to work the
> ground from which he had been taken. After he drove the man out, he
> placed on the east side of the Garden of Eden cherubim and a flaming
> sword flashing back and forth to guard the way to the tree of life. (Gen

3:23-24)

The cherubim and flaming sword suggest protection FROM something as opposed to punishment FOR something. God is keeping them from the Tree of Life in order to keep them from immortal death.

This is the end of the Garden story, the event that reshaped our perception of the world. It is the story that literally captivates the world. But before we leave, once again we must ask what is NOT there. It is vitally important to call out what is missing.

There is no point in the story where God changes the original declarations or deems humanity worthless. God never says, "You are no longer good," or "I can't love you." God never declares anything has changed to evil. Truth doesn't change, because human activity cannot change God's perspective. The God imagination remains in humanity, but covered.

There is no word of anger, or shame, or disgust from God's perspective. God doesn't sit on high exuding a sense of pent-up loathing. God remains whole in the situation, seeking out the restoration of creation. God consistently seeks out humanity, meeting them in the midst of suffering, as opposed to ignoring them or establishing some barrier between them.

Yet how often have we heard the story from the perspective that God is angry at creation, and is almost ruthlessly bent on punishing humanity? We have to ask ourselves if this story is true, or if this story is a projection of our own image of God. Have we created God in our own image? In the famous words of Voltaire, "If God has made us in his image, we have returned him the favor."

As we progress through the rest of the story, it becomes important to leave behind the things we've picked up along the way, namely our misconceptions and projected assumptions about God. If we do, we can begin to see God consistently working towards our restoration. God's problem is the captivity of humanity, not humanity itself.

Chapter 6 – The Downward Spiral

"Human existence is, in fact, a radical and profound tension between good and evil, between dignity and indignity, between decency and indecency, between the beauty and the ugliness of the world." – Paulo Freire

The Original Sin

Time often slows down when something important is happening. Much of our fascination with stories is how they cut out the fluff and give us the important details that move the story along. We go to movies, not to watch someone get out of bed, brush their teeth, and drive to work, but to see the moment they lose their job and end up discovering life. The story resides in the important details of someone confronting and ultimately resolving conflict.

As the story progresses, we find no further conflict between God and Adam and Eve. The story moves past them to their children. The story is now in how the problem begins to manifest in the subsequent generations. Humanity begins to pass down the story through both nature and nurture. In other words, we're predisposed to nurture the embedded captivating story in our bodies.

In some ways it seems strange to just move on. Why doesn't God immediately create some kind of religious system of atonement for humanity? Why doesn't God create some kind of law in order for the humanity to recognize the problem? None of these issues are even addressed. We cannot ignore the possibility that the story suggests God has moved on. God is either callous, providing no means to cross the chasm, or the chasm doesn't actually exist. But, the body can persist in thinking that it does exist. It can continue to manifest the same problem over and over again.

Life goes on for Adam and Eve and they have sons, who work. That's what men do, right? And for some unknown reason Cain comes up with a strange idea of making an offering to God.

> *Now Abel kept flocks, and Cain worked the soil. In the course of time Cain brought some of the fruits of the soil as an offering to the LORD. But Abel brought fat portions from some of the firstborn of his flock. (Gen 4:3-4a)*

Notice the distinct differences in the offerings. Cain brings a basket of fruit. It's like he just grabs something from the "fruit" of his labor and presents it to God. But his brother brings the fat portion of the firstborn of his flock. The differences are reflective of their judgments. An offering is a reflection of how we see ourselves. Abel arrives with the very best of what he has, as if to say, "I am blessed." The offering essentially presents Abel's view of himself. Cain's offering is the same. It reveals his judgment as well, as if to say, "This is all I've got."

Abel's offering is the recognition of what is already true. He's connected to God in such a way that his offering is a tribute to the God who has created him. He's reveling in what is good in a way that shines. Cain's offering reveals the root problem once again. The subtext is, "See my condition?" And God calls him on it.

> *The LORD looked with favor on Abel and his offering, but on Cain and his offering he did not look with favor. (Gen 3:4b-5a)*

Notice God doesn't say, "I don't accept your favor." It says, "...he did not look with favor." The statement is revealing an outside reflection of how God looked. In other words, we're reading each son's perception of God's response. Abel sees God as approving because he sees himself as approved. He is seeing the world from the God imagination. Cain doesn't see God as approving, because he doesn't see himself as approved.

Cain's response reveals the tension of what it means to be captivated.

> *So Cain was very angry, and his face was downcast.*

*Then the LORD said to Cain, "Why are you angry? Why is your face
downcast? If you do what is right, will you not be accepted?" (Gen 4:5b-
6)*

God's question reveals the means by which we identify the root problem. The
phrase, "do what is right," is calling out the "fruit" or actions of his life. The root
word is "yatab". It means, "to BE good". Abel embodied the idea of "good". He
begins with the idea that he is already acceptable. Cain doesn't. Cain's "fruit"
reveals he doesn't believe it. His actions reveal he doesn't know if he's good. In
other words, our lives automatically reveal the judgment we are holding onto.
God is essentially calling out how we identify the judgment, through actions.
God doesn't approve of Cain's offering because to accept it is to approve of his
perception.

*"But if you do not do what is right, sin is crouching at your door; it
desires to have you, but you must master it." (Gen 4:7b)*

This is one of the clearest examples in the story of God inviting humanity to
participate in one's own restoration. God doesn't rescue Cain. Instead he invites
him to participate in his true purpose, which is to rule over the self – namely,
the judgments he's making about himself.

This is also the first distinction of "sin" in the story. The first use of the term is
in relationship to our perception of God's acceptance. Our offerings reveal our
perception. But the first time it is used is outside the Garden.

This story reveals the true meaning of the term "sin". Sin is rooted in our
judgment of reality, especially in regards to the self. It points back to the
original question in the tree. If we approach original sin as eating from the
tree, or breaking God's commandment during a naïve state, it's impossible to
actually replicate what we historically call original sin. Humanity is cut off
from the Garden, and thus can never eat once again from the same tree.

But if we approach "sin" as replicating the root problem, or getting the question
in the tree wrong, every single human being can consistently reproduce it.
Every human being is left with the same question to consider. Are we good

or evil? We identify our answer through the fruit of our actions. If we get the question right, our lives reveal it. We're engaging the way of life. If we get the question wrong, all hell breaks loose.

The shift in the story then plays out that same question in the second generation. But because the human body is corrupted, humanity is now bent towards getting the question wrong.

~~

The Birth Of Religion

Once again notice what is NOT there. The idea of the offering is Cain's idea. God NEVER requests the offering. The situation consistently reveals where the root problem resides. Cain needs to know how God thinks. The need for approval reveals his perception that he doesn't have God's affirmation. Abel sees what his brother is doing and follows along.

This process of offering is essentially the birth of the religious idea. Humanity makes an offering to God for the sake of gaining approval. This is the moment humanity reveals its construct for dealing with the problem of guilt. Guilt is the feeling that arises from the false judgment we make about our own dignity. When we get it wrong, our body tells us so. We feel it. But if we are the problem, how can we solve it? How can we remove ourselves? Deep within we know something is not right, but we are powerless to solve it because we assume a problem that doesn't actually exist.

Cain's offering is the tangible evidence of his own judgment but it is also a bribe. The offering becomes an exchange of guilt for favor. It's an offering to God in exchange for acceptance. When God doesn't accept it, Cain gets mad. He misunderstands God's response and assumes he's still the problem. He immediately falls into the downward spiral because he now has the evidence of God's rejection to validate his original judgment. It's easy to assume the internal dialog because we've all felt it before. "See, I was right. I'm not approved by God." His anger manifests in a brooding and myopic nihilism. He completely misunderstands God's response, but instead of looking for the truth he becomes captivated by the lie.

The incident with Cain and Abel presents the paradoxical reality of seeing the good in the "other" and not seeing it in the self. Cain now knows God's favor rests on his brother. But from his perception, it does not rest on him as well.

The next level in the downward spiral is then to fully embody death against another human being. Cain needs to kills the other, which reveals what he is not. Abel is the reminder of what has been lost, at least from Cain's perspective.

> *Now Cain said to his brother Abel, "Let's go out to the field." And while*
> *they were in the field, Cain attacked his brother Abel and killed him.*
> *(Gen 4:8)*

Cain kills Abel because he knows his brother is good. Abel's offering was approved. But Cain has no connection to why it was approved. He can't see it. The lingering doubt has perched on the doorstep of his mind and he acts on it. We can easily see this as a rebellion against God, but in actuality it is a rebellion against the true self. Cain takes on the death of a false identity, finding his deepest reality in the removal of the God image in his midst. Abel is the polar opposite, the "other" reminding him of what he wants to be, but is not.

~~

True Justice

Cain kills his brother. This is the first moment the oppressive reality of evil has reared its ugly face. The evidence of guilt is now overwhelming. Where Cain's parents had no reference point, Cain does have a story to reference. He has heard and knows the story of his parents. He must be evil, right?

The obvious question is, "How would God respond?" Would God crush humanity, disposing of it like used garbage, once again securing our notion of a worthless humanity and an angry, wrathful God? Or would God seek out its restoration? And worse, would the lie once again struggle to survive?

God's first response is telling. Once again God doesn't rush in angry, but instead begins with a question. He locates the problem.

Then the LORD said to Cain, "Where is your brother Abel?"

"I don't know," he replied. "Am I my brother's keeper?" (Gen 4:9)

Cain's response is equally telling. Immediately we see one of the dominant protective tactics of the lie. There's no one else around to blame, so when we're caught, deny it. Pretend the evidence doesn't even exist. Cain is annoyed because he wants to deny the reality of what happened. And this is the interesting nature of denial. In order to be seen as believable, it often exposes itself by overdoing the response. It's almost like he's saying, "Don't bother me with this drivel."

So God takes it to the next level. The evidence is so obvious it is literally crying out to God. In other words, we can't hide the evidence from God.

The LORD said, "What have you done? Listen! Your brother's blood cries out to me from the ground." (Gen 4:10)

God's immediate response is to seek confession. And in the absence of confession God presents the evidence and the consequence for him.

"Now you are under a curse and driven from the ground, which opened its mouth to receive your brother's blood from your hand. When you work the ground, it will no longer yield its crops for you. You will be a restless wanderer on the earth." (Gen 4:11-12)

Once again God calls out the curse Cain is under. God calls out a present circumstance that exists because Cain holds onto the lie. It's the same thing God does for Adam and Eve. Cain knows he's guilty but this reinforces the judgment of evil. He's murdered another human being. The evidence becomes so overwhelming all he can do is hide. There's no way to escape what is true.

It's important to recognize the curse directly affects his work. Cain is a farmer. If the ground won't produce anything for him, the curse is seen as taking away any means of self-validation. As long as he holds onto the lie, he's essentially stuck.

But more importantly is God's final response. This is the moment we've been waiting for. This is the moment God will rain down fury and wrath on Cain. This is the moment when God will show up as we've expected. So God does... nothing.

Wait a minute! What do you mean, "God does nothing?" Our sense of justice is awkwardly strained by God's response. Cain has just killed his brother. He's killed the God image in another human being, and God does nothing more than call out Cain's curse.

This first moment gives us one of the most important means to understanding the undeniable extent of grace. There is no limit to it. True justice is not punitive, meaning God doesn't need to kill Cain in order for justice to be served. God doesn't demand an eye for an eye. There is no need for a race to the bottom.

True justice is a perfect blend of truth (acknowledging the reality of the evidence) and grace (acknowledging it doesn't define us). This is restoration. At the basis of truth is the reality of each person's dignity. It is the ultimate truth. Grace holds onto that truth even in the face of horrific evidence. God doesn't treat Cain like a victim or a perpetrator. Killing him serves nothing. There is no violent demand for penance or more offerings. God has the right to be offended, but chooses not to be.

The question then is, who can't get over it?

> Cain said to the LORD, "My punishment is more than I can bear.
> Today you are driving me from the land, and I will be hidden from your
> presence; I will be a restless wanderer on the earth, and whoever finds me
> will kill me." (Gen 4:13-14)

Notice what Cain says, "Today you are driving me from the land, and I will be hidden from your presence..." But God never says this. Cain reveals where the chasm is located — in his perception. Cain reveals what he's thinking life will be like in the future.

Cain's response also reveals the next survival tactic of the lie. When things are going poorly, magnify the consequences beyond what they actually are. Stir emotion and sympathy in hopes of reprieve, as long as there is no focus on the problem. But the consequences are a natural outcome of the lie, not from God. Cain suffers from his own captivity to the lie and won't let it go. Whenever he looks at the ground, he will remember his brother's blood, which will in turn remind him of what he has done.

In a rather stunning display of mercy, God actually protects Cain from any further harm.

> But the LORD said to him, "Not so; if anyone kills Cain, he will suffer vengeance seven times over." Then the LORD put a mark on Cain so that no one who found him would kill him. (Gen 4:15)

Yes, you read that right. God marks Cain as untouchable. God's response reveals the truth of justice. Even when Cain can't see his own dignity God reminds him he is still valuable. His dignity remains. He is still a child of the living God, called very good. He still has purpose. And as a final response, Cain turns his back on God. He's so thoroughly convinced of his own guilt that he cannot remain in God's presence.

> So Cain went out from the LORD's presence and lived in the land of Nod, east of Eden. (Gen 4:16)

In spite of God's grace, Cain turns and runs from God. He continues one of the most punishing traits of the ego: finding a false identity in both the victim and perpetrator. In the absence of a true identity, the ego searches in the midst of circumstances, emotions, judgments and consequences. Cain identifies with the each one. Cain IS a murderer because he killed his brother. Cain IS a failure because he feels intense regret and shame. Cain IS unlovable because there is no way a murderer can be loved. Cain IS evil because he thinks the ground will forever remind him of his transgression. The ego, or the wounded self, finds its identity in the intense substance of Cain's circumstantial reality. He sees himself as a victim of circumstance, and perpetrates his own punishment.

We do this too, don't we? We get so convinced of our perceptions we fail to see what is really going on. We turn our back on what is true in order to hold on to what is false. This act of running becomes the final survival tactic of the lie. It compels us to leave God's presence, not because God can't accept us, but because we can't accept our false identities. We refuse to let go of the lie.

Nobody initially seeks out a false identity like victim or perpetrator. We may use it to our advantage, but we don't start out wanting to be known as a victim or perpetrator. It happens by default because instead of facing the circumstances and emotions of the event, we run from them. And in running from them we empower the lie by giving it authority over us. The act of running validates the judgment. We give it credibility and credence. We process the data and emotions over and over, stewing on it and fixating on it in our minds. We reconstitute it as true. We judge ourselves as evil, and worthless, and impossible to love. Fear reinforces the story we have about it. We play into our own demise without even realizing it.

The only way to overcome the false identity is to call it out and to reject it. And that means seeing the entire event differently. It means letting go of the false identity and reclaiming the one that is true. It doesn't alleviate the actual circumstances, but it does change our capacity to deal with them.

~~

The Shadow Of Death

The original consequence of the tree was the loss of the true self. It was first of all relational. Humanity could lose sight of its own dignity, identity, and purpose. But Cain's murder of his brother revealed it was also physical. Human beings could actually die a physical death. This moment creates the dark shadow of death. It confirms the reality of the second death and God's original words. At some point in each human's life, we would die. The evidence is now on the table.

Suddenly humanity is confronted with the possibility of dying. The person next to them could kill. Cain did, so why couldn't someone else? This shadow of death pervades the human story almost incessantly.

The shadow of death creates the tension of a very twisted logic. Each person we meet holds the possibility of being evil. If the "other" is evil, their presence represents the possibility of death. That person(s) must be eliminated. In order to protect the self, humanity must potentially become the very death it seeks to avoid. The only way to stay alive is to completely embody death.

The prophet Zechariah eventually writes a song that includes a reference to the shadow of death.

> "...to shine on those living in darkness and in the shadow of death, to guide our feet into the path of peace." (Lk 1:79)

The only way to mitigate the shadow of death is in finding the delicate balance of allegiance with the "other". These allegiances begin with family and neighbors. They are the people with whom we have enough history to trust they won't kill us. Over time these allegiances grow into tribes based upon shared agreement of mutual engagement and protection. Tribes are social contracts typically based on generations of families that eventually become territorial. To leave the tribe is to risk one's life.

~~

The Embedded Captivating Story

The question in the conflict between Cain and Abel is, "How could this happen?" We see no real evidence of the story leading up to the offering. We don't get to really know the story feeding longing for approval. All we know is that he sought out validation through the offering.

Science is now teaching us how the brain works, and the data reveals something fascinating. When we examine the problem of judgment from a physiological framework, it is very easy to see why humanity becomes captive. The brain is predisposed to seek out evidence to support the conclusions it has already made. In other words, we're biased.

When our judgments are well developed, we exert what is called confirmation bias. We confirm our perceptions by selectively collecting evidence to support our assessments. This bias plays out in three ways. We can reinforce existing conclusions by selectively collecting new evidence, interpreting evidence in a biased way, or selectively recalling information from our past.

Confirmation bias actually creates a barrier for competing information to get through. We're predisposed to see the information supporting our conclusions, and predisposed to ignore evidence negating our conclusions. What this means is a body, which is corrupted, is predisposed to getting it wrong. Over time, this corruption process can actually grow. We can begin to collect evidence to suggest a very deep story confirming our answer to the question in the tree. We can even assume everyone thinks and acts just like us.

In the absence of reliable information about what a person thinks or a group of people think, we project a story. Scientists call this "false consensus bias". We cast our story onto other people and assume they think like we do.

Over time God even points this out. Humanity destroys itself by fixating on the evil part.

> *The LORD saw how great man's wickedness on the earth had become,*
> *and that every inclination of the thoughts of his heart was only evil all the*
> *time. (Gen 6:5)*

In other words, humanity consistently reinforces its own judgment that it is evil.

> *Now the earth was corrupt in God's sight and was full of violence. God*
> *saw how corrupt the earth had become, for all the people on earth had*
> *corrupted their ways. (Gen 6:11-12)*

In nine generations, and over 1,200 years, humanity develops a deeply embedded captivating story. It's self-reinforcing and predisposed to a judgment of evil. It is bent towards getting it wrong, and suffers the consequences of this perspective.

The embedded captivating story is continually reinforced by inherited stories passed down through generations, deeply embedded at a physiological and psychological level. And once this judgment enters the body, it seeks to reinforce itself. It predisposes humanity to an incorrect judgment.

The curse, the shadow of death, and our predisposition to get it wrong creates a perfect storm of problems when engaging relationship. If we can't relate to ourselves, how can we relate to God or each other? If we can relate to those closest to us, how can we relate to the larger world? The downward spiral of violence distorts everything.

What humanity doesn't have is the overwhelming evidence allowing it to cross the chasm back to God. It needs a body of undeniable evidence shattering the captivating nature of the lie. Those who can reverse what Cain started are the extreme exception, not the rule.

~~

The Flood

How do you respond when humanity becomes so captivated by false judgment it is literally killing itself? If our instincts are true, we are tempted to simply remove all evil. And as the story progresses, we are confronted with what easily seems like God doing just that.

The next great event in the story is the flood. And it is here we see confirmation bias in full play. The flood is God cleansing the earth. But we don't typically see it that way, do we? We read into the catastrophic event what we want to see.

The flood is another one of the great misconceptions in the story. Our assumptions lead us to believe that God floods the earth because God is angry. But if we read the story, there is NO word of anger. God's expression of emotion is one of great sorrow.

> *The LORD was grieved that he had made man on the earth, and his heart was filled with pain. So the LORD said, "I will wipe mankind, whom I have created, from the face of the earth—men and animals, and creatures that move along the ground, and birds of the air—for I am grieved that I have made them." (Gen 6:6-7)*

It's so easy to read anger into this moment, isn't it? We see evil and we want God to get rid of it. We want God to act just like we would. But God's response is not anger. It is sorrow. No matter how humanity acts, this is still God's creation. We need to know how God feels the moment humanity is at its worst. We need to know God won't lose sight of what is true. God still remains whole once. God holds onto the idea that humanity is worth fighting for, that humanity is worth saving.

The word anger, from God's perspective, is never used in the story for the first 2,500 years. The first time God expresses "anger" is against Moses because he won't get with the program of God's mission.

We actually need the flood for several reasons. We need God to give humanity another chance. We need to know God's response. We need a new story.

The flood is rarely seen for what it actually is – a do-over. The flood is the moment when God restarts everything. By cleansing creation, God is allowing humanity to begin fresh once again. But in so doing, humanity loses its capacity to ever say, "But if I just had another chance." The flood reveals that even when we start over, the problem is still the same. We're still compelled by our sense of destructive patterns, created by the root problem.

God even gives humanity a head start by beginning with Noah, a man who knows God. Noah will likely tell a different story of a God who exists. He will tell his children they don't have to walk away from God. History reveals, though, that it doesn't turn out that way. Within several generations, humanity is right back where it started.

~~

The Exception

Noah poses a problem. If there is one person who creates a problem for our traditional assumptions about the chasm, and there are actually many in the story, it is Noah. Like Abel, Noah is the exception to the embedded captivating story. He found a way to cross the chasm and engage relationship with God.

But Noah found favor in the eyes of the LORD. (Gen 6:8)

Once again notice the way the story presents the evidence. This is not God coming to Noah and saying, "I like you," or "I approve of you." This is Noah discovering favor in the face of God. Much like Abel, Noah looks into God's face and sees what is already true. Like Abel, he sees the true heart of God. He sees the love shining through God's eyes. There is no condemnation, no disdain. There is only favor.

If our traditional notions of the chasm are true, Noah presents a paradox. If God creates the chasm, it would be impossible for Noah to cross it. There are no atonement, no sacrifice, and no religious priests to make Noah whole. So how can this be? What does Noah do that makes him the exception?

> *This is the account of Noah. Noah was a righteous man, blameless among the people of his time, and he walked with God. (Gen 6:9)*

The word blameless is the word, "*tamiym*". *It means*, "complete, whole, entire, sound." But its meaning resides in what Noah is not doing. He's not blaming anyone. He's not throwing the problem out there onto someone else. In other words, Noah gets it. He sees what God sees. He discovers the God imagination. He looks into the face of God and sees the truth of his own dignity.

To do this, he simply takes the risk to discover who God really is. He walks with God. He puts it all on the line and approaches God with the courage to challenge the prevailing assumption that God would crush him. This is faith on display. It's not making something true by our actions. It's aligning our internal image of reality to what is already true.

Faith is simply opening the door to possibility, to hope, and to a transcendent life. It's taking the risk to challenge the preconceived assumptions and embedded captivating stories. And because of this risk, he sees what is true. He transcends his own perceptions and subjective judgments. He overcomes.

Chapter 7 – The Way Of The World

"It's easier to run. Replacing this pain with something numb. It's so much easier to go. Than face all this pain here all alone." – Chester Bennington

The Way Of The World

We cannot ignore the virtual silence of God for much of the first 2,100 years. With the exception of Noah, and a brief interaction at the Tower of Babel, the story presents virtually no interaction between God and humanity. God is silent in matters of human affairs. Although much of our understanding of the Mesopotamian culture comes out of the history of religion and anthropology, we cannot ignore that religion developed long before God ever begins to proactively engage.

Instead of simply looking into the face of God, like Noah, the human response is to consistently search for some form of alternative validation using subjective means. Humanity constructs patterns that are strikingly obvious when we look for them. These patterns of operating eventually become known as "the way of the world". Each is based on a subjective attempt to solve the root problem. God's silence gives humanity the opportunity to explore these patterns. It gives us the part of the story that reveals our human efforts don't work.

The story suggests the dominant pattern for solving the problem is pride, which is simply an attempt at self-validation. It also offers four other derivatives that are all human inventions: social comparison or class, relationship, the law and religion.

Each system represents a different method of validation using different means. Pride is the original mechanism of self-validation. It is a means of playing judge. Social comparison or class is a means of creating evidence that suggests approval based on comparison. Relationships are the means of seeking approval from someone else, especially those in authority. The law is any attempt to find validation in keeping a moral agreement. Religion is any attempt to find validation and justification from a manufactured god or gods.

These systems of validation suffer from an easily observable problem. They are attempts to solve the problem using subjective means. The standard used to define what is good is always subjective, culturally based, and changing. Someone has to make the subjective judgment of what makes someone good. The judge can be any relationship we can encounter: God, self, other, or world.

~~

Pride

The first way of the world is pride. Pride is essentially an attempt at self-validation using a subjective standard. It is the original means that Adam and Eve were tricked into. It is a natural outcome of trying to be like God by judging what is good and evil. We instinctively know we want and even need to be qualitatively good, but the means we use eventually crumbles under the weight of scrutiny.

Pride is alluring because it feels like something we're already supposed to do. We're supposed to value ourselves, aren't we? But it doesn't work because the basis of our value is in our own subjective judgments, not in God's declaration of dignity.

God's central concern with pride is that it doesn't work. It fails to produce life. Pride is a natural extension of the root problem. It's predicated on the idea of becoming. The only person who needs to become is someone who is not yet sufficient. Pride is then an attempt to solve a problem that technically doesn't exist. Humanity is already good, but trapped under the lie that it is potentially evil. By attempting to become good or prove that they are good, they continuously begin with and thus validate the idea they are not good enough, or not yet. This leads to a downward spiral that always ends in despair.

Pride is self-referential because when we begin with "not yet good" the mind is continuously drawn to what we have failed to do. In avoiding failure, we are drawn to it. In creating the false dichotomy of validation based on something subjective, we cannot ignore even the slightest evidence that implies our guilt. No matter how many "good" images we create, we are always reminded of the broken ones, the events where we lied to our neighbor, stole a piece of candy, or lashed out at our friend. And if we fail to see these moments, the world will remind us of them.

Once we accept the judgment, which is based on something subjective, we must also subject the basis to scrutiny. We can process it internally, and even come to the conclusion that we are good based upon our own internal criteria. We can even convince ourselves of this truth even if we don't quite believe it. We need to believe it's true. But in order to truly validate it, we must subject it to external scrutiny. And once we do, we invalidate our own response because the world will remind us it just won't accept anything less than perfection. And someone else's basis will always be different.

Pride instinctively produces an unpleasant aroma of arrogance because the means of validation is always subjective--our judgment. Internally we hold the judgment that we are good for no other reason than that we need to. Pride inflates the value of the evidence attempting to make it bigger than it really is. It flaunts it, which immediately leads one to question its value. And the more we try, the sillier we look.

The one moment God steps out of silence is to address the self-destructive issue of pride. Humanity builds a monument to its own grandeur known as the Tower of Babel.

> Now the whole world had one language and a common speech. As men moved eastward, they found a plain in Shinar and settled there.
>
> They said to each other, "Come, let's make bricks and bake them thoroughly." They used brick instead of stone, and tar for mortar. (Gen

11:1-3)

Bricks are important because they represent the progression of human creativity. Bricks, which are a mix of mud and straw, can be molded and stacked. Rocks require cutting and moving, sometimes distances. Bricks can be created right at the construction site. Bricks by themselves are an amazing invention, a fabulous use of creativity.

The initial desire is for a city. The tribe is the common social structure of a small group of people who would live together. The city is a natural extension of that. It is a larger group of people banding together. Cain actually built the first city almost immediately after leaving God. It seems natural that a man with experience of death would seek out protection from death through a communal agreement not to kill.

The city has one important characteristic that requires bricks: a wall. The city wall becomes a means of defining and protecting the people. It becomes an objective barrier to let people know where the city starts but also where it ends. But where a wall keeps people out, it also traps people in. The desire for protection also becomes the constant reminder of a defined limitation. In many ways it becomes the next generation of the covering.

Once trapped inside the wall they still need to solve the problem. And the story presents a fascinating account of how they attempt this. They build a monument up to the heavens. And what is their reason?

> *Then they said, "Come, let us build ourselves a city, with a tower that*
> *reaches to the heavens, so that we may make a name for ourselves and*
> *not be scattered over the face of the whole earth." (Gen 11:4)*

The tower is essentially a monument to their sense of grandeur. They're trapped within a defined limit but they still need to prove they can be like the gods. Heaven is where the gods reside. But the humans create this tower in order to understand and validate themselves. The only people who need to make a name for themselves are people who have forgotten their identity, or those who have never been told who they are. In other words, the tower exposes the root problem.

God's response is especially curious. There is no anger. There is no retribution or wrath. God actually protects them from their own devices.

> *But the LORD came down to see the city and the tower that the men were building. The LORD said, "If as one people speaking the same language they have begun to do this, then nothing they plan to do will be impossible for them." (Gen 11:5-6)*

In many ways this is God's first response to empire, the collective gathering together as a community to validate itself through might and creative force. God recognizes that language is a connection point to ideas and possibilities. Speaking the same language calls out the reality of their agreement on an idea. But the means of their effort is destructive.

This is the problem with pride. By engaging it, it produces the exact opposite effect we are looking for. It completely distorts our perception of what is possible. We become captivated and even galvanized by a sense of grandeur, that anything is possible. We become fascinated by the possibility that we can actually solve the problem through human means, that we can gain the favor of God by human effort.

To protect humanity, God intervenes on their behalf.

> *Come, let us go down and confuse their language so they will not understand each other." (Gen 11:7)*

Over and over again God protects humanity from itself. The original idea of a "city" is essentially a collective human effort to organize around human agreement not to kill each other. From there it can begin to design rules or laws that define social interaction. City is what happens when enough people collectively agree to work together. Instead of physical resources being used against each other, they can be used with each other.

City is the precursor to the fullest embodiment of pride, which is "empire". Empire is what happens when that collective group becomes a force to be reckoned with. Empire reveals the possibility of assembling and validating ourselves through sheer mass and force.

The implications of empire are staggering because it does provide an initial sense of peace and protection. The idea that "we are bigger than you" keeps the "other" from attacking. The collective agreement centralizes trade, food distribution and the arts. It provides a military to protect and even expand the borders. Community protection exists because there is always someone managing order.

But the protection comes at great cost. Empires require extensive taxation, create classes of wealth, and can require conscription to an army. Slavery is common and human rights are entirely subjective. Most people are subject to a ruling class. The greater an empire grows the more people become afraid of it, which potentially increases the risk of attack. Those who are defeated in battle become subjects of the new empire.

Empires require someone to be in control. The empire must be managed. And that control almost always comes through the force of might. Those who rise to the top of the empire are considered gods in the flesh, kings of kings and lords of lords. Very early in the story empire becomes the primary means of oppression. Egypt, one of the earlier empires, even ends up becoming one of the central locations in the story for human oppression.

~~

Social Comparison

Pride uses a subjective means of comparison for validation. The natural extension of that and the one men are bent towards is social comparison, which is a subset of pride. It is any arbitrary standard used to judge people. We define what is good and then do whatever it takes to acquire those elements. We locate something resembling perfection and then create a standard based on that perfection. Social comparison is perhaps the dominant means we use to bolster pride.

The standard is typically based on something tangible like attributes, assets, and skills, which provide a sense of gratification. The more immediate the gratification to a larger group of people, the more valuable it becomes. The more valuable it becomes, the more it is good. But the opposite is also true. The more immediately it gratifies the sooner it loses value.

Social comparison works on a scale. We search for someone better than us to give us hope about what we can "become", but we validate ourselves predominantly be reminding ourselves of those behind us. In many ways those in front of us are just as troublesome, consistently reminding us of what we have yet to become.

Social comparison is entirely subjective and subject to time. What is valuable in one time period can change in the next. If we lose the tangible element that provided the value, we become invalidated. We see this in fashion, automobiles, and even art.

Perhaps the most immediate sense of gratification is beauty. Beauty is visual and can be judged immediately. Attitudes in one culture about what is beautiful can be entirely different in another culture. Even within tribes, the standard can vary widely, and often does. Beauty is in the eye of the beholder. The data used for comparison can be entirely arbitrary. It only requires that a large enough group of people want it.

To posses beauty is intoxicating because we understand its value in the world. Yet somehow even the "most" beautiful fail to overcome their insecurities. Their lives reveal the same want for validation. The prophet Ezekiel laments the perils of beauty.

> "So you were adorned with gold and silver; your clothes were of fine linen and costly fabric and embroidered cloth. Your food was fine flour, honey and olive oil. You became very beautiful and rose to be a queen. And your fame spread among the nations on account of your beauty, because the splendor I had given you made your beauty perfect, declares the Sovereign LORD.
>
> But you trusted in your beauty and used your fame to become a

prostitute. You lavished your favors on anyone who passed by and your beauty became his. You took some of your garments to make gaudy high places, where you carried on your prostitution. Such things should not happen, nor should they ever occur." (Ez 16:13-16)

The problem with beauty is that it eventually becomes an asset we are prone to prostitute. Fundamentally we understand that we are more than our beauty. Our beauty is seen as the something separate from the self, something which can be sold. So we become managers of our own prostitution, selling it at every turn. And if we lose our beauty, which everyone does with age, our sense of validation disappears with it.

At a deeper level of comparison are tangible assets like physical possessions, money, and social capital. In most cultures this becomes a class system of haves and have-nots. Those who have control the system, simply for the sake of keeping what they have.

Assets create the illusion of material blessing, which is that "I must be blessed because I have." Within the human story is a myth that God blesses only those who are good and doesn't bless those who are evil. Yet the story consistently reveals God's blessing is not based on performance. Jesus completely obliterated this idea.

"(God) causes his sun to rise on the evil and the good, and sends rain on the righteous and the unrighteous. " (Mt 5:45)

From God's perspective everyone is part of creation. We can see ourselves as evil or good, but it doesn't change God's judgment of us. Wisdom is God's perspective about humanity that it is good. True wealth is the capacity to trust in God's wisdom. It is the realization of the God imagination.

Physical assets suffer from an important problem. We eventually lose them, spend them, or somebody steals them. And if we die with them, we can't take them with us. It is not uncommon for people to see the folly of assets during periods of suffering. In the shadow of death or persecution, we instinctively recognize that our "stuff" can't validate us. Job wrestled with the search for wisdom in physical assets as he lamented his situation with God.

> *"But where can wisdom be found? Where does understanding dwell?*
> *Man does not comprehend its worth; it cannot be found in the land of*
> *the living. The deep says, 'It is not in me'; the sea says, 'It is not with me.'*
> *It cannot be bought with the finest gold, nor can its price be weighed in*
> *silver. It cannot be bought with the gold of Ophir, with precious onyx or*
> *sapphires. Neither gold nor crystal can compare with it, nor can it be had*
> *for jewels or gold. (Job 28:12-17)*

In the midst of an experience that strips away Job's possessions, an event that must have felt like death, Job understands that assets can't solve the root problem, expressed as a loss of wisdom. In our most pressing moments things can only further the illusion.

At an even deeper level is knowledge and skill. Basic knowledge and skills include the capacity to grow food, construction, or tend animals, skills that keep people alive on a sustenance level. The more valuable skills are those that are complex or can protect people, such as strategy, rhetoric, architecture, and combat. In a tradition-oriented culture, knowledge and skill become very valuable because they can't be stolen.

The problem with skill is that our identity and validation is dependent upon the continued ability to perform that action. Once we cease our "performance", we lose the means of our validation. We see this in professional performers like athletes, actors, and musicians. As long as they can perform in a way that is pleasing to the crowd, they are good. But once they fail, or stop performing, the applause ends.

King Solomon laments the problem of knowledge and skill. At the end of the day, all of our knowledge and skill goes to waste.

> *So my heart began to despair over all my toilsome labor under the sun.*
> *For a man may do his work with wisdom, knowledge and skill, and then*
> *he must leave all he owns to someone who has not worked for it. This too*
> *is meaningless and a great misfortune. What does a man get for all the*

toil and anxious striving with which he labors under the sun? (Ecc 2:20-22)

Solomon understood that much like beauty and possessions, knowledge and skill have a finite limit.

~~

Relationships

Even if we believe we are validated, we still have that nagging sense of wanting to validate our own opinion by seeking the approval of others. We just can't help it. In most cases, it's just easier. This leads to the third common attempt, and the one toward which women are often bent, which is validation through relationships. Pride eventually reveals its limitations. The easiest thing to do is find someone to tell us we're good. This is the basis of relationships as a means of self-validation.

The initial means of validation in relationships resides in the parents. We hear the stories they tell about us and over time it generates a sense of understanding about our worth. We are loved or we are not. We are good or we are not. The judgment we end up with does not even have to be the actual judgment the parents express, because the judgment is a complex story of both positive and negative experiences. Like Bob, it is just as easy to assume the final judgment based on our perception of that judgment.

The relationship to the parent initially assumes the parent knows the answer. But if the parents were told a different story, it is likely they will pass that story of invalidation to the child – not because they want to, but because it is the only story they know. A child experiences invalidation as the norm because the parent was invalidated. If one or more parents are absent, the child is often compelled to invent a story.

Over time and as we grow older, we begin to experience relationships with friends, neighbors, classmates, co-workers, bosses and even spouses. The social connection of friends, or better yet, a best friend, is powerfully exhilarating. Each of these "others" becomes a possible representation of our value. When they call us, spend time with us, and desire friendship with us, it becomes validating. When that same friend abandons us, it calls into question the entire relationship, and more importantly offers evidence that supports our validation. Rejection stings because it directly affects our sense of validation.

When we discover romantic love, it is often experienced as rapturous delight. We marvel at the possibility that someone in the world could actually see beyond our frailty, brokenness, and hidden secrets. We wonder at the idea that someone would share their body and even the responsibility of parenting. But if this validation is lost, the experience is often equally if not more devastating. The loss of love brings into question our original hopes.

The value of relationships is in the concept of authority. Someone may just be an expert on what is true. We seek out the authority on a subject because she has earned the respect of the larger crowd. There are two specific relationships, outside of parents, that hold tremendous power of authority: the teacher and the preacher. When our parents send us to school, they invariably grant the teacher authority in our lives. The assumption is that teachers know what is true. This authority grants them the right to instruct us, but it also grants them the authority to make judgments about our conduct and skill. They grade us and even award us. These judgments shape our perceptions of the self in very deep ways.

The second and arguably the most powerful external relationship is the preacher. In some cultures this would be the rabbi, shaman, yogi, priest, or imam. Preachers are typically seen as the representative of the knowledge of God, an idea that is more granted than presented. Their role is to figure it all out for us and to tell us what the answers are. And of principal concern is our value. So if the preacher tells us God is angry at humanity and can't get over it unless there is sacrifice, we take notice.

The problem with finding our validation in relationships is the same as pride or social comparison. The basis for validation is always based upon something subjective. The basis for value is rooted in subjective feelings, circumstances, experiences or judgments, which can easily change on a whim or over time. If someone calls us good but then exhibits evil, is their authority in question? If that person removes their validation, was it ever true?

Human relationship is arguably our most dominant system of validation because it is the most fundamental. Social interaction, connection and even intimacy are essential to seeing the God image in our midst. Relationships reflect the God image to us, often informing us about who we are, even when we don't realize it.

But the responsibility of validating another human being is a terrible and even impossible weight to hold. We feel this tension in relationships with people who show up as needy or wanting. The act of validating reveals itself to be insufficient.

~~

The Law

The fourth common attempt to validate the self is a form of social agreement called the law. This is a socially accepted list of practices used as a basis for judgment of one another. The assumption is that evil will eventually reveal itself through social encounters. The opposite is also true. What if someone could perform such perfect action that one could render oneself approved? What if that person could fulfill the social agreement for acceptable action in such a perfect way that the gods would be forced to grant favor?

The law develops because within community is the potential for a downward spiral of retribution. For example, when David accidentally kills John's cow, John is forced to consider his response. He can do nothing, which might lead David to believe he can do anything he wants to John and his property. Or he can do something that teaches David never to do it again. By escalating his response John creates fear. Instead of killing David's cow, he kills three of his oxen, which now affects David's family's ability to eat. David buys into the escalation of violence and instead of killing three oxen, kills John's family. John continues the escalation of violence and enlists the help of his tribe, killing David and his entire tribe.

This downward spiral of violence has no real end other than human annihilation. It arguably finds support in the myth of redemptive violence, which suggests the gods favor those who conquer. Might makes right. It incites the imagination.

Niccolò Machiavelli, a sixteenth century Italian statesman, eventually crafted a poetic articulation of retribution.

> *"Upon this, one has to remark that men ought either to be well treated or crushed, because they can avenge themselves of lighter injuries, of more serious ones they cannot; therefore the injury that is to be done to a man ought to be of such a kind that one does not stand in fear of revenge." (The Prince, p11)*

Machiavelli understood that in order to truly quell violence we had to eliminate the other person's capacity to respond. We had to go all the way. And the only way to go all the way involves a violent form of death.

To create a sense of equilibrium that allows people to live together, humanity creates a standard of what is acceptable for human interaction. But in order for these ideas to work, it requires agreement between two parties. These agreements create the basis of the law. These laws could only be enforced through the power of the tribes. The power isn't then in the law but in the agreement with the law.

In order for humanity to create the law, someone had to sit in the seat of judgment and define the law. In other words, the law was humanity's attempt to turn the subjective into the objective through social agreement. If enough people agree, it must be true. The law became the standard of life. It included what to do and what not to do. And that standard was entirely arbitrary, dependent on the person sitting in the seat of judgment and defined the law, typically the tribal leader. That person didn't need to be right. He just needed others to agree he was right.

The law was a tool to cement the collective agreement of action to reduce violence. Two people standing next to each other are harmless until they take up arms against each other. The law initially didn't have to produce justice. It just had to keep people from killing each other and seeking an escalated form of revenge.

The law eventually determined the response. The term "eye for an eye" actually prevented a man from engaging an escalated form of violence. It created an exacting form of punishment on the perpetrator. God's law to his people would later include this idea of "eye for an eye".

But contrary to common perception, the Ten Commandments were not the first set of organized laws within humanity. In Mesopotamian culture, a man named Hammurabi created what is considered the first organized legal code. Hammurabi's Code contained 282 laws and existed almost 500 years before the Ten Commandments. The code was considered a marvel of community establishment. Most of the codes dealt with the subject of theft, agriculture, property rights, slaves, murder, and injury.

But the problem with the law is that is becomes infinitely complex. Every circumstance has an infinite number of parts. Each specific circumstance must then be judged individually even if there is a law. The weight of judgment is not in presence of the law but in the sheer magnitude of the law. To play the game of law is to play God because it presupposes enough information about any event to define what is right in any given circumstance.

But what if God were to define the law for us? What if God offered up a basic set of laws that would help humanity define social interaction? The Ten Commandments provided a basic framework for social interaction from God's perspective. But within God's law is a provocative possibility. What would happen if we could keep them? All of them? Would that person be complete? Could that person judge oneself, or be judged as acceptable or good? Would we gain the favor of God?

This creates the distinction between character and personality. Personality is the public face. Character is the private one. It eventually becomes obvious that one wouldn't need to actually be good in private, as long as one could project goodness in public.

This is the fundamental tension of seeking validation in the law. To fulfill the law is to suggest completeness. God even speaks about the law as a way to live.

"Hear now, O Israel, the decrees and laws I am about to teach you. Follow them so that you may live and may go in and take possession of the land that the LORD, the God of your fathers, is giving you." (Deut 4:1)

The first purpose of the law was to produce life. If humanity followed it, they wouldn't kill each other.

Unfortunately the law has a nasty side effect. It has a distinct way of revealing that we can't keep it. The Apostle Paul explored this idea in his letter to the Romans.

Therefore no one will be declared righteous in his sight by observing the law; rather, through the law we become conscious of sin. (Rom 3:20)

The law was added so that the trespass might increase. (Rom 5:20)

The law is then not primarily a system for morality. God provides the law so that "the trespass might increase." The law is in essence a constructive mechanism for revealing the root problem. It's very counterintuitive. To attempt to follow it is to break ourselves over it. It reveals our sense of lusting and pride, the want that cannot be fulfilled. The law is only as good as when we agree to it. Once we break it, it reveals the fallacy of our capacity to keep it.

To engage the law is to reveal the evidence that supports our own judgments. The law is self-condemning.

"But your iniquities have separated you from your God; your sins have hidden his face from you, so that he will not hear." (Is 59:2)

Notice the perspective in which Isaiah speaks. It is the sin, or incorrect judgment, that separates us from God, not God. We see our own brokenness and we assume we are unlovable. We condemn ourselves. We assume God will not hear us because we have broken the law.

The question then becomes, "Why do we hold onto an idea that eventually condemns us?" The allure of the law is the capacity to catch, to control, and to condemn the "other". We hold onto the law because it also serves to protect us. We use it to our benefit in order to keep the other from killing us. When we judge those around us, we condemn, allowing us to keep people at bay.

And this is where the law becomes a trap. To place our faith in the law is then to become subject to its full demands. The moment we create and agree to a subjective standard is the moment we become subject to it. This is fine for the other. But the moment we're guilty, we're the first ones who want the exception. We want mercy instead of punitive justice. We feel the full weight of its measure.

We cannot ignore the fact that God doesn't begin the story with the communal law. God's law is not revealed for 2,500 years and only after human beings create a common code. Its primary purpose is to reveal the root problem and the eventual problem of guilt. Guilt leads us to one final means of validation: religion.

~~

Religion

The final common attempt to validate the self is through religion. Religion is a human invention and is largely a process for dealing with guilt through an exchange. The exchange is a subjective and relative offering of tangible value to gain favor or to appease the gods' anger or wrath against the person. Virtually all god-based religions share this same construct. Only the assumption of what the god looks like changes.

Religion begins with a sense of guilt. We do something we judge as evil, which forces us to construct an understanding of God's response. But as Adam and Eve, and later Cain revealed, the judgment is self-perpetuated. Without a clear understanding of God, we naturally project our own sense of anger back onto God. We assume God can't get over it. Instead of discovering the truth, we walk away from God. The farther away we walk, the less informed we are of

God's actual response. It means we no longer know God. Over time, we can only assume what God is like.

If our perception is that we are detached from God we still need an image of God. Instinctively we understand something controls everything, even if we don't know what "it" is. All we know is the god(s) control things that make living possible. Perhaps it's one god. Perhaps it's multiple gods. God's image is then a manifestation of what we think God looks like as opposed to who God really is. God becomes a reflection of ourselves, ruthless and demanding, bloodthirsty and evil. God then needs satisfaction because we need satisfaction. Humanity is then forced to gain favor or appease the gods.

Not surprisingly, the gods always looks like us. Inevitably, humanity begins to wonder and eventually cast out what it thinks God looks like. Is there one god? Are there multiple gods? Are there multiple versions of the same god? Humanity begins to notice really important things like rain, and seasons have a deep effect on its capacity to eat and live. If the rain doesn't come, or the neighboring villages pillage our crops, does that mean the god(s) are angry? If circumstances don't turn in our favor, does that mean the god(s) are somehow not on our side? If a crop produces a bounty of food, does that mean the god(s) s have shined on us? If the gods are somehow angry, we needed to appease them.

The fullest physical representation of our projection is the idol. Religion requires a god(s) to validate. But detached from god, humanity is compelled to do what it does best. It casts its image of god outward and creates a physical representation of that god as an idol. We create a tangible representation or form of our imagination and then we bow down and worship it. But in order to tangibly deal with and talk about this image, we have to create language around it. We give these images names like Anu, Ishtar, and Molech.

"These myths were metaphorical attempts to describe reality. These dramatic and evocative stories of gods and goddesses helped people to articulate their sense of the powerful but unseen forces in the world."
(Karen Armstrong, A History of God, p5)

The source of these gods is our imagination. They look somewhat like us because they are like us. They reveal our distorted perceptions of what we think God looks like. They often end up as strangely fat, unshapely, and mean. They are true because we believe they are true and real and powerful enough to affect our lives.

Idols represent the fullest expression of the power of the lie. The idol represents the lie's ability to manifest something outside of the self to which we become subject. We cast it onto something tangible and then become subject to its demands. These projections will demand our death over their own, subjecting us to all kinds of sacrifice, punishment and shame. And because we believe they are real, we will follow right along.

The idea of creating idols is actually a natural expression of our design. God creates a reality and then we do the same. God projects an image onto us. The idea of image-casting is then a natural extension of that design. The image we cast is an expression of the mental image we are holding. So if we cast an image of God, we're creating a limited understanding of who God is. Idols aren't just our interpretations of God. They are the representation of anything that validates us, anything that plays the role of God in the religious system.

God's eventual prohibition against creating an idol is then a protective mechanism to keep us from limiting our understanding of God and ourselves. It was so important that it became one of the original Ten Commandments.

> "You shall not make for yourself an idol in the form of anything in
> heaven above or on the earth beneath or in the waters below." (Ex 20:4)

The prohibition was essentially God protecting us from limiting ourselves. The problem with idols is the same as the false identity. Once we create an understanding of God, we become subject to that god, in all of its forms. We limit what is possible in God because we create a limiting construct. We limit ourselves in terms of what is possible.

If we are truly reflections of God's image, then our capacities are much larger than we can possibly even imagine. Jesus intimated this to the disciples.

Jesus replied, "I tell you the truth, if you have faith and do not doubt, not only can you do what was done to the fig tree, but also you can say to this mountain, 'Go, throw yourself into the sea,' and it will be done." (Mt 21:21)

The problem isn't our capacity. The problem is our ability to create naturally limiting barriers for ourselves. But if we limit ourselves, then we become prisoners of our own design. We create obstacles that keep us from realizing the God image in ourselves.

Guilt produces a strange problem. It's easy to experience guilt simply because we assume we are guilty. If God's response is directly related to how we act, then we have to be conscious of what we do. This wonder can compel us to admit our guilt, but it can also drive us mad wondering if we have committed something we're not even aware of, or to search where nothing exists. What if someone in the family has done something "wrong"? What if the discretion is hidden?

The problem then is not actual guilt. The problem is our lack of knowledge about God's response. God's primary response is to show mercy and to seek restoration through confession. But standing in the way of our restoration is our projected assumption about how God will respond if we admit guilt. We assume God is angry. The problem then is our basis for understanding God's response. Instead of asking for God's response, we invent one that is entirely subjective.

Religion assumes God's favor or appeasement can be bought. If the god'(s) anger is stirred, then maybe it would accept something in exchange for holding back that anger. What if we could stave off retribution through a bribe? This same idea can also be turned around. If the god(s) would accept an offering for guilt, would they also accept an offering in exchange for favor in things like harvest, pregnancy, and war? What was once an intimate relationship of love and validation becomes nothing more than a transactional business relationship.

If the god(s) will accept an offering, the question is then, "What do we have that has value?" In a developing Mesopotamian world, possessions were of tangible value. Things like food and animals were important for survival. So someone would set out an offering to a god and wait. And then an interesting question would arise. If the crop manifested a good harvest, did the original offering work? The process became subjective. The bribe didn't have to be true to work. It just needed enough people to think it was true.

In an age of information scarcity and myth, the idea of appeasing the gods through sacrifice is somehow born. What is a possibility in one generation becomes true in the next. Ideas spread not because they are true, but because humanity believes them to be true, because humans observe that one instance that works just enough to make us believe they are true. Over generations, these religious constructs gain a foothold because they are traditions passed down by unsuspecting and even concerned parents.

The religious process becomes self-reinforcing. The easiest move to make when we are born into a world that already practices religion is to simply accept the religion. It's what is given to us as a tradition. To question the tradition is to reject the society into which one is born.

What if there were people who knew what would appease the gods and who could tell us what bribes they would accept? Over time, the development of the religious priest is born. Someone would tell another person, "If you just offer a tenth of your grain, the god of the sun would be appeased, granting you favor." People would pay someone to make the sacrifice for them.

Within the Mesopotamian culture, the religious system produces a multitude of different gods for different things. Different gods control different things. So when a person needs to know how to appease a specific god, it goes to the religious priests for that god. Each god demands different things to bestow favor or to be appeased.

The question is then how far the gods will go to require favor or demand being appeased. What do humans possess that holds true value in order to release guilt or gain favor? It doesn't matter that the demand is extreme. It only matters that the demand is met.

Within a tribal culture, the most valuable thing a person has is one's life. But to offer the self doesn't solve the problem. It only makes it worse. The most valuable thing to a person then is not the food, or possessions, but the child that will carry the name of the family, who will protect the tribe, and work in the field. And the sacrifice doesn't just extend to the child's capacity to work off the transgression. True sacrifice comes in the form of blood, in losing the child permanently.

But within that system is another measure. What if the child was just a frail son, or worse, a son of ill repute? This would not do. A true sacrifice would be a son that mattered, that reflected the best of what humanity had to offer. The ultimate sacrifice would be a perfect son.

As brutal and horrific as this idea sounds, this is exactly what ends up happening. Humanity reaches a point where it is willing to sacrifice its own children to save itself. Molech, for example, demanded the death of children. Humanity literally subjects itself to horrific manifestations that demand the death of one's own child. Death takes on such a deep form that humanity is willing to kill its own reflection to satisfy its own sense of guilt.

Even if it is not as demanding, we see this in our own world. We create an assumption about God that demands appeasing. We assume God can only love us if there is a proper sacrifice. Or we assume that God's favor can be bought through that same sacrifice. How often do we say, "God, I will do this, if you give me this." We barter with God in a way that makes the relationship transactional.

The primary problem with the religious construct is that it is a temporary and individual solution to each transgression. If we do something to anger the god(s) again, we have to produce another sacrifice. The religious process is essentially endless and often bloody. It is important to reiterate that like the law, religion is deeply embedded in the Mesopotamian culture long before God ever uses it in the nation of Israel.

If the religious process is our understanding of god's response, it exposes our need for punitive action. We need blood to satisfy our own sense of guilt. We see this enacted over and over again when someone is murdered. We demand the murderer be killed. We confront death by becoming death itself. We need a harsh penalty to satisfy our own demands.

This is the immense power of the lie. Religion is a human construct primarily designed to solve the problem of guilt. It is an attempt to make meaning where none exists. But in the process of reading God through the covering, humanity ends up serving gods of its own creation. It bows down to a manufactured invention. It didn't really matter that the gods were fickle, ruthless, and demanding. It didn't matter that they looked just like us. All that mattered was that they be appeased or that we could gain favor. Much of the criticism against religion, especially by atheists, is warranted for this very reason.

The allure of religion is similar to the law. It holds the immense capacity to control the "other". True religion, in its essence, requires a subjective god who is in some way fickle and prone to respond in human ways. If a priest tells someone god is angry, and the person believes it, the priest can actually control the person. The person becomes subject to the priest's visions. The priest can literally become one of the most powerful people in the land. God becomes a mechanism to control the people based on naïveté. The priests can command inquisitions, torture, and even war in the name of God.

~~

Lust

The central motivating force that drives each of these systems of validation is the root problem. Humanity holds onto the idea that it is incomplete and needs validation. It grasps onto the role of judge and gets the question wrong. And as long as we seek to "become" good based on human effort, we will always be wanting. This want is the insatiable force called lust. We want for something that cannot be fulfilled because we believe the lie that we need it. We buy into the lie that something will fulfill us.

Lust is the physical force that arises from the insatiable need for validation. Lust is not a power in the sense that it produces something creative or meaningful. It is a force, compelling us to acquire better, more, faster, and stronger for the sake of validation, even at great cost.

The Apostle John talks about a lusting with our eyes, and with our flesh. We see something and we assume it will fulfill us. We create a story of what is true, about that thing's ability to validate us. We literally crave it in our flesh because it is a manifestation of our judgments.

We see lust played out in each form of validation, with pride, social comparison, relationships, the law, and with religion. Over and over again, humanity seeks to fulfill a want with something that cannot fulfill.

> *Do not lust in your heart after her beauty or let her captivate you with her eyes, (Pr 6:25)*

> *You burn with lust among the oaks and under every spreading tree; you sacrifice your children in the ravines and under the overhanging crags. (Is 57:5)*

> *She gave herself as a prostitute to all the elite of the Assyrians and defiled herself with all the idols of everyone she lusted after. (Ezk 23:7)*

> *For everything in the world—the cravings of sinful man, the lust of his eyes and the boasting of what he has and does—comes not from the Father but from the world. (1 Jn 2:16)*

History provides endless stories of the insatiable drive for more. Alexander the Great, Greek king of Macedon, was famous for conquering the Ancient world and ended up lamenting the insatiability of it.

> *"When Alexander saw the breadth of his domain, he wept for there were no more worlds to conquer." (Plutarch's AD 46-126, Life of Alexander.)*

Lust is destructive because it eventually convinces us to play an endless game of acquisition. We assume that if we are beautiful enough, or have enough, or boast enough, we will then be fulfilled. But enough is an arbitrary number. It's subjective, and because enough is subjective it is never enough.

Lust compels us to find meaning and value in a thing which is eventually manifested in a form or an idol. But in that search we eventually prostitute ourselves, surrendering our dignity for the sake of acquisition. We become like the thing, a product, something to be sold. For women this comes in the literal form of prostitution. For men it is subtler, coming in the form of slavery. The lusting turns us into the marketer of a body for the sake of validation. We become our own worst enemies, peddling flesh to the highest and sometimes the lowest bidder.

Worse yet is when we attain something that creates a false sense of perfection. We gain rock star status and become blinded by the lights. We believe our own press, at least for a while. We think we've arrived as we buy into the idea that we actually are good by our own means. And the higher we climb, the farther we fall. Beauty fades. Possessions break, decay, or get stolen. Skills wither. The audience becomes fickle. The law reminds us of that one thing we've done wrong. Our sacrifices were for that old problem. This is a new one. We wonder if God has abandoned that which once shone like the stars.

What is astounding about lust is how it survives as a force. The moment we attain something, we typically or inevitably experience a letdown regarding the object of our affection. We see that it has no real power to validate. It's just an inanimate object. The problem inside is revealed once again. But instead of ceasing our search, we simply replace it with something new.

Lust typically leads to the idea of possession. To possess something means we find our identity in that thing. We possess the bigger, the better, the stronger, and the faster; hoping it will becomes the means of validation. Lust is more seductive than possession because lust carries a story of possibility and hope. It fuels our imagination because we have yet to make it a reality. Possession always begins the slow, progressive experience that kills hope because stuff ultimately can't validate us.

Lust is the fuel that informs our search for validation. But we cannot ignore the deep influence and social value which religion, and even some of the human constructs for validation, have on culture. The temptation is to simply want to shut off and fall into a depressive state of paralysis. It is there that we can turn to understand why we hold onto them. They are in essence coping mechanisms. They are a means of making sense of our own reality, from a blind perspective.

As long as we point to the constructs and try to eliminate them, without addressing the underlying root problem, we will be shooting ourselves in the foot. To call them out as coping mechanisms allows us to sit with them for a while and begin the slow process of letting them go so we can see what remains underneath them.

If God's primary concern is consequence, we can draw the conclusion that God's concern for lust is primarily in how it affects us. The problem with lust is not necessarily that it is morally wrong, but that it captivates us in a way that destroys us. It blinds us to our own self-destruction. To lust after something means we are captivated by the idea that a thing, a person, or a sense of circumstance will actually validate us. And if this idea is true, we will do anything it takes to acquire that fulfillment. We will lie, cheat, steal and beg to get that one thing.

Lust represents the created order ruling over us. The physical world is controlling us, producing a want that distorts our perception of reality and compels us to fulfill a need that comes at the expense of our own humanity.

~~

The Unfolding

Up to this point, the story begins to reveal a remarkable fact. Much of the story so far is about humanity's downward spiral and God simply reacting. For 2,100 years the story focuses on God's interaction with only five individuals: Adam and Eve, Cain and Abel, and Noah. In each case, God is not the primary focus of the story. God is simply interacting with humanity to address human problems.

The dominant events in the story are humans eating from the tree, being expelled from the Garden, the first offering and subsequent first murder, the downward spiral of humanity resulting in the cleansing of the earth, and the birth of empire resulting in the confusion of language.

Humanity's primary response to the problem is the search for validation through five human constructs, which are fueled by lust: pride, social comparison, relationships, the law and religion. Religious practice becomes the norm rather than the exception. Empires begin to develop and even flourish. God has so far provided only one prohibition – do not murder – and consistently meets humanity in the midst of its situation.

The stark reality is that God is remarkably silent for much of history. If this were a movie we'd begin to ask if God is even the main character in the story. This relative silence strains our collective imagination. Does God's silence or relative inactivity mean God doesn't care? Or could it mean that God has a reason?

The silence is strange if the root problem is God's demand for justice, or if humanity has sold itself into captivity to Satan. We would imagine an immediate, stern rebuke or a list of demands that must be met in order for God to interact with us. Or we would expect some form of dialog between God and Satan. But both just don't happen. If the silence seems to suggest anything it is that God doesn't actually care about humanity. Maybe God really did abandon humanity. Under these circumstances, it creates a strange lead-in to God suddenly taking an interest in Abraham.

As brutal and strange as God's silence may seem, it is entirely consistent with God's original structure of grace and freedom. Humanity gets to walk away. It gets to explore alternative means of validation and solutions to the problem. It gets to explore evil in its entirety. This sense of freedom God gives us is unnerving because we assume that it has consequences that can change what is true. We assume that humanity can reach a point where it actually is no longer "good". But it doesn't. Humanity can't change what is already true. But it can suffer the consequences of its attempt.

The first 2,100 years are then an exploration into our own imagination. Like the Prodigal Son story we needed the time to give it a shot. We needed the space to run and hide, devise our own plans, give them a try, and discover they just don't work. Much like an alcoholic who has yet to discover his destructive patterns don't quite produce the redemptive quality he is seeking, God's silence is actually allowing humanity to discover that its own means of validation don't really work. What if God understands that humanity has to reach the collective and proverbial bottom? Much of our frustration with God's silence is often misguided attempts to blame God for circumstances that reveal our self-destructiveness.

The only way to get over evil is to fully explore it and come to the realization that it just doesn't work. It actually does produce death. And we need to know that, don't we? We need to know that our human effort pales in comparison to God's reality. Waiting allows this reality to be exposed.

Religion is arguably the most important human invention because it includes a transactional quality for dealing with guilt. It reveals the conditions of the contract that will satisfy the human soul, allowing it to release itself from guilt and cross the chasm. In other words, the religious process, which is a human invention, is humanity declaring:

> "This is what it would take to release us. We need a sacrifice of blood.
> And not just anybody, but perfect, human blood."

Religion is humanity's attempt at reconciliation with God. It is steeped in violence because it is designed through the covering. It is demanding because it is projected through a bent perspective that thirsts for nothing short of human blood. It is the fullest embodiment of death.

Chapter 8 – The Missio Dei

"I will make you into a great nation and I will bless you; I will make your name great, and you will be a blessing." - God

Sign Me Up

God does not remain silent forever. Once the human construct for dealing with the root problem has firmly revealed itself, God begins to act. Instead of inventing something entirely new that humanity won't understand, God uses what they have already invented. The religious process reveals the demands and conditions for humanity's own release. Humanity wants perfect human blood. What is more surprising is that God complies.

It is here that the story shifts in a dramatic way. God begins to proactively engage for the sake of humanity. Some scholars call this response the Missio Dei, or mission of God. It is the long, slow, painful, and often laboring process of redeeming humanity by fulfilling the human contract. And oh, what a response it is.

The first thing God does is to reach down into the world of religion and pick out the son of a man who actually makes idols. The Jewish Midrash suggests Abraham doesn't just know what religion means. He has lived his life watching his father serve its commands. An early tale of Abraham and his father Terah, told by the second century Rabbi Hiyya, gives us insight into the type of person he is. It reveals an insightful sensitivity to the religious.

> *"Terah was a manufacturer of idols. He once went away somewhere and left Abraham to sell them in his place. A man came and wished to buy one. 'How old are you?' Abraham asked him. 'Fifty years,' was the reply.*

'Woe to such a man!' he exclaimed, 'you are fifty years old and would
worship a day-old object!' On another occasion a woman came with a
plateful of flour and requested him, 'Take this and offer it to them.' So
he took a stick, broke them, and put the stick in the hand of the largest.
When (Terah) returned, he demanded, 'What have you done to them?' 'I
cannot conceal it from you,' he rejoined. 'A woman came with a plateful
of fine meal and requested me to offer it to them. One claimed, "I must
eat first," while another claimed, "I must eat first." Thereupon the largest
arose, took the stick, and broke them. 'Why do you make sport of me,' he
cried out; 'have they then any knowledge!' 'Should not your ears listen
to what your mouth is saying?' he retorted. (Midrash Genesis Rabbah
38:13)

Abraham knows that the religious process is a sham. And his trick reveals that his own father knows it too. In terms of religion, Abraham could be better described as an atheist. He's rejected the human projection of God. But watching his father serve, even consciously aware that it is a sham, must have ingrained in him a desire for something better, something more.

So when God arrives at Abraham's (initially called Abram) door with an offer, he jumps at it.

The LORD said to Abram, "Leave your country, your people and your
father's household and go to the land I will show you. I will make you
into a great nation and I will bless you; I will make your name great,
and you will be a blessing. I will bless those who bless you, and whoever
curses you I will curse; and all peoples on earth will be blessed through
you." (Gen 12:1-3)

This moment is often called "the blessing." The initial invitation must have been surreal. Instead of showing up with demands that must be appeased, God offers blessing to Abraham. But it's not really new. God isn't establishing what is becoming true. God is reiterating what is already true. God's first act after 2,100 years of virtual silence is to restore the God imagination into humanity. God is giving Abram hope by addressing the root problem. God cuts to the chase and electrifies the God imagination within him. He awakens something deep within Abraham's soul that is in fact already there.

For Abraham, here is a God unlike anything his father has ever manufactured. The story provides no assumption or evidence that there was any relationship with God before this. In other words, God is NOT choosing to give Abraham a God imagination because he's done something to earn it. God just shows up and makes the offer because it's already true.

The trick with his father revealed that the idols were just human constructs, but here was a God actually speaking to him. And the words are not like other gods. Instead of Abraham being called to earn God's favor, God is already giving favor. God arrives with gifts already in hand. And it's not just any favor, but a blessing; something that speaks to the deepest recesses of his soul, something that addresses the root problem.

God's voice provides an amazing sense of promise, but notice who is doing the validating. "I will make you…" "I will bless you…" "I will make you…" God is adamantly reorienting Abraham back to the original structure. God is giving Abram a renewed sense of dignity, identity, and purpose based upon God's declarations.

God is fundamentally shifting Abraham's orientation. He's giving him a way of seeing life through dignity. He's giving him a holistic perspective of how to see the world that is not subjective, but objective. All he has to do is embrace it.

What will Abraham do with this? He's likely going to question the reality of what he's hearing. He's not going forward as a blind follower. He's already shown that with his father. Instead he's going to think about it, and wrestle with it, and question the sanity of it. What if Abraham is the perfect person to begin with for this reason? To follow means Abraham actually believes there is a God there to follow.

Contrary to the other gods', this God's promise is also interested in humanity's greatness. In other word, this God is willing to share the glory. God includes humanity in the fullness of it. The God imagination is so great that it must be shared.

To experience, or fully realize, these things Abraham has to do one thing. He has to leave his place of origin. He has to separate himself from his story, his identity, his tribe, his foundation, and his sense of security. He has to leave his protective shell, his covering. In other words, God is pulling him out of a false sense of foundation in order to give him one that is true. This process reiterates one of the most consistent themes in the entire story. Humanity must leave the false self in order to embrace the true self.

~~

An Intrinsic Mobilizing Story

Abraham represents the beginning of what storytellers would call the turning point in the story. God interacts with humanity in such a unique way that the story turns toward hope and possibility. Contrary to the way of the world, which is imprisoned by an embedded captivating story, this new imagination gives Abraham an intrinsic mobilizing story. It works because it is true.

So Abram left, as the LORD had told him; and Lot went with him. (Gen 12:4)

Abraham takes the risk. The story is so meaningful it mobilizes him to action. He crosses the chasm to engage God. Abraham doesn't leave because he has to. He leaves because he gets to. To leave is to be human again. It is to discover what is true.

It is also important to remember that for God, who operates from kairos, there is no sense of time. The idea that "I will…" is strictly for humanity. Abraham has no reference to future events to sustain him. "I will…" then serves to speak to what will be true for Abraham, but is already true for God.

This new imagination is the means to faith. It is God-breathed, or what some would call Spirit-led. God is simply reminding Abraham of the story already written into the fabric of his being. He doesn't have to invent it. God is the one who made it happen. All Abraham has to do is to step into it and realize it.

The act of leaving makes it real in Abraham's world through trust. To leave is to realize it one step at a time. It is to discover the love that is already true. God's love, or validation, has always been there. Abraham just can't see it yet because he has no reference point in his long-term memory.

The Apostle Paul spoke of this spiritual realization process to the ecclesia in Corinth.

And now these three remain: faith, hope and love. But the greatest of these is love. (1 Co 13:13)

Faith is not inventing something. It is taking the risk to release the self from a state of perpetual captivity to the false image in our heads. It is opening our eyes to the God imagination in our lives. It is awakening our hearts and minds to the truth of God's perspective. It is reconnecting to the original story of blessing that God establishes in the beginning of the story. We don't have to earn it, or sacrifice for it. We don't have to strive to make it true. We just have to embrace it by surrendering to it through faith.

Once we engage faith, we create a new possibility of validation, one that is meaningful and better than what we are currently experiencing. This is hope. It is the future possibility realized but not yet fully experienced. But it's not something fleeting. It is deeply trustworthy because it is true. Hope mobilizes us to action because something new is possible. Good is true. It fills us with energy, passion and drive. It sustains us when we run into obstacles and it breathes life into our steps.

But as Paul said, the greatest of these is love. Love is the fullest realization of the God imagination. It is experiencing it in the moment, through friends and family, circumstances and events, emotions and thoughts. It is seeing everything from God's perspective, as true in the moment. It is being fully awake and alive to the reality of God's infinite, undying love. This gift of love is the God imagination in us. It is seeing that God has never left, never abandoned, never lost touch – and never will. Love is then the fullest realization of what has always been true.

Paul also understood that unleashing the God imagination was often developmental. It was something that grew to what he called a "full measure."

And to know this love that surpasses knowledge—that you may be filled to the measure of all the fullness of God. (Eph 3:19)

Much of the God imagination is then a process of discovering what is already true as we slowly take off the covering. We open ourselves to "leaving" the old constructs that create the false self. They are deeply embedded constructs that are typically released over time. These include our judgments of each relationship with God, the self, our neighbor, and the world around us.

~~

A Confrontation With Fear

The God imagination comes with a unique trait. The only way to sustain it is to continually practice discovering it in our minds. The God imagination is true, but the experience of it deepens over time. This means that we must learn to hold it even in the face of our worst fears. In other words, the fullest experience of the God imagination comes in the face of the worst possible fear that it might not be true.

As Abraham leaves his country, it is fair to think that he is somewhat sustained by a tangible understanding of blessing. He immediately experiences God's tangible favor in travels, wealth, allies, and even war. But the original promise includes being the father of a great nation, and that means one important element: a son. Over time, it becomes quite a staggering promise for an old man with no children. The God imagination is simply an image of hope, but not yet fully realized. So Abraham begins to doubt.

But Abram said, "O Sovereign LORD, what can you give me since I remain childless and the one who will inherit my estate is Eliezer of Damascus?" And Abram said, "You have given me no children; so a servant in my household will be my heir." (Gen 15:2-3)

We do this, don't we? We're bent towards doubt because our mind has so few reference points. We invent alternatives that seem a little more rational, a little more plausible to the evidence of our surroundings. We question what we hear and wonder if our hope is even possible.

God brings Abraham in direct confrontation with his fear. He's old. He's waiting, and waiting, but his wife is not producing a child. Maybe this God thing is just a figment of his imagination. Maybe he invented it. It's just too good to be true. Maybe the trick he played on his father has come back to haunt him. Maybe he's delusional. The lie rears its ugly head once again.

> *Then the word of the LORD came to him: "This man will not be your*
> *heir, but a son coming from your own body will be your heir." He took*
> *him outside and said, "Look up at the heavens and count the stars—if*
> *indeed you can count them." Then he said to him, "So shall your offspring*
> *be." (Gen 15:4-5)*

Faith inevitably leads to confrontation with our previous story, the one that our minds use to define us. The purpose is restorative. Rewriting our stories requires reconstitution. It requires pulling out the old reference points so we can rewrite them. But the act of pulling them out reminds us of what used to be true. It feels like doubt all over again. But we pull them out not so they can overwhelm us, but so we can overcome them.

In order to fully realize the God imagination, we must pass through fear, worry and dread. We must be subjected to the one doubt hiding in the shadows that we know exists: the worst-case scenario. Deep in our minds we hold onto the idea that we are the exception. We are the one person God is playing a trick on, and we fall for it. In order to release it, Abraham must actually confront his fear in his mind so he can let it go.

And what happens next is the moment of truth.

> *Abram believed the LORD, and he credited it to him as righteousness.*
> *(Gen 15:6)*

Abraham gets it right. Righteousness is not about fulfilling a contract. Reconciliation is not about covering guilt. It's about opening ourselves to the reality of God's perspective in our lives. All Abraham does is accept what is already true. He embraces the God imagination, God's original declaration of what is true.

Abraham presents serious problems for the traditional notions of atonement. God's declaration of righteousness comes before any means of religious reconciliation. His act of reconciliation is in believing what is already true, not embracing a religiously symbolic covering of blood.

God confirms this sense of reconciliation by changing Abraham's name, a practice God consistently uses throughout the story.

> *"No longer will you be called Abram; your name will be Abraham, for I have made you a father of many nations. I will make you very fruitful; I will make nations of you, and kings will come from you." (Gen 17:5-6)*

By engaging faith, Abraham is becoming a new kind of exception. He's becoming the exception to the way of the world. He's participating with God in rewriting the story, not just for himself, but also for all of humanity. This is why Abraham is the father of a great nation. He chooses the God imagination over his own. He holds onto the hope even in the midst of fear and doubt.

Abraham has changed. He is beginning to discover the God imagination within. He is discovering his dignity. He's realizing who he is and what he is called to do. His primary purpose is to engage the rule over himself by engaging the blessing. To engage reconciliation is to overcome his imagination. With God filling his imagination, he is now ready for the new reality. Twenty-five years of waiting are about to be realized.

~~

The Promised One

If we examine Abraham's life and we're honest, everything up until this point could simply be luck or fate. His blessings, wealth, and good fortune could be chalked up to timing, or the setting of the sun, or whatever we want to call it. The God imagination could simply be a God delusion playing with his mind.

But the child – now this is another matter.

Abraham is the perfect choice once again because he's too old. The idea of a child is not just unlikely, it's laughable. If he were young, having a child could qualify as fate, but not in this case. Abraham and Sarah, his wife, are now well beyond child bearing years. This is what makes Abraham's decision to trust even more ridiculous, and what, in fact, usually makes trusting God ridiculous. The deck is usually stacked against him.

This is the problem with faith. It is not realized until we develop tangible evidence that constitutes the embedded captivating story. As human beings we need real, observable evidence that gives us logical reason to rewrite the story. We can't see around the corner until we actually turn the corner. And just like that, we're around the corner.

> *Sarah became pregnant and bore a son to Abraham in his old age, at the very time God had promised him. (Gen 21:2)*

This is the moment in the story when everything changes, when the God imagination begins to develop and grow, when it becomes not just possible, but true. Abraham has confronted his fear and Isaac is the tangible evidence of a new story realized.

The temptation of the moment is to think this is about the birth of a child. But what is also happening is the birth of love into the human story. Abraham is realizing that God actually is real, alive, and wanting and willing to bless him. At this point, God is becoming true all over again. Abraham is discovering that all of his faith and hope has led him to the fuller realization of love.

But with great love also comes great responsibility. Just when we think the old story is gone, God seems to return to it once again. Lingering within the old story is the terrible notion of the demands of God. Deep within the human imagination is a transactional question. "What is the real cost of all of the blessings?" In other words, what does God really want?

> *Some time later God tested Abraham. He said to him, "Abraham!"*
> *"Here I am," he replied.*

Then God said, "Take your son, your only son, Isaac, whom you love, and
go to the region of Moriah. Sacrifice him there as a burnt offering on one
of the mountains I will tell you about."

Early the next morning Abraham got up and saddled his donkey. He took
with him two of his servants and his son Isaac. When he had cut enough
wood for the burnt offering, he set out for the place God had told him
about. (Gen 22:1-3)

"Finally!" the critics shout. It's the moment our sense of doubt has been waiting for. "See, God is just like the rest of them!" It is hard to read this without wondering, "What kind of test is that?" God even appears to be mocking Abraham with "your only son." The idea of sacrificing a son after twenty-five years of waiting must have felt like a punch in the gut. Yet, here's no emotion or trepidation on his part. Abraham immediately complies.

To really understand this moment, it is important to remember that religion is the primary means of appeasing guilt or gaining favor from the gods. Sacrificing what was most important is not only acceptable, it's normal. In the back of Abraham's mind, the gods make these kinds of requests. And in order to rewrite the story, God has to first call it out.

Abraham took the wood for the burnt offering and placed it on his
son Isaac, and he himself carried the fire and the knife. As the two of
them went on together, Isaac spoke up and said to his father Abraham,
"Father?"
"Yes, my son?" Abraham replied.
"The fire and wood are here," Isaac said, "but where is the lamb for the
burnt offering?"

Abraham answered, "God himself will provide the lamb for the burnt
offering, my son." And the two of them went on together. (Gen 22:6-8)

It's hard to know whether Abraham is being dishonest with his son, or if he actually believes God will provide an alternative. But his statement leaves open the possibility that Abraham is beginning to discern how God will act, even in the face of conflicting evidence. He's beginning to construct a reality about the true nature of God.

> *When they reached the place God had told him about, Abraham built an altar there and arranged the wood on it. He bound his son Isaac and laid him on the altar, on top of the wood. Then he reached out his hand and took the knife to slay his son. (Gen 22:9-10)*

This is realistically one of the more important moments in human history. The hand is raised. The knife is ready. With the death of Isaac, so goes the imagination. To bring the knife down is not just on his own son, but also on himself. The father of faith has been asked to give up the very thing that helped rewrite his own imagination.

We rub up against the brutish nature of the act, but in the act of sacrificing his own faith, Abraham actually solidifies it. In placing his own faith on the altar, he reveals it. With this act of trust so great, he begins to take part with God in truly rewriting his own story, and the human story at the deepest levels. For it is only in the face of such horrific violence upon his old story, of revisiting the scene of the crime per se, that Abraham can discover his own reality.

The point is not to kill Isaac. God releases Abraham.

> *But the angel of the LORD called out to him from heaven, "Abraham! Abraham!"*
> *"Here I am," he replied.*

> *"Do not lay a hand on the boy," he said. "Do not do anything to him. Now I know that you fear God, because you have not withheld from me your son, your only son."*

> *Abraham looked up and there in a thicket he saw a ram caught by its horns. He went over and took the ram and sacrificed it as a burnt offering instead of his son. (Gen 22:11-13)*

It's still very easy to wonder why God would resort to such a horrific act. Why the need for violence? Many scholars reel at this story, interpreting it as the moment Abraham proves himself worthy to God. But the story reveals God doesn't need it. God stops him. If anything, it is Abraham that needs it. Abraham needs to know his own faith. The God imagination is already in him, but he needs to discover it. The evidence of the moment is then not for God, but for Abraham.

This moment reveals the nature of God's tests. We often think of tests as a proving ground for the teacher or the test-giver. But if God is outside of time, God doesn't need to know. God already knows. Tests then are not for the test-taker. They are for humanity. We need to know. We need the evidence of faith within ourselves. We need the evidence of God's interaction in the midst of our faith. Tests become the intersection of reality, where we shift from what we think is true, to become aware of what is already true.

As we wrestle with our own emotions about the event, which contribute to our own God imagination, it's easy to skip over how Abraham must have felt. The test doesn't produce anger at God. It produces awareness. The moment is so profound that he sets up an altar to remind himself of how God showed up.

So Abraham called that place The LORD Will Provide. And to this day it is said, "On the mountain of the LORD it will be provided." (Gen 22:14)

It is only in the risk of engaging our faith, even in the face of violence, that we rewrite the story. It is only when we take a step of faith even into the face of suffering, expecting God to show up in profound ways, that we are transformed and restored. God's defining act is not in the test but in rewriting Abraham's understanding of what God is really like. This God does not require human sacrifice. Unlike the other gods, this God does not require the blood of a human being in order to be satisfied.

This event also foreshadows what will become the defining moment in the story, the sacrifice of Jesus. It places us in direct conflict with some of our traditions, which see God as requiring the sacrifice to satisfy a punitive sense of justice.

~~

The One Who Wrestles

Abraham begins the long process of a large group of people discovering, forgetting and re-discovering the God imagination. If God is going to reconcile humanity, it will require creating an exceptional story within humanity that contrasts with the way of the world. The covenant with Abraham begins what could be likened to a control group. What would happen if a select group of people discovered the God imagination together? What would that look like?

God begins with Abraham in order to establish a new story that people can hold onto. The story of reconciliation begins with the idea of acceptance. It begins with reconciliation. The story is not based on becoming accepted. It's based on trusting that we already are accepted. In other words, the fabric of the nation begins with the idea of reconciliation.

Much like a control group, the children of Abraham create a long-term counter-story of redemption. They are the scribes of humanity's interaction with the living God. They reveal not only the embedded captivating story, but also what it looks like to discover an intrinsic mobilizing story. Over and over again, they continuously find their way into captivity only to see God bring them out again.

But curiously the people of God are not named after their forerunner. Abraham's son Isaac has two sons, Esau and Jacob. And it is Jacob's journey that will reveal the war raging inside the heart of the people of God. Jacob's story begins with an auspicious prophecy.

> The LORD said to her, "Two nations are in your womb, and two peoples from within you will be separated; one people will be stronger than the other, and the older will serve the younger." (Gen 25:23)

As much as this prophecy is actually about Jacob and Esau, it is also about the human problem of duality. The two sons represent the two sides of the war raging inside of the heart of the humanity. Esau is the mighty one. He represents everything pride has to offer. Jacob is the smart, and eventually trusting, one. He represents the younger path of faith. The prophecy reveals that faith is stronger than might.

The problem is that Jacob consistently wants what his brother has. Jacob steals not only Esau's birthright, but also his blessing. In order to do this he literally attempts to become his brother. He dresses up in skins to trick his father.

> He went to his father and said, "My father."
> "Yes, my son," he answered. "Who is it?"
>
> Jacob said to his father, "I am Esau your firstborn. I have done as you told me. Please sit up and eat some of my game so that you may give me your blessing."
>
> Isaac asked his son, "How did you find it so quickly, my son?"
> "The LORD your God gave me success," he replied.
>
> Then Isaac said to Jacob, "Come near so I can touch you, my son, to know whether you really are my son Esau or not."
>
> Jacob went close to his father Isaac, who touched him and said, "The voice is the voice of Jacob, but the hands are the hands of Esau." He did not recognize him, for his hands were hairy like those of his brother Esau; so he blessed him. "Are you really my son Esau?" he asked.
> "I am," he replied. (Gen 27:18-24)

Jacob becomes his brother because he longs for his father's blessing. The subtleties of what is going on are easy to miss unless we understand the root problem. The problem isn't about stealing. The problem is he doesn't believe he has the blessing. Jacob becomes the father of the nation because he is the symbol of the control group. Engaging the God imagination will always include the tension with our previous story. Discovering means we have previous knowledge of the way of the world, and sometimes it just looks better, more appealing. We'll lust after it. Jacob reveals the constant internal struggle to return to the old means of validation.

Jacob's story reveals that it doesn't work. Esau finds out and determines to kill him. Jacob ends up doing what anyone living a lie ends up doing. He runs.

Instead of living in the land of his fathers, he has to live in self-imposed exile, one of the more apt metaphors in the story.

But the moment he leaves, God once again instills in him the God imagination.

> *He had a dream in which he saw a stairway resting on the earth, with*
> *its top reaching to heaven, and the angels of God were ascending and*
> *descending on it. There above it stood the LORD, and he said: "I am*
> *the LORD, the God of your father Abraham and the God of Isaac. I will*
> *give you and your descendants the land on which you are lying. Your*
> *descendants will be like the dust of the earth, and you will spread out*
> *to the west and to the east, to the north and to the south. All peoples on*
> *earth will be blessed through you and your offspring. I am with you and*
> *will watch over you wherever you go, and I will bring you back to this*
> *land. I will not leave you until I have done what I have promised you."*
> *(Gen 28:12-15)*

The dream is virtually the same image Abraham received at various times in his life. Once again God reiterates the idea, "I will bless you." God reminds Jacob that validation comes from God alone. The idea of a dream reveals that it sits in the back of his imagination. It's instilled but not quite at the forefront of his mind.

To bring it to the forefront, to realize the blessing, Jacob has to remember who he is. He must confront the past. He must return to the scene of the crime. But it takes Jacob more than twenty years. He finally sends word to his brother to meet with him. And on his way, he experiences the internal struggle between the false self and the true self.

> *So Jacob was left alone, and a man wrestled with him till daybreak. (Gen*
> *32:24)*

Some scholars hold that the man was God. Some hold that it is an angel. But the story doesn't say that. It says "a man." A more likely scenario is Jacob wrestling with himself about God. The story reveals he's alone, yet there are really two people there. There is the man Jacob thinks he is, sitting at the forefront of his imagination, and the man he really is, sitting in the back of his imagination. The story reveals the original tension of the prophecy. The war is within the self about the self.

> *When the man saw that he could not overpower him, he touched the*
> *socket of Jacob's hip so that his hip was wrenched as he wrestled with the*
> *man. Then the man said, "Let me go, for it is daybreak."*
> *But Jacob replied, "I will not let you go unless you bless me." (Gen 32:25-*
> *26)*

Some mystic healing traditions suggest that problems in the hip socket mean a resistance to accepting present experiences. This is the fight of Jacob's life, a fight for his soul. He's resisting the idea of facing the truth.

This is the central tension for Jacob, of the entire human story. He's stolen his father's blessing by becoming someone he's not. And it doesn't work. In many ways this wrestling could be likened to a conversation in the mirror. We are the "other," spelling it out to ourselves. And in true fashion, the self responds in a remarkably fascinating way that drives right to the core issue.

> *The man asked him, "What is your name?" (Gen 32:27a)*

Think about that. Of all the questions the man could have asked, he drives straight to the lie. He calls his bluff because Jacob understands that what got him in trouble in the first place was in trying to be someone else. The man doesn't even answer Jacob's request because he instinctively understands that blessing, or validation, is originally rooted in discovering one's true identity.

> *"Jacob," he answered.*

> *Then the man said, "Your name will no longer be Jacob, but Israel,*
> *because you have struggled with God and with men and have overcome."*
> *(Gen 32:27b-28)*

Once Jacob is truthful with himself, once he can see who he really is, the man gifts him with knowledge of his true purpose. Israel can mean, "one who rules with God". But it can also be taken to mean "one who wrestles with God". Jacob has wrestled with God and himself and overcome. He has ruled over the created order in his own mind.

In this simple scene we see the discovering of the God imagination. In the midst of running, God reminds him of his true blessing. It captures his attention enough that he is willing to address what binds him, which is the lie. But to realize it, Jacob has to come out of hiding and face his fears. He has to discover the false identity and embrace what is already true. And once he does, the man once again roots him in his original purpose, which is to rule. He reminds him of what is already true. The act of renaming roots his purpose in the act of overcoming the struggle within himself.

The nation of Israel is not named after the one who has faith, but on the one who wrestles and overcomes. It's easy to see why God does this. The act of wrestling is the more revealing label for humanity. Where Abraham immediately trusted, Jacob doesn't. His journey is far more typical of the human struggle, which is to wrestle with our fears in order to overcome.

To answer the central question in the Garden – Are we good or evil? – we must wrestle. To discover the answer we must be brutally honest with the self. We must literally wrestle with the self and overcome the root problem of the lie. To discover the answer is to overcome the struggle.

~~

Into And Out Of Captivity

If the need for validation were the root problem, it would seem obvious that this would also be the one thing leading to the captivity of the people of God. And you'd be right. Jacob has sons. A lot of them. Twelve, to be exact. God's original promise is beginning to unfold. But it is a gift of favor that reveals how deeply embedded the root problem is even in the control group, in the people chosen by God.

Now Israel loved Joseph more than any of his other sons, because he had been born to him in his old age; and he made a richly ornamented robe

for him. When his brothers saw that their father loved him more than any
of them, they hated him and could not speak a kind word to him. (Gen
37: 3-4)

The tension was not in the robe but in what the robe represents: the father's
favor. It is the means of reminding the brothers what they don't think they
have. Joseph is the youngest, which suggest he's not the mightiest of the bunch,
but he has his father's love.

To make matters worse, Joseph has a series of dreams that reveal he will one day
rule over the brothers. It doesn't help that Joseph shares the dream with them.
In a world in search of validation, this must have stung the other brothers. Their
response is telling. They first desire to kill him, but instead they literally sell
him into captivity. Those who are missing validation must remove the presence
of the one who has it.

If Abraham risking it all is the first turning point, this is the second. Of all the
moments the story could present, it consistently points back to and reveals the
root problem and the subsequent consequence of captivity and death.

And wouldn't you know it? The story once again points towards empire. Joseph
is sold into a caravan that takes him straight to Egypt. God allows captivity to
take place in the one context that represents the fullest manifestation of the
root problem.

In a dramatic turn of events Joseph's dream actually comes true. The king of
Egypt elevates Joseph and he ends up ruling over his brothers. But instead of
leaving, Israel ends up staying in Egypt and in the center of captivity.

For 200 years, Israel lives in the center of empire. They drink deeply the cost
of what it means to be held captive. They are in essence living out the root
problem. They are not living in the land of their fathers. Captivity becomes
one of the central themes of the Israel. It's not if they find themselves in it, but
how God ends up getting them out of it. Over and over again, Israel needs to
be rescued.

As much as the story reveals human activity that leads to captivity, it cannot be ignored that God allows it. Our emotions bristle against the idea that God allows Israel to end up in the space of suffering. But captivity reveals the central underlying problem. Humanity is captivated by a lie and as a consequence, is already suffering. Empire just represents the fullest expression of that captivity. Egypt simply draws attention to it.

But what if it's even deeper than that? If captivity is the central underlying consequence, Israel needs to understand it. Egypt gives them a personal story of enslavement. They can speak from experience about the problem and how horrific it really is. And if Israel is going to truly become the priesthood, they have to know what the root problem is. They have to relate to it. This relationship of Israel to the empire is a foreshadowing of one of the central moments in the process of reconciliation. Israel will become the priest for the empire. The awkward relationship of captive to captor will be revealed at Golgotha.

God is also not silent on the matter. Israel is not left alone. Central to the problem of captivity is the issue of participation. If the problem lies within humanity, what happens if God just lifts humanity out of captivity? What happens if God solves the problem for them? The easiest thing God can do is simply rescue humanity. But is rescuing the best option?

God chooses Moses, a man who grew up among the royalty of empire, to lead Israel out of captivity. But Moses must face the Pharaoh, the ideas of human rule, and essentially the spokesperson for empire. Initially, Pharaoh refuses.

The story reveals a series of strange plagues that beset the empire in the face of the Pharaoh's opposition. It becomes important to consider that Pharaoh represents a construct as much as a position. Empire is the dominant human construct of social order and control. It is the ultimate human system of keeping people in line. The plagues remind us of how stubborn pride can be. We typically see the obstinacy of the Pharaoh but they also reveal how relentless God is in the face of pride.

This is not just a war of empires. It is the central work of God. And in the face of God, pride crumbles. The exodus, or story of God rescuing the people out of captivity, becomes the central unifying story of Israel. It becomes the one unbelievable piece of evidence that God is capable of anything.

The Exodus requires one very important element. Israel has to actually leave. Exodus requires leaving captivity. And much like Abraham, they have to leave everything they've ever known. They have to leave a way of life that looks much more like death than anything. Their initial response is to leave immediately. But once out of captivity, they immediately start to grumble. Over and over again they express their urgent desire to return to captivity.

> *In the desert the whole community grumbled against Moses and Aaron. The Israelites said to them, "If only we had died by the LORD's hand in Egypt! There we sat around pots of meat and ate all the food we wanted, but you have brought us out into this desert to starve this entire assembly to death." (Ex 16:2-3)*

> *That night all the people of the community raised their voices and wept aloud. All the Israelites grumbled against Moses and Aaron, and the whole assembly said to them, "If only we had died in Egypt! Or in this desert! Why is the LORD bringing us to this land only to let us fall by the sword? Our wives and children will be taken as plunder. Wouldn't it be better for us to go back to Egypt?" And they said to each other, "We should choose a leader and go back to Egypt." (Num 14:1-4)*

Almost immediately the people begin to reveal the central problem with rescuing. If God simply lifts them out of captivity with no real effort on their own part, it allows them to blame God for anything that goes wrong. The exodus isn't smooth and easy, unlike Abraham's. It's brutal and messy – more like Jacob's. It's deeply immature people struggling to make sense of what it means to leave the only thing they've ever known. It's filled with fear and anxiety, pain and want. Like a drug addict in remission they are their own worst enemy.

To understand the problem of rescuing we turn to the work of Paulo Freire, a Brazilian theorist on the subject of oppression. Freire, once a political prisoner of a military government, argued in Pedagogy of the Oppressed that the process of coming out of oppression requires an intrinsic, self-developed, cognitive awareness of one's own oppression AND dignity. To simply lift someone out of oppression prevents the person from discovering their own dignity in the process. True emancipation requires recognition of one's oppression and the willingness to participate in one's own liberation for the sake of dignity. Freire also argued that emancipation was a community endeavor. No one liberated the other or themselves all alone. Liberation is only possible through the community working together.

Freire argued for two sequential ideas. Liberation first requires the conscious reality of oppression and suffering. This is essentially an awakening to the reality of the root problem. The story reveals this first reality.

> During that long period, the king of Egypt died. The Israelites groaned in their slavery and cried out, and their cry for help because of their slavery went up to God. (Ex 2:23)

Liberation also requires the intrinsic and developed initiative of the oppressed to emancipate themselves from the oppressors, specifically through asking the simple question, "Why?" The awareness of one's own dignity in the space of suffering invites the person to seek out liberation from the suffering.

The grumbling of the people immediately suggests they are conscious of their suffering but have no developed awareness of their dignity. So why does God rescue humanity from the empire? The initial possibility is to display the power of God. The point is to show the people that God is real. God is stronger. God is present and capable of overpowering the other religious systems. It is also likely that the people would not have left unless God had displayed a sense of charged power. The exodus story provides the people with an initial sense that God is real. It's filled with real experience that cannot be ignored. The exodus gives the people a tangible reference point in their story that God has the power to act for the sake of liberation. They needed God to be this direct.

But the less apparent answer is that God rescues them to reveal that participation is required. Humanity needs to know what happens if they just allow God to do everything. They need to know the devastating consequences of God simply solving the problem for them. The immediate grumbling, and subsequent desert experience, reveals what happens when someone is simply rescued.

This problem plays out over and over again in people who are rescued from drug and alcohol addiction. Rescue takes the person out of the problem without engaging his purpose, which is to wrestle with it for the sake of overcoming. To liberate someone from oppression, without an awareness of her own dignity, is to actually continue the oppression.

We can contrast the exodus rescue with two important events: Israel's captivity to Babylon and Jesus' call to follow. When Israel becomes captive to Babylon, God doesn't rescue them a second time. He leaves them in the midst of their captivity in spite of their cries. Liberation is not simply from physical captivity to freedom. It is the deep process of wrestling with the root problem, for the sake of overcoming. Israel refuses to do that.

Jesus' call to follow reiterates the requirement of participation. Jesus doesn't rescue the people from the physical captivity of Caesar. He calls them to observe their own dignity in the midst of suffering, and participate with God in the liberation of their own dignity within the model of shared community. He then calls them to participate with God in that same process outward to the larger community. But that process is not a call out of the empire. He calls them to live in the world but not in the way of the world. He calls them to transform the world in which they already live, even to transform the oppressor.

Freire essentially came to the same conclusion as Jesus. True liberation is not simply the overthrow of oppression. The fullest extent of liberation is to see the dignity of the oppressor restored as well. It is love incarnated to the enemy.

~~

Passover

As God is bringing Israel out of captivity, the story reveals an astonishing event that will become pivotal to understanding God's response to the root problem and essential to understanding the nature of reconciliation. God reveals the nature of atonement already exists.

As the Pharaoh refuses to let Israel go, God sends plagues upon the empire of Egypt. The plagues are very specific to the religious structures in Egypt. Each plague confronts a particular god. But the final plague is the worst. To release the people from captivity, God allows the death of the firstborn son.

Scholars wrestle deeply with this moment. How could God commit such a horrific act upon the people of the empire? Most arguments fail to consider that if captivity is true, Egypt represents it. It is the fullest expression of the search for validation and the subsequent captivity. The plague on Egypt is reminding them of the cost of bondage. To provide allegiance or safety to the empire is to validate it, which we don't want God to do unless we want to remain captive.

The final plague reveals at whom the plague is directed.

> *"On that same night I will pass through Egypt and strike down every firstborn—both men and animals—and I will bring judgment on all the gods of Egypt. I am the LORD. The blood will be a sign for you on the houses where you are; and when I see the blood, I will pass over you. No destructive plague will touch you when I strike Egypt." (Ex 12:12-13)*

God's primary concern is with the gods of Egypt and with Egypt itself. God's actions are a direct challenge to the construct of captivity and empire that oppresses humanity.

The Passover is a statement of allegiance. To protect Israel, God requires them to post the blood of a lamb on their doorposts as the plague is descending on the city. This sign provides protection from death. The Passover then speaks deeply to the root problem. To those without the Passover, death still prevails. It still takes hold, even to those in the empire. In other words, the Passover reveals who it is not protecting as much as who it is protecting.

The Passover also reiterates the original perspective of God. Before there is any priesthood, or law, or religious practice within Israel, there is already reconciliation and protection. The Passover provides us with one of the clearest symbols that the atonement was not for God, but for humanity, for those who chose to participate with God in faith. It reiterates the idea that grace is already true. In order for God to provide the atonement metaphor, the idea of atonement must already be true. This idea of grace outside of time presents a problem to traditional notions of atonement that assume grace becomes true at the cross.

Chapter 9 – Entering Into The Suffering

"I am concerned about their suffering." - God

A Kingdom Of Priests

The Mission of God is about restoration. But in order to engage that restoration, humanity needs someone who knows how to enter into and redeem the space of suffering. It needs someone who can sit in the midst of guilt and realize what it means to not be defined by it. This is the specific purpose of Israel, to reveal the way into and eventually through pain and suffering.

Once in the desert, God calls Moses up to Mt. Sinai to receive what could be considered the defining vision of Israel. And it is in this vision that we see the true calling of Israel. They shall act as the priesthood for humanity, and even for empire.

> *Then Moses went up to God, and the LORD called to him from the mountain and said, "This is what you are to say to the house of Jacob and what you are to tell the people of Israel: 'You yourselves have seen what I did to Egypt, and how I carried you on eagles' wings and brought you to myself. Now if you obey me fully and keep my covenant, then out of all nations you will be my treasured possession. Although the whole earth is mine, you will be for me a kingdom of priests and a holy nation.' These are the words you are to speak to the Israelites." (Exodus 19:3-7)*

This is the defining vision of Israel. The central responsibility of Israel is to serve as priests to humanity, which is represented in empire. A priest is someone who enters into the space of suffering and helps the person redeem it. The priest would be responsible for hearing people's worst crimes and then conferring grace. They will become a people who reveal what reconciliation and wholeness looks like, what the way of redemptive life looks like, and that humanity can live in relationship with God. They would, if they participated, serve as a contrast to the way of the world around them.

This idea of priests is not new in any way. It is already deeply established in Mesopotamian culture. They are intimately familiar with and understand the role. In other words, God is using a construct that humanity already understands, but is redeeming it. Their central responsibility is to facilitate reconciliation.

Restoration from captivity to the lie is never meant exclusively for Israel. It is for all of humanity. This idea is presented all throughout the story of Israel.

All the nations you have made will come and worship before you, O Lord; they will bring glory to your name. (Ps 86:9)

Give thanks to the LORD, for he is good; his love endures forever. (1 Ch 16:34)

"And afterward, I will pour out my Spirit on all people." (Joel 2:28)

The LORD will lay bare his holy arm in the sight of all the nations, and all the ends of the earth will see the salvation of our God. (Is 52:10)

And the glory of the LORD will be revealed, and all mankind together will see it. For the mouth of the LORD has spoken." (Is 40:5)

You open your hand and satisfy the desires of every living thing. (Ps 145:16)

"I revealed myself to those who did not ask for me; I was found by those who did not seek me. To a nation that did not call on my name, I said, 'Here am I, here am I.'" (Is 65:1)

Gather together and come! Approach together, you refugees from the nations! Those who carry wooden idols know nothing, those who pray to a god that cannot deliver. (Is 45:20)

O you who hear prayer, to you all men will come. (Ps 65:2)

Restoration is meant for all of creation, but Israel must first be established in order to serve as the priest to all of creation.

~~

God's Version Of The Law

To become a nation of priests, Israel would have to learn how to enter into spaces of suffering and redemption. To create an awareness of the root problem, God provides a set of commands and religious observations. They would have to be the ones to lead the way for the rest of the world. Like Jacob, they would have to learn how to confront the root problem in themselves.

It is up on the mountain that God begins the process of revealing God's version of the law and the religious system. The law would serve to expose the root problem. The religious system would provide a way of redeeming the root problem.

The original law was a set of Ten Commandments which focused on relationship to God, to the self, and to the world around them. And once again, God doesn't provide demandments, but commandments. The law only works if the people live into it.

> "Hear now, O Israel, the decrees and laws I am about to teach you.
> Follow them so that you may live and may go in and take possession of
> the land that the LORD, the God of your fathers, is giving you." (Deut
> 4:1)

God's design for the law is, "Follow this so that you may live." Within the law is life. It represents a construct that keeps people from killing each other, and directly addresses the root consequence of death. God uses the law to stop the downward cycle of death.

The Hebrew phrase "that you may live" here is "chayah." It means, "to remain alive, sustain life, live prosperously, live forever." Most of the law is relational, which means that the law was about how to relate to each other. It directly addresses the tension of living in the shadow of death.

It is important to reiterate that humanity is living in the shadow of death. Humanity is beginning on the defensive with God, which means that trust is something that requires work. This also means that at some point the people would recognize they are not living in accordance with God's laws. So they would need a way to address the root problem.

The law, by nature, has several glaring weaknesses. First, it can only reveal the root problem. The law provides a mirror that exposes our brokenness. It cannot solve the underlying root problem. The writer of Hebrews intimates this problem.

> *The former regulation is set aside because it was weak and useless (for the law made nothing perfect), and a better hope is introduced, by which we draw near to God. (Heb 7:18-19)*

Without a means of restoration, the law becomes something that perpetually reveals but does not restore. To attempt to keep it perfectly is to attempt the impossible. This is the problem of subjective moral systems. They cannot solve the problem. They can only identify the problem and create guilt. This is what the law is designed to do.

Second, the nature of the law reveals an infinite complexity. Each circumstance, no matter how similar, always has uniquely different conditions. The events leading up to the circumstance are different. The people are different. The consequences are different. So the law would have to be interpreted for each situation, taking into account the differences. The original Mitzvot, the original Jewish precepts, included only 613 laws, but it could literally expand forever.

Finally, the 613 laws didn't cover absolutely everything, so someone would have to determine how the law applied to the specific circumstances that seemed to fall in a middle ground. Each circumstance required a judge, or third party who was hopefully impartial, to determine guilt. The need for a judge reveals the subjective nature of our interpretation of the law. The original Garden state did not include the law because humanity was not living under the lie.

Our bodies were not corrupted. Humanity was not bent towards getting the question wrong, so it didn't need a construct to identify the problem. The Garden assumed grace because it began with the idea that humanity was always more important that what we might do to one another. It began with an entirely objective standard of "good."

~~

The Name Of God

One of the intriguing issues that God has to address is the actual name of God. The original identification God provides in the story is Elohim, which is actually a plural distinction. But after the Garden, God seems to hesitate in giving a name to humanity. The risk with providing a name reveals the tension of perception. If we know the name of God, do we know the whole image of God? If a name is meant to describe or even define an image, can a name accurately do the same for God? If we assume we know the whole of God, are we equals with God?

As Moses interacts with God, Moses asks the question. What is your name?

> Moses said to God, "Suppose I go to the Israelites and say to them, 'The God of your fathers has sent me to you,' and they ask me, 'What is his name?' Then what shall I tell them?"

> God said to Moses, "I am who I am. This is what you are to say to the Israelites: 'I AM has sent me to you.'" (Exodus 3:13-14)

Although Moses' intentions are likely good, this act of seeking out a name is a means to wrap his head around this God. But God refuses to play along. What if God understands that humanity will create a limiting construct with the name of God? The purpose of the name is to construct a reality of what something is, something tangible…so that we can control it. In refusing to play the name game, God keeps humanity from being able to limit itself.

God uses the expression, "I AM", which is a rather intriguing response. It's called the "Tetragrammaton", and is considered unutterable because it is four letters without vowels. The four letter letters are "YHWH." Pronouncing the four letters together doesn't seem to make sense. But another possibility may express a deeper insight into the meaning. Mystics in the contemplative tradition see the letters as a breathing pattern. Each letter seems to follow the pattern of inhale, exhale, inhale, exhale.

This idea is deeply consistent with how God is revealed in the story. It communicates the idea that God is found in the unseen. We feel God moving in and out and through us, filling our lungs with God's presence. Once again God chooses an expression of presence. God is always present no matter how far humanity appears to run away. No matter how far we go, we can never escape the reality and presence of God. We can hide, but even in our hiding God finds us.

When we look at the world our eyes are instinctively drawn to the tangible, or to what we can see. It is our realization. But if we draw our attention to the space around the tangible, something like the wind, we begin to experience the unseen. In other words, God is drawing our attention outside and beyond our own traditional realizations.

God consistently identifies with the concept of breath, or the unseen, as the beginning of life throughout the story.

> *The LORD God formed the man from the dust of the ground and breathed into his nostrils the breath of life, and the man became a living being. (Gen 2:7)*

> *The Spirit of God has made me; the breath of the Almighty gives me life. (Job 33:4)*

> *So I prophesied as he commanded me, and breath entered them; they came to life and stood up on their feet—a vast army. (Ezk 37:10)*

> *And he is not served by human hands, as if he needed anything, because he himself gives all men life and breath and everything else. (Ac 17:25)*

God even paints a counterintuitive picture for the prophet Elijah. We typically see God in the dramatic forces of nature, but instead God chooses the whisper.

> The LORD said, "Go out and stand on the mountain in the presence of the LORD, for the LORD is about to pass by."
> Then a great and powerful wind tore the mountains apart and shattered the rocks before the LORD, but the LORD was not in the wind. After the wind there was an earthquake, but the LORD was not in the earthquake. After the earthquake came a fire, but the LORD was not in the fire. And after the fire came a gentle whisper. (1 Kings 19:11-12)

It's as if God is saying truth comes by releasing our imagination to the unseen. It begins with releasing control of our realizations into faith. And once we do, we can begin to see the God imagination at work, breathing life into us.

~~

The Tabernacle

God's mission is all about restoration and reconciliation. As Israel leaves captivity, God establishes the Tabernacle, one the more restorative images in the kingdom. Instead of an elaborate building of worship, which is common among traditional religious practices, God chooses to reside among the people in a tent. The tent doesn't just suggest humility. It suggests family. The tent would have been the common means of dwelling for the people, especially during their sojourn in the desert.

The tabernacle is centered in the middle of the camp, which reveals presence as opposed to absence. Three tribes would camp on each side. But the presence of God is not determined by human action. God doesn't leave when humanity sins. God remains present even in the midst of their brokenness. No matter how many people come with a sacrifice, God doesn't leave.

The tabernacle's design suggests the root problem. A wall surrounds the tabernacle. Just inside the entrance is an altar for sacrifice. Just past the altar is the laver, which is a washbasin used before entering the tent. The tent is divided into two sections: the Holy Place and the Most Holy Place. Separating the two rooms is a thick curtain. One would initially think that the presence of the wall, the altar, the washbasin, and the thick curtain between two rooms suggests God might be trying to keep people out. If restoration requires participation, and if the central problem is the assumption of separation, the tabernacle is a consistent reminder of both.

The tabernacle is a symbolic representation of the restorative process. . The act of entering requires facing the truth about one's actions as well as one's fear about approaching God. Entrance then requires going through a wall, which is representative of a false identity. Once inside, the person is required to address guilt through an atonement process. The person symbolically washes one's self before entering. Each act communicates responsibility. God wants the people to know they are clean. But once inside, the heavy curtain represents the root problem of the covering. To see the God imagination one must pass through it.

The primary responsibility of Israel is to be the priests, eventually for the empire. It needs to learn how to overcome the root problem in humanity. The tabernacle serves as a practice ground for doing that. The chief priest, initially represented in Aaron, is the representative of the people. But his articles of clothing included two incredibly important symbols: the breastpiece and the turban.

> "Whenever Aaron enters the Holy Place, he will bear the names of the sons of Israel over his heart on the breastpiece of decision as a continuing memorial before the LORD. Thus Aaron will always bear the means of making decisions for the Israelites over his heart before the LORD." (Ex 28:29)

The breastpiece symbolizes the people. The chief priest is granted authority to represent the people before the Lord and is charged with going through the reconciliation process on their behalf. Each time they have to go through the wall, the offering, the washing, and the curtain and into the presence of the Lord. This shift becomes deeply important later because it allows Jesus to become the final representative. It creates the foundation for a final atonement.

The turban, which is a hat, is part of an elaborate wardrobe conveying honor and dignity. The priest is literally covered in gold and fine linen. God provides a covering that communicates the God imagination…before the atonement. But where does the turban go? Over the head.

> *"Make a plate of pure gold and engrave on it as on a seal: HOLY TO THE LORD. Fasten a blue cord to it to attach it to the turban; it is to be on the front of the turban. It will be on Aaron's forehead, and he will bear the guilt involved in the sacred gifts the Israelites consecrate, whatever their gifts may be. It will be on Aaron's forehead continually so that they will be acceptable to the LORD." (Exodus 28:36-38)*

God creates a hat for the man that represents the people, which includes the answer to the root question…in their mind. Once again the priest puts it on before entering. The statement is not, "Holy IS the LORD". The statement is, "Holy TO the LORD." The turban is perhaps more metaphoric than anything. It's an imaginative way of literally putting on the God imagination.

~~

The Mercy Seat

Within the Tabernacle, God also provides one of the more profound symbols of grace in the story. The law is placed inside a protective housing called the "Ark." But on top of the Ark is an ever-present symbol of grace.

> *"Make an atonement cover of pure gold—two and a half cubits long and a cubit and a half wide. And make two cherubim out of hammered gold at the ends of the cover. Make one cherub on one end and the second cherub on the other; make the cherubim of one piece with the cover, at the two ends. The cherubim are to have their wings spread upward, overshadowing the cover with them. The cherubim are to face each other, looking toward the cover. Place the cover on top of the ark and put in the ark the Testimony, which I will give you. There, above the cover between the two cherubim that are over the ark of the Testimony, I will meet with you and give you all my commands for the Israelites." (Ex 25:17-22)*

The ark is a deeply symbolic and profound reminder of God's perspective of justice. The law provides the means to determine the problem. It provides a powerful mechanism for self-examination using actions, which humanity uses to become aware of the root problem. The ark also provided a "covering" or means of solving the problem. Early translations reveal the nature of the covering, translating it as "mercy seat."

The ark provides a story for Israel. The law was inside the Ark, but the covering reminded the people that God meets them in grace. God doesn't ignore the truth. True justice requires confession. God just sees humanity through the lens of mercy and holds onto the reality that they are not defined by their actions. The ark is then a representation of grace and truth, both of which are required for true justice.

The atonement engaged the person in a physical experience. It took them through a physical reminder of their own release from judgment. The atonement is then FOR humanity. Over and over again God gives a means to engage its own restoration.

> *He shall burn all the fat on the altar as he burned the fat of the fellowship offering. In this way the priest will make atonement for the man's sin, and he will be forgiven. (Lev 4:26)*

> *He shall remove all the fat, just as the fat is removed from the fellowship offering, and the priest shall burn it on the altar as an aroma pleasing to the LORD. In this way the priest will make atonement for him, and he will be forgiven. (Lev 4:31)*

> *He is to bring to the priest as a guilt offering a ram from the flock, one without defect and of the proper value. In this way the priest will make atonement for him for the wrong he has committed unintentionally, and he will be forgiven. (Lev 5:18)*

The atonement is not just FOR us, but for US. The declaration states, "he will BE forgiven". It points to an internal reality or state of awareness. It points to where the change is happening. We needed the atonement. We are the ones demanding evidence. We are the ones demanding proof that we are forgiven. We need a symbol so profound that it would give us undeniable evidence that God could overcome our own brokenness. God even creates a yearly festival called the Day of Atonement, to remind the people to seek out their own wholeness.

The distinctions of offerings or sacrifices are called the "korbanot". While the term korbanot refers to the exchange, some Hebrew scholars suggest that the root, which is "Qof-Reish-Beit", offers a better understanding of the purpose of the sacrifice. Qof-Reish-Beit means, "to draw near to God." The sacrifice draws the person back towards God for the sake of reconciliation.

The idea is deeply consistent with the overall story. It suggests that even God's original covering for Adam is a means of helping people deal with the problem. Over and over God's desire is always to draw people towards God. The problem is not in God. The problem is in humanity. We won't recognize our own false reality so that we can let it go. The very nature of our brokenness is to conceal that we are broken and instead blame someone else.

~~

The Means Of Restoration

The root problem creates a perpetual problem of judgment leading to guilt and shame. We assume that our actions can change reality and judge the self as outside of God's love. Instead of addressing the evidence and the subsequent judgments, we hide from them under the protective covering. We assume God's response by projecting our sense of anger back onto God. Solving the problem of guilt becomes one of the central aspects of God's mission.

Guilt can be deeply restorative or deeply oppressive. Guilt is first of all the judgment that we've stepped outside of God's design for life. Breaking God's will or design is a destructive act that has consequences. Guilt identifies the destructive action. Our bodies are designed to produce signals that let us know, which we would call the conscience. The intentionally destructive act can only follow the lie so it is the recognition that something wrong is embedded in the self. Guilt then is the body's initial response to address the problem.

If the state of guilt leads to an awareness of the destructive act and the underlying judgment creating it, it becomes a means of restoration. It leads us to confession. Facing the evidence and the problem leads us to discovering that it actually doesn't define us. If we are grounded in the God imagination, with a deeply developed sense of dignity, identity and purpose, we're likely to see guilt this way, as a helpful mechanism.

The problem is that frequently guilt appears to reinforce the underlying judgment. The lie automatically produces destructive fruit, or evil actions. Actions are the tangible evidence we use to judge the original question of good or evil. They reveal the underlying judgment we hold about ourselves. If we assume we are the problem it produces shame, which is the body's physical response to the false judgment of value. Guilt and shame typically go hand-in-hand because they are parts of a natural progression happening in the body. If guilt becomes the primary identity it feeds the downward spiral. If the state of guilt leads one to confirm the original lie – that we are primarily evil – then it actually deepens the original problem.

This is the central problem with God's use of the law. It runs the risk of perpetuating the problem. The law simply exposes the underlying judgment that produces the action. The real problem isn't then the action, but the original root judgment that perpetuates the resulting "fruit" problem. But to get to the root problem, we have to first deal with feelings of guilt the judgment creates.

Where the law reveals the root problem, and the tabernacle was a space of addressing the root problem, what keeps people from coming is still the problem of guilt. The question is then how to get people to change their minds and see guilt for what it is.

Guilt requires a judgment. But to get there, God has to help humanity learn how to effectively judge guilt.

"If a member of the community sins unintentionally and does what is forbidden in any of the LORD's commands, he is guilty." (Leviticus 4:27)

The law then helps humanity continually identify how to determine it is in breach of the law. It reveals the inward, self-condemning state of the person. The verse states, "he IS guilty." In other words, the law reveals the inward relational state of judgment the person is holding about the self.

The story consistently and overwhelmingly reveals that humanity is the one doing the judging. As much as we think God is our judge, humanity is responsible for identifying its own transgressions. God does address the larger community in general through the prophets, but individuals are required to identify their own guilt. God doesn't send around the police looking for people who break the law.

Guilt becomes restorative when it serves as a means of reconciliation. The only way to address the underlying problem is to identify it and call it out. The principal means of restoration is then to guide the person towards confession, in order to release the person of guilt.

> "When anyone is guilty in any of these ways, he must confess in what way he has sinned…" (Lev 5:5)

So who does the judging? We do. The law becomes like a mirror reminding us of where we are getting it wrong. Once we become aware of the law, humanity instantly judges itself and becomes aware of the guilt. The judgment is inward.

And it is here we see God use the human construct in a way that is restorative. Where the original religious system served to appease the human projection of the anger of the gods, or gain their favor, God uses the system as a means of addressing the guilt. In other words, it serves to address the initial fruit problem that keeps the person from engaging God.

> "And, as a penalty for the sin he has committed, he must bring to the LORD a female lamb or goat from the flock as a sin offering; and the priest shall make atonement for him for his sin." (Lev 5:6)

God uses the primary system with which they are already familiar to speak directly to them. The purpose of the sacrifice is to communicate to the person that the guilt of the transgression has been covered. It addresses the inward state of anger at the self and the projected image of God's anger, by communicating the problem has been covered. Humanity needs a clear means of knowing when it is released from the state of guilt.

The central purpose of the atonement is the same as the Passover. It is for humanity. In every case the atonement sacrifice is mentioned, the primary purpose is to address the problem in humanity, not in God.

~~

The Promised Land

As hard as the journey becomes, Israel reaches their destination, the Promised Land. Canaan is theirs to take if they will trust. But remarkably, they don't! The moment they have the physical representation of the Kingdom of God before them, they refuse to take it. The Promised Land needs to be cleared of literal giants. In other words, to experience what God has to offer requires facing the final obstacles in their path.

As much as we like to think of this as simply fear of confrontation, the event suggests a deeper issue at play. To enter into the Promised Land speaks to the profound issue of value and worth. To live in God's kingdom means that God actually thinks they are worth blessing, that something deep within still has value. The giants are there because God allows them, but the purpose is to call out something within Israel. To fight the giants is to align one's heart to the idea that humanity is worth fighting for. To fight for the Promised Land is to buy into the idea that God would actually bless humanity.

History unfortunately reveals that Israel turns away in fear. Humanity has yet to wrestle through the conflict and discover its own dignity. As much as the destination seems to reveal the point, it is the proverbial desert journey that will transform them. The long stretches in the desert and the constant struggles and wrestling are what change them.

Israel is literally and figuratively changed. It literally takes a new generation to embrace the Promised Land. For forty years, Israel wanders the desert. This powerful symbol of wandering reveals the nature of refusing God's blessing. Transformation requires letting go of the old self. When we refuse to engage what it true, the act of wandering is all that is left.

Those who have been born outside of captivity engage God's blessing. They cross the river Jordan and embrace what God has for them. But on the doorsteps of the kingdom God has them perform what is arguably one of the strangest strategies of war, EVER.

Instead of simply attacking the city gates and hoping for the best, God has them march around the WALL for six days, blowing trumpets.

> *Then the LORD said to Joshua, "See, I have delivered Jericho into your hands, along with its king and its fighting men. March around the city once with all the armed men. Do this for six days. Have seven priests carry trumpets of rams' horns in front of the ark. On the seventh day, march around the city seven times, with the priests blowing the trumpets.*
>
> *When you hear them sound a long blast on the trumpets, have all the people give a loud shout; then the wall of the city will collapse and the people will go up, every man straight in." (Joshua 6:2-5)*

If you are Joshua, who is now leading the people, what do you do with that? To march around the city could be suicide. The people could pick the soldiers off from high atop the wall. It's so counter-intuitive that it is bewildering.

But it works.

The people need an undeniable moment. They need evidence to create a reference point in their story. This is an entirely new generation, and they know of the exodus but not the experience of the exodus. This is their moment to revel in the power of what God can do. But it comes through faith.

The central tension in the Promised Land is that God allows Israel to kill other nations in order to expand the kingdom. It directly confronts the idea later expressed in the Great Commandment to "love your neighbor." God uses death in order to expand the kingdom. Reconciling this tension becomes important to being honest about what it means to engage God.

The expansion of the kingdom cannot be understood outside of the root problem. If God is simply killing for the sake of pleasure, this is an absurd ego trip. We cannot ignore the fact that if God creates life, God can also take life, but at God's discretion.

> *On the plains of Moab by the Jordan across from Jericho the LORD said to Moses, "Speak to the Israelites and say to them: 'When you cross the Jordan into Canaan, drive out all the inhabitants of the land before you. Destroy all their carved images and their cast idols, and demolish all their high places." (Numbers 33:50-52)*

The primary purposes of expansion are to reveal the power of God and to reveal the inheritance. If this original root problem is true, the nature of these other kingdoms is inherently destructive to humanity. It cannot be ignored that death already reigns in the surrounding kingdoms. Death is inevitable in humanity. So when God instructs Israel to destroy the surrounding people, like Egypt, it is first a direct response to the systems of might and religious idols that inhabit them. It is not a judgment on the people participating in them.

By expressing God's might, God is directly revealing the only Kingdom that has true power. It is important to remember that when Israel forgets, especially in the process of battle, they always lose. The point is to reveal where true power lies, and that is with the kingdom of God. Once again it becomes a statement of allegiance. To align with God is to experience life and profound blessing. To align with the other gods is to suffer the consequences of the death that is already present.

The second reason is inheritance.

> *Take possession of the land and settle in it, for I have given you the land to possess. Distribute the land by lot, according to your clans. To a larger group give a larger inheritance, and to a smaller group a smaller one. Whatever falls to them by lot will be theirs. Distribute it according to your ancestral tribes. (Numbers 33:53-54)*

Expansion represents humanity's inheritance. It's the symbolic idea of God actually blessing humanity with tangible elements when they are ready for it. Everything is God's anyway. God is just giving it to those who are in the kingdom. It doesn't mean God exclusively gives to those in the kingdom. God is just using this moment for this specific purpose in the story.

~~

Back Into Captivity

The sad reality is that as long as Israel remains in relationship with God, they flourish in the land. But over time, the inevitable bent towards captivity continues to show up. They forget what God has done and begin to seek out the ways of the world.

> *After that whole generation had been gathered to their fathers, another generation grew up, who knew neither the LORD nor what he had done for Israel. Then the Israelites did evil in the eyes of the LORD and served the Baals. (Jdg 2:10)*

Even Israel returns to their own projected gods. The destructive bent reveals that humanity would rather serve an oppressive god than one that seeks restoration. So God gives them a unique system of leadership. Instead of using the surrounding construct of kings, God provides judges, whose principal responsibility is to listen to God's perspective.

> *Then the LORD raised up judges, who saved them out of the hands of these raiders. Yet they would not listen to their judges but prostituted themselves to other gods and worshiped them. Unlike their fathers, they quickly turned from the way in which their fathers had walked, the way of obedience to the LORD's commands. (Jdg 2:16-17)*

God's principal mechanism of governing is directly related to the issue of judgment, not something that will fuel their pride. Israel is given a governing system that directly addresses the root problem in the mind. As long as they live by it they flourish. But if they don't, they flounder.

*Whenever the LORD raised up a judge for them, he was with the judge
and saved them out of the hands of their enemies as long as the judge
lived; for the LORD had compassion on them as they groaned under
those who oppressed and afflicted them. But when the judge died, the
people returned to ways even more corrupt than those of their fathers,
following other gods and serving and worshiping them. They refused to
give up their evil practices and stubborn ways. (Jdg 2:18-19)*

God gives them the one means of leadership that will provide God's perspective
in matters of justice and social governance. Judges serve as direct representatives
of God's will, or perspective, in the land.

It is only when the judges are not actually appointed by God that the people
begin to seek out the need for a king. In the latter days of Samuel's life he
appears to circumvent God's process and appoints his own sons to the role of
judge. Inevitably they become corrupt.

*When Samuel grew old, he appointed his sons as judges for Israel. The
name of his firstborn was Joel and the name of his second was Abijah,
and they served at Beersheba. But his sons did not walk in his ways.
They turned aside after dishonest gain and accepted bribes and perverted
justice. (1 Sam 8:1-3)*

This gives Israel an excuse to seek out other means of governance. Israel seeks
out the means of governance that is a direct reflection of empire.

*So all the elders of Israel gathered together and came to Samuel at
Ramah. They said to him, "You are old, and your sons do not walk in
your ways; now appoint a king to lead us, such as all the other nations
have." (1 Sam 8:4-5)*

The request for a king is a human need. They see what the stronger empire
has and desire it. It's Jacob and Esau all over again. The overriding drive is for
something that fuels pride. It's the consistent and overwhelming need to seek
out the strong path, as opposed to the weaker one.

God's final words, given to the prophet Malachi, provide a commentary about this endless drive.

> *"I have loved you," says the LORD.*
> *"But you ask, 'How have you loved us?'*
> *"Was not Esau Jacob's brother?" the LORD says. "Yet I have loved Jacob,*
> *but Esau I have hated, and I have turned his mountains into a wasteland*
> *and left his inheritance to the desert jackals." (Mal 1:2-3)*

God first reveals a love for humanity. And this is at the worst possible moment of captivity. But then God reveals something peculiar. God reveals a hates towards Esau. At first glance it appears he's actually speaking about Esau. But perhaps God is actually speaking about the two sides of Jacob, the one that seeks out his true purpose, and the one that seeks out the false identity.

God doesn't hate Esau. God hates what Esau represents, which is the continuous search for validation that is already there. Esau's path is to seek validation outside of God's perspective. It destroys humanity and always leads to captivity. Jacob's path is to seek validation in God's perspective by facing the truth.

The periods of judges and kings are stark contrasts in styles. Expansion and profound blessing mark the period of judges. With a few exceptions, conflict, strife and drama mark the period of kings. The downward spiral of Israel reveals the false identity. Israel sees its validation coming from the limiting identity of being Israel, the one that is a force to be reckoned with, not from a God that establishes Israel.

Within the period of kings God consistently provides the prophetic imagination. God reveals through prophets what is going to happen to Israel before it even happens. Yet instead of listening, they rebel. The destructive covering blinds them to their impending doom.

> *O LORD, do not your eyes look for truth? You struck them, but they felt*
> *no pain; you crushed them, but they refused correction. They made their*
> *faces harder than stone and refused to repent. (Jer 5:3)*

The period of kings ends in comic-tragic captivity. The kings forget God and once again end up captive to the Babylonian empire. One doesn't know whether to weep or say good riddance. But the physical cycle of "into captivity, out of captivity, and back into captivity" brings together the two opposing kingdoms one last time.

~~

The Egoless God

Throughout the story, we cannot overlook the evidence of God's anger and jealousy. God often appears to have an inflated sense of ego that looks identical to the other gods. If we handpick certain sentences (or verses) out of the story, God can easily seem petty, demanding, and downright mean.

Much like expansion, anger and jealousy can only be understood in light of the whole story. But we have to be open to seeing it. Unless we see the story that informs the emotions, we will miss how they fit within God's overall process of redemption.

The root problem creates a distortion in our judgment of the self, which creates guilt and shame. So instead of dealing with the root problem, we're largely dealing with the secondary problem of our perception of God's response. We see God as angry. When God commands our attention, even for the sake of our own restoration, it is easy to see God as jealous and demanding. We cast our wounded ego back onto God and assume God needs validation. We read statements of God's anger and jealousy through our own bent perception. We create a response that doesn't technically exist. Instead of dealing with the root problem we're now dealing with our ability to trust our perception. Each layer adds to the complexity leading to a state of distrust and confusion.

In many ways, this is bias confirmation at its finest. We see what we want to see. This is arguably the point of seeing the grand narrative in context. We can't simply pluck certain things about God and expect to come to a true understanding of the image of God. We have to see God in light of the whole story.

The first time we actually see God's anger expressed violently is at the empire.

In the greatness of your majesty you threw down those who opposed you.
You unleashed your burning anger; it consumed them like stubble. (Ex
15:7)

God's anger is restorative if the empire is the fullest expression of captivity. We want and even need to know how God feels about it. Empire is the tangible expression of our trapped state.

But as God enters the story in a very active way, God begins to deal with the people's downward spiral directly. At first glance the words of God seem harsh and punishing. God is not afraid to express punishment and wrath.

> *"'But if you will not listen to me and carry out all these commands, and*
> *if you reject my decrees and abhor my laws and fail to carry out all my*
> *commands and so violate my covenant, then I will do this to you: I will*
> *bring upon you sudden terror, wasting diseases and fever that will destroy*
> *your sight and drain away your life. You will plant seed in vain, because*
> *your enemies will eat it. I will set my face against you so that you will be*
> *defeated by your enemies; those who hate you will rule over you, and you*
> *will flee even when no one is pursuing you." (Lev 26:14-17)*

> *"Therefore wait for me," declares the LORD, "for the day I will stand up*
> *to testify. I have decided to assemble the nations, to gather the kingdoms*
> *and to pour out my wrath on them—all my fierce anger. The whole world*
> *will be consumed by the fire of my jealous anger." (Zeph 3:8)*

> *But this is what the LORD, the God of Israel, says: "I will surely gather*
> *them from all the lands where I banish them in my furious anger and*
> *great wrath; I will bring them back to this place and let them live in*
> *safety." (Jer 32:37)*

We first have to place these statements in context. God's expression of anger and wrath come centuries after God begins the mission. They are predominantly directed at a chosen people who are responsible for a critical role in God's mission of restoration and reconciliation. They come after the people have continuously returned to a state of captivity, serving the gods of their own imagination.

These expressions of anger can only be understood in light of the problem they are solving. Much like a parent who is relentlessly trying to protect a child, God's anger is the only thing addressing the problem. Like a white-hot iron, as long as the people hold onto the root problem, they become the recipient or object of that anger and wrath. They feel it because they are embodying it.

God is then not angry AT humanity, but FOR humanity. God's primary motivation is not compliance to some cosmic system of justice but instead humanity's restoration. But the people won't participate. They keep returning to their own systems of validation that just don't work.

These perceptions of God also ignore the relative brevity of God's anger, which is primarily found in the exodus and the era of the kings. They also ignore God's own statements about the nature of anger.

> For men are not cast off by the Lord forever. Though he brings grief, he will show compassion, so great is his unfailing love. (Lam 3:31-32)

> I will not accuse forever, nor will I always be angry, for then the spirit of man would grow faint before me—the breath of man that I have created. (Isa 57:16)

God is entirely bent towards mercy, not anger and wrath. But we can't see that until we let go of our projections.

The other distorted perception is that God has a tremendous ego, as though God is just like other gods, and needs to be first on the list. This is largely due to the fact that God directly reveals a sense of jealousy in the Ten Commandments.

> "You shall not make for yourself an idol in the form of anything in heaven above or on the earth beneath or in the waters below. You shall not bow down to them or worship them; for I, the LORD your God, am a jealous God, punishing the children for the sin of the fathers to the third and fourth generation of those who hate me." (Ex 20:4-5)

But once again these are commandments, not demandments. They are invitations to life in relationship to God. The response of jealousy is much like anger. God is not jealous of other gods. God is jealous for us. We are God's precious creation. We reflect the God imagination. When humanity bows down to a false god, it corrupts itself. It enacts deeply destructive violence on the soul. If the problem is real, we don't really want God to let us bow down to other gods of our imagination. We want God to create some kind of understanding of what is killing us. In this way God's jealousy is a restorative response.

The idea that God is angry and jealous persists because it is a powerful mechanism for control. An angry God is a punishing God. A jealous God is a demanding God. And a demanding and punishing God can be used to keep people from killing each other. This distorted image of God can actually be used as a governing system to curtail the problem of death.

~~

Exhausting Possibility

The long, slow progression of God interacting with a chosen group of people reveals an astonishing idea. God establishes and uses the human constructs in Israel to exhaust their possibility. God allows Israel to explore pride, social comparison, relationships, the law, and religion to see that they don't work.

As a nation, they are at their best when they find their dignity, identity, and purpose in the God imagination. They are at their worst when they find their dignity, identity, and purpose in their own imagination. As they compare themselves to the empires around them, they cannot help but see their own splendor. But at the same time they continually lust after what others have. Over time, their relationships with surrounding empires eventually corrupt their imagination and take them captive. The law does nothing but reveal their transgressions. Religion becomes an endless ritual of spilling blood and an oppressive task of removing the same judgment of guilt over and over.

This is where we see the true nature of God at work. We don't like the idea that God will allow us to explore our own destruction. But what if that is the exact thing we need in order to discover our own limits? If humanity really thinks of itself as evil, self-destruction is inevitable. Humanity needs to explore its own ideas and imagination. It needs to see that they don't work. It needs to prove to itself the depths of its own imagination, apart from God. Israel's journey into captivity, rescue, and back into captivity reveals how deep the problem runs. But now they have a story to tell.

The response strikes at the heart of the inevitable question, "Why does God allow suffering?" This vexing problem has haunted humanity forever. We wonder why God allows us to create wars, mechanisms of war, and manifestations of death. Yet we often forget that this is the consequence, not the underlying root problem. The story of Israel provides us with that evidence. As hard as we try to solve the problem on our own, we can't.

Suffering is then deeply redemptive because it reveals the problem. It shines a spotlight on the very thing that captivates us. It calls us to address it by participating with God in redeeming it. But because that problem is embedded in us, we don't like looking at it. We assume we are the problem and thus assume we have no recourse to solve it.

It can also be argued that God uses punishment and the threat of anger for much the same reason, to exhaust their validity as an incentive mechanism. As economists continue to study the mechanisms of incentive and motivation, they are now realizing that control mechanisms can actually increase lawlessness. By establishing the cost and consequence, we're just as likely to consider the cost for experiencing the consequence.

The purpose of punishment is to provide a controlled consequence. It's designed to be restorative. We assume it works. Yet the story of Israel reveals that it really doesn't. No matter how much anger or vengeance God expresses towards the people, no matter how many prophets he sends, they don't return. Even under the full weight of anger, wrath, and jealousy, the people continue to walk away from God.

If the expressions of God's anger reveal anything, they show what God is capable of doing, but for the most part chooses not to. The base incentive mechanism in anger and punishment is fear. But if the fear of God does anything, it pushes people away. Instead of controlling people, it reminds them of the very thing they are trying to come out of. We cannot ignore that God is trying to root out fear.

> *There is no fear in love. But perfect love drives out fear, because fear has to do with punishment. The one who fears is not made perfect in love. (1 Jn 4:18)*

The delicate balance of using anger and punishment to drive out fear for the most part just doesn't work. Fear may produce compliance but it rarely produces repentance. One of the problems appears to be that Israel realizes God is bent towards mercy. If Israel realizes anything it is that they can get away with it. God can be taken advantage of, at least in the short term.

Yet something inside of us wants God to get angry. We need God to express anger because we want to know God actually cares. We build walls to see if God will tear them down. We get in trouble to get caught. The root problem creates evidence that demands our punishment. But at what point does our need become drama? Or we hold onto the idea of fear as an incentive mechanism because it's just an easier motivator. It doesn't require much more than a threat and a raised hand or a puffed-up chest. We need a God that will punish our enemies. And in holding onto the anger, we subject ourselves to it.

The story reveals that God's use of anger is short lived. The exile from the Garden was not a punishment. It was a protective move to keep humanity from immortal death. The flood was not a punishment upon humanity because it removed virtually everyone. It was a cleansing of the earth and the human story. God' use of punishment is primarily towards Israel during the period of the kings.

It assumes life is possible. God essentially does everything to help the Israel avoid pain and suffering. But pain and suffering could only reveal what didn't work. It could not point the way back to what did. True restoration, which is found in the early origins of the criminal rehabilitation process, is not found in the act of pain or punishment but in the rediscovery of our dignity. Rehabilitation means, "To restore to useful life".

~~

The New Promise

If the story ended with captivity, it would be remarkably depressing. We could easily ask, "What was the point of it all?" But it doesn't end there. God isn't like other gods. God doesn't leave humanity to its own devices. God tips his hand and reveals what would be a response so remarkable that even those within Israel would miss it.

Throughout the era of kings, God consistently sends prophets to communicate God's perspective. These messages reveal that no matter how bad things get, God remains whole. The time of exhausting human methods of validation is coming to a close. So God begins to reveal a new era, one embedded in God's perspective.

> *"The time is coming," declares the LORD, "when I will make a new covenant with the house of Israel and with the house of Judah.*
>
> *It will not be like the covenant I made with their forefathers when I took them by the hand to lead them out of Egypt, because they broke my covenant, though I was a husband to them, " declares the LORD.*
>
> *"This is the covenant I will make with the house of Israel after that time," declares the LORD. "I will put my law in their minds and write it on their hearts. I will be their God, and they will be my people.*
>
> *No longer will a man teach his neighbor, or a man his brother, saying, 'Know the LORD,' because they will all know me, from the least of them to the greatest," declares the LORD. "For I will forgive their wickedness and will remember their sins no more." (Jer 31:31-34)*

To create the new covenant, God would reveal a method of atonement that is so profound, it would literally confound the people it engaged. It would be so unique the people participating in it wouldn't even know it was happening.

God would reveal the second Adam, who would then disclose the definitive answer of God's response.

> *He was oppressed and afflicted, yet he did not open his mouth; he was led like a lamb to the slaughter, and as a sheep before her shearers is silent, so he did not open his mouth. (Isa 53:7)*

As much as captivity reveals the problem, it still serves a larger purpose. Israel now sits deep within the construct of empire, ready to perform one of the most courageous acts imaginable. They will serve as priests in the one task they have been chosen for, the final atonement of humanity.

Chapter 10 – The Imago Dei

"Beauty is in the eye of the beholder." - Plato

A Voice In The Wilderness

For four hundred years, God is once again silent. Israel, the priesthood for humanity, is once again captive to the empire. The prophetic voices that once revealed God's perspective are silent. Israel must wait. And then out of nowhere, a man comes out of the wilderness preaching repentance for the forgiveness of sins.

> *And so John came, baptizing in the desert region and preaching a baptism of repentance for the forgiveness of sins. (Mk 1:4)*

Suffice it to say, it's not the message people in captivity want to hear. Repent is the prophetic voice. It's the harder message. The story of the Israel is about rescue, isn't it? It's about a leader rising up to bring people out of oppressive political captivity. This is what people want to hear. They want God to do the work.

But as Freire argued, this is not what humanity needs. Restoration requires a deep recognition of suffering and oppression, but it also requires an awareness of one's own dignity and the willingness to fight for it. Repentance is not about rescue, but about restoration in the midst of captivity. It's about turning way from what captivates through a change of mind. Israel must once again show the way by engaging its true purpose. It must reveal the way to restoration; this begins with participation.

If we understand the root problem, repentance comes almost naturally. The consistent response of humanity is to run away. This began with Adam and was magnified with Cain. Repent first means to turn around. The only people who need to turn around are those running away. John's message is unconditional. Forgiveness is already there. All humanity needs to do is turn around to realize it.

The act of turning requires something, though. It requires a change of mind. Turning around means embracing a new way of seeing things. It means embracing the God imagination. Repentance is a change in our perception, not in God's. The act of repentance doesn't change what is true from God's perspective. It changes what is true from our perspective. In order to turn around, humanity must change its perception of itself. Repentance is then addressing the root problem of judgment about oneself.

We see this idea played out in the baptism of Jesus. Jesus goes down to the river to meet John and is baptized. His act is not predicated on changing what is true, but in embracing what is true – that God is pleased. The story gives us a vivid example of God's perspective, realized from Jesus' perspective.

As Jesus was coming up out of the water, he saw heaven being torn open and the Spirit descending on him like a dove. And a voice came from heaven: "You are my Son, whom I love; with you I am well pleased." (Mk 1:10-11)

God is the one validating Jesus. God is already pleased and Jesus just receives His affirmation. It's not predicated on anything other than God's declaration. Jesus hasn't done anything other than embrace what is already true in relationship with God.

Once again we see the story framing God's perspective as already pleased. God takes pleasure in humanity. For someone to follow Jesus in baptism is to embrace that same reality. If Jesus is the true representative of humanity, this statement represents how God feels about all of humanity. It's not conditional to Jesus. If it is conditional, or predicated on a sacrifice or specific actions, then baptism is not yet possible for everyone else. But Jesus models the act for the people around him. In order to receive something it must already be true.

Reception is predicated on something already being there.

The act of baptism is a public and symbolic act of embracing God's perspective, which is true justice. God doesn't need to let the problem go. We do. The symbolism of washing is for the person. Much like the atonement, it is a physical experience that creates a reference point in time of aligning oneself to what is true. We are publicly declaring we have crossed the chasm. By making it public we acknowledge it to the community around us, and can be held accountable for it.

~~

The Word Becomes Flesh

> *In the beginning... (Jn 1:1)*

The story just keeps taking us back to the beginning, doesn't it? The root problem began with a false realization. Something appeared incomplete. Something wasn't right, and then Adam got the question wrong. Humanity began the long downward spiral of death, and in the process completely forgot who it was.

So how do we remember? We've tried everything, exhausting all of our possibilities in the process. Pride didn't and still doesn't work. Social comparison or relationships don't work. Neither does the law, or religion. Humanity needs a God image so present, so completely unlike us that it awakens a long-lost reality within.

> *In the beginning was the Word, and the Word was with God, and the Word was God. He was with God in the beginning. Through him all things were made; without him nothing was made that has been made. (Jn 1:1-3)*

The Word is the original God imagination. It is the true picture of reality. It is God's original perspective of judgment. But from behind the covering all the people have are stories in language that create a projected image of what God could possibly look like and respond. When Jesus suddenly arrives, the God imagination is no longer just words. It is made real. It is present.

The arrival of Jesus is much like turning a new corner and realizing a perspective that was once hidden. It's always been true. We just couldn't see it because we were still behind the wall. Our view was covered under the layers of regret, shame, arrogance and pride. And now, it suddenly makes sense.

> In him was life, and that life was the light of men. The light shines in the darkness, but the darkness has not understood it. (Jn 1:4-5)

The arrival of Jesus marks the beginning of the next turning point in the story. Suddenly and without warning, the God imagination is among the people. They don't have to wonder or make sense of their own distorted imagination. They can see it embodied in Jesus in front of them. They can touch it and interact with it. It is present and tangible. No longer is it a distant memory or story. It is among the people.

Jesus represents the fullest expression of the God imagination in humanity. Somehow Jesus is different. The story reveals that He is born of the Spirit and is unhindered by the corrupted body. In other words, he is not bent towards getting the original question wrong. He's not dealing with all of the secondary problems because He knows who He really is. He is a child of God.

~~

Missional

Jesus announces his participation with God's mission of restoration and reconciliation by quoting the prophets. Once again Jesus makes a rather counterintuitive choice. Instead of choosing quotes from the prophetic voices that remind the people of God's punishment and anger, which is the projected image of God among the people, Jesus chooses a passage that addresses, of all things, the root problem.

> "The Spirit of the Lord is on me, because he has anointed me to preach good news to the poor. He has sent me to proclaim freedom for the prisoners and recovery of sight for the blind, to release the oppressed, to proclaim the year of the Lord's favor." (Lk 4:18-19)

The imagery of the choice is striking. The message is first good news. The choice of good is arguably prescient and even ironic. When it comes down to it, the root problem is a choice between good and evil. Good news suggests a subtle play on words that is easily missed.

The good news is for the poor. Our traditional thought process might initially lead us to the idea of those who are financial or even socially bankrupt. We think of the lower class, or even the beggars in the street. But the idea of poor is larger than that. Poor essentially means, "to have nothing." But the statement follows the good news. Poor is then in reference to the absence of "good news."

The next sentence begins with the idea of participation with God. Jesus is "sent." He's immediately identifying the fact that he's not doing this on his own. He's participating in what God is already doing in history. He is sent to "proclaim freedom for the prisoners." Once again the good news is about release from captivity.

He follows captivity with the statement, "and recovery of sight for the blind." The mission of God begins with the idea that there is something that people can't see. The lie is a covering which blinds humanity from seeing what is true, and because of it, humanity is captive to its own imagination. Jesus then follows with, "to release the oppressed." Once again he returns to the central consequence of enslavement. He draws their attention to the oppressive nature of captivity.

But the last statement is perhaps the most counterintuitive. If our traditions were true, we would expect Jesus to make some connection to the underlying reason he has come. So far it's been about what he's going to do. But he says, "to proclaim the year of the Lord's favor." Jesus establishes the reason for his coming in a way that directly addresses the root problem.

That's it. This is Jesus' mission statement. There is no anger or wrath to appease. God is declaring favor and Jesus is bringing that favor to the people. Then he sits down and says,

"Today this scripture is fulfilled in your hearing." (Lk 4:21)

Jesus doesn't say it's going to be true. He says, "this… is fulfilled." It's already true. Jesus is essentially speaking from kairos here. He's speaking from the awareness that truth resides outside of time and our imagination. All we have to do is embrace it.

~~

Come Follow Me

Jesus leaves the temple and begins engaging the mission. But he follows with arguably parallel to Freire's second observation. He doesn't just call out the suffering and oppression in the world. He invites people to join him in stepping into it for the sake of overcoming it.

"Come, follow me," Jesus said. (Mt 4:19)

The invitation to follow is an invitation to participate in the discovery of the God imagination. It is an invitation to live an entirely different way of life, one that is objective as opposed to subjective. He surrounds himself with a community of people interested in participating in an entirely new way of life.

The Way of Jesus begins with a single presupposition of "good." It begins with getting the original question right. It begins with solving the root problem in the human soul. It begins with discovering what is already true. This single reality creates an immovable foundation for life. To illustrate this idea, Jesus tells a simple story.

"Therefore everyone who hears these words of mine and puts them into practice is like a wise man who built his house on the rock. The rain came down, the streams rose, and the winds blew and beat against that house; yet it did not fall, because it had its foundation on the rock. But everyone who hears these words of mine and does not put them into practice is like a foolish man who built his house on sand. The rain came down, the streams rose, and the winds blew and beat against that house, and it fell with a great crash." (Mt 7:24-27)

To begin with a single objective reality, which is in essence God's perspective, is to address what is creating the underlying tension. When we engage a subjective life, nothing is stable. Everything is changing like the wind. And in the process we inevitably become the exception. These fears are the waves in Jesus' story. Much of our energies are spent trying to get through the fears that spring from our choice for subjectivity.

The Way ended the deep tension by eliminating the subjectivity. There is no exception. Our bodies may continue to reproduce the tension because we hold the residual of the old story, but we rest in the reality of God's perspective, which allows us to get through the fears and create a new story.

So when Jesus invites people to follow, He's inviting them to create a new story. Our bodies need evidence to reference. Our stories are so deep, so riddled with death, that we need the undeniable evidence of God working in our lives. But we can't see it unless we are open to that transformation. The value of following is then in creating the evidence of life that deepens the realization in one's own life.

The Apostle Paul speaks of this idea in his letter to the ecclesia in Rome. The central means of change takes place in the mind. Transformation happens when we rewrite the story.

> *Do not conform any longer to the pattern of this world, but be transformed by the renewing of your mind. (Rom 12:2)*

Living into the way is the process of continuously reconstituting the old imagination with the God imagination. It is living into the reality that is already present. It is stepping into faith on a constant basis so we can discover our dignity, identity, and purpose.

The Way of Life is first present moment. It is here and now, experiencing the reality of God's presence in the now. To create a new story, we need evidence in the here and now. When we eliminate subjectivity, which is primarily the fear of God's response to what we've done and what we can do, we open ourselves to the present. We open ourselves to peace.

To engage the Way, Jesus invited people to live into a life of response to pain and suffering. He called people to give away their money, feed the poor, heal the sick, and pick up a cross. In other words, Jesus invited people to step into pain and suffering for the sake of overcoming them. Jesus used the cross to signify that life is only possible when we've addressed the suffering in our own lives, when we've answered the question. To face death is to discover life.

The temptation is to take Jesus' call to action as the necessary requirement to effect salvation. It's very easy to list out all of the actions Jesus performed or commanded and then go do them, as if these are the actions that must first be performed. The assumption is often that these actions will then produce salvation. If this is true, then Jesus is just another religion. The Way becomes just another means of earning our way across the chasm.

The Way of Jesus answers the fundamental tension between grace and works. The Way is not a specific set of actions that will then make something true. The Way of Jesus is a specific set of actions for realizing what is already true. This is the brilliance of the Way. We don't have to make something true. We can't. Truth is truth regardless of what we think. We can only embrace it or reject it. The act of believing or following, or even loving doesn't make something true. It is simply the realization of what already is true.

The act of salvation is entirely singular to the person and widely varies in the story. Of the more than 25 biblical stories of people coming to faith in Jesus, none follow a consistent pattern. The beginning realization of belief is the starting point. It is the moment a very different possibility for life is created. To follow is to embrace the possibility of good. But it is only by living into the Way of Jesus that we can begin to experience life. We live into faith, which creates hope, so that we can experience love.

This love is the awareness of the true answer to the original question. From God's perspective, we have always been good. We just couldn't see it. This opening of ourselves to truth can be seen as an awakening, or the sudden capacity to see. We're not creating the reality. We're simply experiencing it for the first time.

~~

Humility

Throughout the life of Jesus we can begin to see him addressing the specific methods of validation common to the world. Jesus consistently rubs up against the pride of the Pharisees, but instead of just calling it out, he specifically reveals the alternative of humility.

> *As he looked up, Jesus saw the rich putting their gifts into the temple treasury. He also saw a poor widow put in two very small copper coins. "I tell you the truth," he said, "this poor widow has put in more than all the others." (Lk 21:1-3)*

> *"When you fast, do not look somber as the hypocrites do, for they disfigure their faces to show men they are fasting. I tell you the truth, they have received their reward in full. But when you fast, put oil on your head and wash your face, so that it will not be obvious to men that you are fasting, but only to your Father, who is unseen; and your Father, who sees what is done in secret, will reward you." (Mt 6:16-18)*

> *"Everything they do is done for men to see: They make their phylacteries wide and the tassels on their garments long; they love the place of honor at banquets and the most important seats in the synagogues; they love to be greeted in the marketplaces and to have men call them 'Rabbi.'" (Mt 23:5-7)*

Pride can be so tangibly hard to deal with that it is easy to miss the compassion in these statements. Jesus understands that pride is simply an attempt to validate the self. It blinds the person from seeing what they're doing. Everyone around the person can see it but the person herself cannot.

It's why we bristle against arrogance, but then attempt it ourselves. Fundamentally we need a form of validation. We need to answer the original question. We try and we try to no avail because we must. The body is designed for it.

Jesus' own life consistently reveals a life informed by the God imagination.

He embraces the idea of humility, which resists the need for self-validation. This idea is played out in the humbling moment of Jesus washing the disciples' feet. This cultural idea is so backwards, so completely against the grain that the disciples can't handle it.

> *So he got up from the meal, took off his outer clothing, and wrapped a towel around his waist. After that, he poured water into a basin and began to wash his disciples' feet, drying them with the towel that was wrapped around him.*
> *He came to Simon Peter, who said to him, "Lord, are you going to wash my feet?"*
> *Jesus replied, "You do not realize now what I am doing, but later you will understand." "No," said Peter, "you shall never wash my feet."*
> *Jesus answered, "Unless I wash you, you have no part with me." (Jn 13:4-8)*

Jesus consistently and completely inverts the ladder but for a very good reason.

> *"But many who are first will be last, and the last first." (Mk 10:31)*

> *"And whoever wants to be first must be slave of all." (Mk 10:44)*

Jesus isn't saying to consider the self as worthless. To step down the ladder is only possible in suicide or in the act of embracing our true value. To identify with the lowest is to see there is no scale or ladder to climb. We don't need to seek validation because God already validates us. Our validation is not in the self. Our center is not in our own subjective judgment. It is in God's perspective.

The Apostle Paul speaks to this idea in his commentary on Jesus. He even calls out the original temptation to seek equality with God.

> *Your attitude should be the same as that of Christ Jesus: who, being in very nature God, did not consider equality with God something to be grasped, but made himself nothing, taking the very nature of a servant, being made in human likeness.*

And being found in appearance as a man, he humbled himself and
became obedient to death— even death on a cross!
Therefore God exalted him to the highest place and gave him the name
that is above every name." (Phil 2:5-9)

The act of humility is in essence denying the ego's need to be the objective center. Jesus is refusing to judge himself. He's refusing to do what Adam did. He's holding onto the judgment of God as opposed to his own. And without that baggage, he can see there is no ladder. He can speak to the wealthy or the poor. He can move freely because he is not driven by a need for validation.

The act of washing the disciple's feet or even dying on the cross is not an attempt to say, "Look at how good I am." It is the natural extension of the good that is already in him. It is an act of reinforcing the dignity that is already present in the other. Giving his life becomes the fullest extension of love. So to embrace humility is not to embrace the act of lowliness, but to fundamentally change the underlying system of judgment about the self.

~~

Kingdom

For human beings struggling to make sense of a world they are born into and without a choice in the matter, figuring it all out just seems impossible. Life is captivity. No matter how hard anyone tries, it somehow leads to death and conflict and general mayhem. Empires rule the world, war is a common threat, slavery is everywhere, and the world just doesn't seem to work.

When Jesus arrives on the scene, he presents a fascinating idea of a Kingdom unlike anything anyone has ever seen. This kingdom is in direct opposition to the empire because it is based upon God's objective rule. But instead of spelling it all out for them, he paints wildly imaginative pictures and invites people to search for their meaning. In other words, he doesn't just rescue them.

Then Jesus asked, "What is the kingdom of God like? What shall I compare it
to? It is like a mustard seed, which a man took and planted in his garden. It
grew and became a tree, and the birds of the air perched in its branches."

Again he asked, "What shall I compare the kingdom of God to? It is like yeast that a woman took and mixed into a large amount of flour until it worked all through the dough." (Lk 13:18-21)

"The kingdom of heaven is like treasure hidden in a field. When a man found it, he hid it again, and then in his joy went and sold all he had and bought that field."

"Again, the kingdom of heaven is like a merchant looking for fine pearls. When he found one of great value, he went away and sold everything he had and bought it." (Mt 13:44-46)

Over and over again he describes a kingdom that is hopeful and valuable. In God's kingdom, people matter. They have dignity and identity. They have purpose and meaning. These images are part of the God imagination, a world where hope resides. It is not intrinsic to the way of the world but at the same time it is near, and even within.

Jesus said, "My kingdom is not of this world. If it were, my servants would fight to prevent my arrest by the Jews. But now my kingdom is from another place." (Jn 18:36)

"The kingdom of heaven is near." (Mt 10:7)

Jesus replied, "The kingdom of God does not come with your careful observation, nor will people say, 'Here it is,' or 'There it is,' because the kingdom of God is within you." (Lk 17:20-22)

Jesus sparks their sense of curiosity about it by not explaining it to them. He engages their sense of wonder by creating provocative images of something valuable.

The central image of "kingdom" speaks to the idea of rule, a space of judgment and reign. Rule is the idea of a space where someone makes the final judgment about important matters. God's kingdom is painted in terms that are in direct conflict with the way of the world. Rule is important because it draws our attention back to who gets to make the rules. Israel lives in a state of captivity to a foreign rule. Someone else is making the rules.

Jesus understands the captivating nature of rule, which is a judgment. It's intoxicating because it means control. But the moment we create a standard of rule, it can then be used on us.

> *For in the same way you judge others, you will be judged, and with the measure you use, it will be measured to you. (Mt 7:2)*

The Kingdom of God is a place where God establishes the rule. And if we look at the story of creation, it essentially comes down to a single question, which is embedded in the Tree of Knowledge. Are we good or evil? To see the kingdom means surrendering our judgment to this one question. Unless we surrender our broken perceptions, we can't see the kingdom. It doesn't come by our looking for it. It comes by surrendering the obstacle that keeps us from seeing it. And as the poets would eventually say, surrendering means coming over to the winning side.

So when Jesus paints an image of kingdom, He's awakening the God imagination that is already within. To embrace the kingdom is to apply a new rule. It is to follow in the Way of Jesus and get the original question right. It is to live by an objective standard that is so diametrically opposed to the human construct, it can only be considered an entirely new way of life.

~~

The Clarifying Image

Jesus presents the reality of what it means to live by God's rule, and in doing so He becomes the clarifying image of both humanity and God. Jesus is the fullest expression of the God imagination in humanity. He is fully alive as a human being. He's the best expression of what humanity looks like fully connected in relationship to God. Jesus also provides the whole expression of God reflected to humanity. He represents the embodied understanding of God's response to humanity.

Jesus first presents the possibility of the God image made real in a human being.

In Jesus, there is no judgment of evil. There is no covering or hiding. There is only love, which is the judgment of good.

> *"Believe me when I say that I am in the Father and the Father is in me."* *(Jn 14:11)*

Jesus essentially shows us what humanity looks like with the God imagination fully uncovered. The true humanity is revealed in the realization that there is no false dichotomy. There is no distinction of good and evil in the created order. Humanity is already in God and God is already in humanity. There is no separation.

Jesus doesn't just assume God likes him. He assumes God is in complete relationship with him. He begins with the idea that God is fully connected and fully informed in him. There is no covering to take off, no separation or chasm to cross. Jesus fundamentally understands he doesn't have to earn what he already has. It just is.

This idea directly confronts the root problem. When Jesus assumes he is connected to God, he is assuming that he is acceptable to God. He is continually embracing God's original declaration of value established right from the beginning. Jesus gets the original question right.

Jesus continuously surrenders himself to the objective rule of God, even in the face of overwhelming evil. He applies it universally to the created order, to the people around him, even to the least of these and the enemy. He assumes humanity's dignity. There is no exception. He is able to love others because God first loves him.

To answer the original question, we have to be connected to God. The root problem distorted the image of the self, but it also distorted the image of God within our own perception. It left us wondering, what is God's response? Answering the question, "What does God really look like?" became deeply important.

Jesus deals with this in a rather provocative way. He makes a statement that is easily misunderstood.

Jesus answered, "I am the way and the truth and the life. No one comes to the Father except through me. If you really knew me, you would know my Father as well. From now on, you do know him and have seen him." (Jn 14:6-7)

Some have taken this to mean that humanity is actually excluded from God's presence unless they accept Jesus as a personal savior. Yet the story reveals that both God and Jesus are more than willing to meet people exactly where they are.

Another way to understand Jesus' statement is to see it from humanity's perspective. When Jesus says, "No one comes to the Father..." he's offering the reality that we're bent towards running from God, not towards God. Jesus is actually stating that we can only fully understand God's response is through the clarifying image of his life.

So when people seek out God through other paths, they are not excluded from God because God is already present as the very breath that gives them life. They just don't have the lens for understanding what is God's true response to the root problem, which will draw them away from God. What this means is that anyone can come to God through any path, but they will always be rubbing up against the subtle underlying tension of the root problem. And without a clarifying image, they won't be able to answer the question effectively. To know Jesus is to know God's response to the question in the tree.

So when Jesus says, "No man comes to the Father except through me..." he's addressing the basic idea that humanity will forever live in the question unless it has undeniable proof. Humanity can come to the Father. Noah and Abraham proved this. All too often, though, humanity won't. Most of Israel proved this. Humanity will be constantly rubbing up against the evidence of its own realizations. It will be fighting a sense of guilt and shame. And it won't be able to cross the chasm because it will condemn itself, over and over and over again.

Jesus is the God image made real. He's God's response to humanity in the flesh.

And in revealing God's response, he's presenting the possibility that we can understand God by looking at Jesus. We're not seeing the entirety of who God is. We don't need to. What we need is the answer to the original question. We need to know God's response to our experience of evil. We need to know if God is like us, or if God is whole. Jesus presents the reality that God's response is one of compassion, true justice, and mercy, not punitive justice and rejection.

If we accept God's response as fully present in Jesus, it changes our perception of the chasm. We can change our reference point that creates it. We can reconstitute our image of God and come home. There is no chasm. When all is said and done, when the evidence of our transgression is on the table, God still holds onto love as a response.

To make the claim that Jesus gets it right, we have to deal with Jesus' own words on the matter. And surprisingly, Jesus initially appears to contradict this idea. The one time Jesus does talk about the original distinction of good, he presents what seems like an odd response.

> As Jesus started on his way, a man ran up to him and fell on his knees before him. "Good teacher," he asked, "what must I do to inherit eternal life?"
>
> "Why do you call me good?" Jesus answered. "No one is good—except God alone." (Mk 10:17-18)

At first it may seem like Jesus is actually denying He is good in the root sense. But if that is true then He is disqualifying himself from what He is called to do in the story. The statement would be contradicting God's original declaration in the garden, and much of the reason he has come. It would then place Jesus in a state of captivity.

A more logical conclusion is that Jesus is actually drawing out the man's own method of validation. Jesus asks him, "Why do you call me good?" Jesus is calling out the connection between the man's validation and the action. He has already drawn a conclusion of good about Jesus' capacity to teach.

The man comes to him looking for what specific actions he must do to inherit life. In other words, he's following the traditional methods of the world. In his mind, he must perform an action that will then make him acceptable. The statement, "No one is good except God alone," can be taken two ways. Jesus is either asking the man if he thinks Jesus is a child of God, or he's calling out the man's judgment that no one is good. Unless the man shifts from his own way of thinking, he won't be able to see the difference.

~~

God The Father

Jesus doesn't just change how we see God. He completely obliterates any previous notion of it. God is not like the projected gods of our imagination, which are removed, fickle and typically angry. Jesus doesn't see God as someone to be feared. He sees God in the most intimate and relational of terms: Father.

> Jesus said to them, "I tell you the truth, it is not Moses who has given you the bread from heaven, but it is my Father who gives you the true bread from heaven." (Jn 6:32)

> "Abba, Father," he said, "everything is possible for you. Take this cup from me. Yet not what I will, but what you will." (Mk 14:36)

Jesus' approach to God is one of deep respect and intimate connection. He's deeply aware of God's power but is not afraid to approach God in moments of need.

The distinction of father is so important that Jesus instills it in others. It's not something exclusively for Jesus. It is for everyone.

> He said to them, "When you pray, say: "'Father, hallowed be your name, your kingdom come.'" (Lk 11:2)

> "And do not call anyone on earth 'father,' for you have one Father, and he is in heaven." (Mt 23:9)

The purpose of this shift is first that it is inherently true. Jesus is aligning humanity to the original structure of creation. Adam had no father other than

God. Each and every human being is a child of God. It is written in the fabric of our being. Identity always first resides in this original distinction, but the covering hides it.

Second, although God is not exclusively represented in male form, he connects the people to the role of the father because it is deeply important in the Mesopotamian and Jewish culture. Jesus understands that in the way of the world, it is the father that bestows the blessing. This is still true in most cultures. It is the father who holds authority, and who validates the child in the family. By drawing a direct connection to that role, Jesus is bringing them back to the one who actually can validate them.

Jesus completes that circle by calling out the God imagination in himself. By calling God his father, he is revealing the answer to the question in the Garden. He's confronting the false dichotomy that is created by the lie. The prevailing assumption is that only those who are good can be children of God. The tension of this idea plays out in a remarkably harsh exchange with the Pharisees.

> *"I am telling you what I have seen in the Father's presence, and you do what you have heard from your father."*
>
> *"Abraham is our father," they answered.*
>
> *"If you were Abraham's children," said Jesus, "then you would do the things Abraham did. As it is, you are determined to kill me, a man who has told you the truth that I heard from God. Abraham did not do such things. You are doing the things your own father does."*
>
> *"We are not illegitimate children," they protested. "The only Father we have is God himself." (Jn 8:38-41)*

Jesus has an amazing way of drawing out the inward reality. In about ten seconds they've claimed two fathers. In other words, they don't really know who their father is. They're grasping for straws and trying to win an argument because they are supposed to be the smart ones. That is their false identity. Jesus just cuts through the smoke and mirrors.

Jesus said to them, "If God were your Father, you would love me, for I came from God and now am here. I have not come on my own; but he sent me. Why is my language not clear to you? Because you are unable to hear what I say. You belong to your father, the devil, and you want to carry out your father's desire. He was a murderer from the beginning, not holding to the truth, for there is no truth in him. When he lies, he speaks his native language, for he is a liar and the father of lies." (Jn 8:42-44)

It is deeply important to understand that Jesus is not adding to the false dichotomy by the statement, "You belong to your father, the devil." Jesus is calling out the truth of their reality, or the image in their heads. They too are children of God, but their own lives reveal the judgment they are holding onto. And to prove it, he holds up a mirror to their faces using their own method of validation, which is based in actions. They want to kill him. They want to embody death all over again.

Yet because I tell the truth, you do not believe me! Can any of you prove me guilty of sin? If I am telling the truth, why don't you believe me? He who belongs to God hears what God says. The reason you do not hear is that you do not belong to God." (Jn 8:45-47)

The sad reality is that they can't see it because they are captivated by the lie. They've spent their entire lives living out a false identity of having the "right" answer. Up until now it's worked, at least in public. And now someone is telling them something else. And because their entire identity is so completely wrapped up in having the right answer they become trapped. They can't let it go because it is the only thing they've ever known.

Chapter 11 – Engaging The Root Problem

"Not everything that is faced can be changed. But nothing can be changed until it is faced." - James Arthur Baldwin

The Fruit

Throughout Jesus' ministry, he makes a very deep connection to the human construct of seeking validation through action. But instead of drawing it out, he uses metaphorical language. Over and over again, Jesus keeps mentioning the idea of fruit, drawing our imagination to a tree. And where does the root problem reside? In a Garden. In a tree.

> *"You did not choose me, but I chose you and appointed you to go and bear fruit—fruit that will last. Then the Father will give you whatever you ask in my name." (Jn 15:16)*

> *"Make a tree good and its fruit will be good, or make a tree bad and its fruit will be bad, for a tree is recognized by its fruit." (Mt 12:33)*

> *"No good tree bears bad fruit, nor does a bad tree bear good fruit." (Lk 6:43)*

It's very possible that his audience draws the connection to the Tree of Knowledge, or maybe they don't. But he makes one point very clear: fruit is an indicator of something, not the determiner of something.

Historically we approach sin as the problem of things we do, like actions, words, and even thoughts. These are the fruit of our lives. We see the consequences they create for ourselves, our neighbors and our friends, and are continuously struck by the potency of their evidence. They demand judgment. We're bent towards using them to judge the self or the other. In this way we are using the fruit to determine what kind of tree we are.

If we make that judgment, we are left with the question of God's response. And because our judgment is subjective we end up make the same mistake Adam did. We assume God is angry. Then we spend most of our energies trying to cut out the fruit, or to hide the evidence. Or we simply ignore God and live with the cost regardless. We're human beings. To err is human, right?

Jesus is taking it deeper than that. Jesus understands that fruit is an indicator of the root problem. The fruit does have consequences, often devastating ones, but it is a byproduct. If we spend our time picking it, it will just grow back because the tree is designed to produce fruit. It is a natural response of the tree that is producing it. To focus on the fruit is the wrong issue.

What Jesus is saying is that the fruit cannot survive without the tree that is producing it. The real problem lives in the tree that produces the fruit. It resides in the underlying root problem that creates the fruit in the first place. The tree is the organizing system. The trunk, which resides above ground, cannot survive without the root system supporting it. The strongest root is the taproot. In many trees the root system is as big if not bigger than the tree. To kill the fruit we have to kill the root.

We don't ignore the fruit either. Jesus uses the metaphor because fruit is the clearest indicator of how we have answered the root question. We use fruit, or the action of our lives, to determine the root judgment embedded in the self.

There are only two fruits: those that produce death and those that produce life.

> *The acts of the sinful nature are obvious: sexual immorality, impurity and debauchery; idolatry and witchcraft; hatred, discord, jealousy, fits of rage, selfish ambition, dissensions, factions and envy; drunkenness, orgies, and the like. (Gal 5:19-21)*

Notice how Paul calls them the acts of a sinful nature. Underlying the action is a base construct, or paradigm. So if we produce destructive fruit, it is a clear sign that we're holding onto the wrong judgment, not proof positive that we are evil.

The strongest indicator that we have gotten the question right is the fruit of the Spirit, which is an outpouring of the God imagination.

> *But the fruit of the Spirit is love, joy, peace, patience, kindness, goodness, faithfulness, gentleness and self-control. Against such things there is no law. (Gal 5:22-23)*

The fruit of the Spirit is so powerful and so filled with life it will never conflict with the law. It will be so consistent with the rule of God that it will reflect the Kingdom of God. The only way to produce the fruit of the Spirit is to address the root problem.

Jesus is essentially using the human construct but flipping it on its ear. He's once again turning it back around. Instead of using fruit to determine value, we use fruit to indicate the value judgment that has already been made, so we can correct it. The brilliance of it is that we can't ignore it. Fruit just shows up whether we like it or not. Fruit essentially calls our bluff. It stares us in the face and calls our pretension. It is redemptive only when we see if for what it is, a revelation of the judgment we make about ourselves.

Jesus also seems to suggest that although the shift of judgment is a single question, it is also a growth process that takes place over time. It might even seem painful. Once again he returns to a plant metaphor.

> *"I am the true vine, and my Father is the gardener. He cuts off every branch in me that bears no fruit, while every branch that does bear fruit he prunes so that it will be even more fruitful. You are already clean because of the word I have spoken to you. Remain in me, and I will remain in you. No branch can bear fruit by itself; it must remain in the vine. Neither can you bear fruit unless you remain in me." (Jn 15:1-4)*

Jesus uses the vine, a metaphor for something that grows wild and free. But true life begins with connection. In order to grow, we have to remain connected. In order to grow into a healthy plant we also require pruning. We have to continually cut out that which doesn't produce life. We require careful care and nourishment.

~~

The Sinner And The Saint

Within the social fabric is the class system, a common form of validation using social comparison. There are the haves and the have-nots. It doesn't really matter what someone has, as long as someone else doesn't. Embedded within this process is the idea that health and wealth are signs of favor from God. The haves have it and the have-nots don't. God is punishing or has simply forgotten the poor and the diseased. This issue exists even within Israel.

Jesus turns this idea on its ear. He travels with, dines with, and interacts with both classes.

> While Jesus was having dinner at Matthew's house, many tax collectors and "sinners" came and ate with him and his disciples. (Mt 9:10)

> Jesus replied, "Go back and report to John what you hear and see: The blind receive sight, the lame walk, those who have leprosy are cured, the deaf hear, the dead are raised, and the good news is preached to the poor." (Mt 11:4-5)

Jesus allows a woman to anoint him. He meets with a wealthy Pharisee named Nicodemus. It is likely that women financed much of Jesus' ministry. For Jesus there is no distinction of class or favor. Everyone is favored. But he does seem to favor the poor simply because they are the most open to seeing their own need.

> "The King will reply, 'I tell you the truth, whatever you did for one of the least of these brothers of mine, you did for me.'" (Mt 25:40)

At the heart of Jesus' ministry is the idea of transforming our perception of human dignity through the God imagination. Jesus played the role of priest, consistently stepping into the space of pain and suffering and healing those around him. The act of healing directly confronts our fear and loathing of the sick and broken.

> *When he came down from the mountainside, large crowds followed him. A man with leprosy came and knelt before him and said, "Lord, if you are willing, you can make me clean."*

> *Jesus reached out his hand and touched the man. "I am willing," he said. "Be clean!" Immediately he was cured of his leprosy. (Mt 8:1-3)*

The act of healing the sick is largely addressing an embedded idea within culture. How could God heal the unlovable? Sickness is a sign of God's rejection. By healing people, especially the leper, which is culturally the lowest of the low, Jesus is confronting their perception. He's forcing them to question embedded reality. If the lowest of the low can be healed, is God then with *them* too?

By identifying with the least of these, Jesus is also directly addressing social comparison. Things like race, creed, color, and gender are not identities but expressions of something deeper. They are not a good basis of comparison because once we apply them, we become subject to them. Someone is always richer, or prettier, or stronger, or lighter. Before someone is a sinner or a saint, before someone is a male or female, that person is first of all a human being.

Jesus breaks down the false dichotomy and the idea of social comparison behind it by seeing the God image in everyone. Behind the poor, the less than, the forgotten, and the oppressed is a human being created in the image of God, called "very good."

These interactions are a natural extension of the God imagination. Jesus is grounded in the idea that all of humanity is good. Everyone is part of creation and has been endowed with dignity. They may not know it, or they may be trapped behind the covering, but Jesus consistently reminds them of their dignity.

Perhaps the most important example of this is his encounter with the adulterous woman. The adulterous woman represents someone caught in the act. With the leper, one has to guess what the person has done. But with the adulterous woman, everyone knows what she's done. Jesus turns justice on its ear.

The teachers of the law and the Pharisees brought in a woman caught in adultery. They made her stand before the group and said to Jesus, "Teacher, this woman was caught in the act of adultery. In the Law Moses commanded us to stone such women. Now what do you say?" They were using this question as a trap, in order to have a basis for accusing him. (Jn 8:3-6a)

What the Pharisees are doing is a common practice in social comparison. We don't need someone better than us. We just need someone worse than us. It deflects negative attention off us. The teachers and Pharisees had every right to stone her, according to Jewish law.

But Jesus bent down and started to write on the ground with his finger. When they kept on questioning him, he straightened up and said to them, "If any one of you is without sin, let him be the first to throw a stone at her." Again he stooped down and wrote on the ground. (Jn 8:6b-8)

Jesus cuts to the heart of the matter by using the system against them. He holds up a mirror to their own reflection and they crumble. He uses the law for its intended purpose – to reveal the problem.

At this, those who heard began to go away one at a time, the older ones first, until only Jesus was left, with the woman still standing there. Jesus straightened up and asked her, "Woman, where are they? Has no one condemned you?"

"No one, sir," she said.
"Then neither do I condemn you," Jesus declared. "Go now and leave your life of sin."
(Jn 8:9-11)

If ever there is a moment Jesus reveals God's view of judgment it is now. Jesus has every right to condemn her, but instead he holds onto true justice. He lives out God's perspective of true justice. He calls out what is true, but then offers her radical grace. Justice doesn't mean ignoring the evidence. It means transcending it.

This moment is the problem in the Tree played out. The woman is producing undeniable evidence of her brokenness. And if the people are to live by the law, they are to stone her. How can she be good when there is ample evidence to suggest she is evil? Jesus transcends the moment by revealing the rule of God, which is to hold onto her dignity even in the face of the overwhelming evidence.

Jesus holds her dignity but also reminds her of it. He calls out what is true in the midst of grace. To call her to leave her sin is not about leaving her act of adultery. Adultery is a fruit of the underlying root problem. It is the consequence of the covering and forgetting who she really is. Jesus calls her to remember her dignity and identity as a human being, created in the image of God. To leave sin is to discover her true self.

~~

Satisfying The Insatiable

The original purpose of humanity is to rule in a way that produces life. The original distinction was a call to rule over the created order, specifically "over all the earth". Part of this distinction is a call to rule over our lusts, especially our need for material things. This idea of ruling over the created order is so central to our humanity that God embeds it into the Ten Commandments.

> "You shall not make for yourself an idol in the form of anything in heaven above or on the earth beneath or in the waters below. You shall not bow down to them or worship them." (Ex 20:4-5)

An idol is any projected, tangible representation of what validates us. We see something and agree to the idea, "If we just have that, then we'll be good." We project a story onto the object and lust after it. What validates us can be anything we determine, but behind the idol is the granted power to validate us. This idea of idols is not limited to what we think of as gold statues. It applies to the tangible things that we assume give us validation – namely, our stuff.

We accumulate wealth, represented in things, as evidence of God's favor. In the system of social comparison, wealth plays a huge part in continuing the idea the gods favor the wealthy. The gods give stuff to those they like. Stuff becomes a symbol of god's favor. So to have stuff is just another form of validation.

The problem is that humanity ends up finding its identity in stuff, as opposed to in the giver of the stuff. It also holds onto it at the expense of the neighbor. The class system of haves and have-nots exists because of this reason. Stuff takes value over the need of the other because it validates the person holding it. We see this tension played out in Jesus' encounter with the rich man.

> Now a man came up to Jesus and asked, "Teacher, what good thing must I do to get eternal life?" (Mt 19:16)

The assumption we can make is that the man doesn't yet believe he has eternal life. He asks because he assumes he doesn't have it yet, but he wants it. We can also assume that what he already has is not producing that life, or he wouldn't need to ask.

Jesus' answer is extremely revealing. At first he calls out the standard possibility of following the law.

> "All these I have kept," the young man said. "What do I still lack?" (Mt 19:20)

Even though the man has followed the law he still doesn't really believe it. Something is still lacking.

> Jesus answered, "If you want to be perfect, go, sell your possessions and give to the poor, and you will have treasure in heaven. Then come, follow me." (Mt 19:21)

The distinction of "perfect" essentially means to be whole or mature. Jesus is leading him towards the real purpose of the question. But then he calls out the true problem. "Go and sell your possessions." The key word is possessions. Jesus is addressing his primary means of validation. The man can't let go because he possesses his stuff. In other words, he finds his identity and validation *in* his stuff. They are proof of his validation, even though he still doesn't believe.

It's easy to see Jesus' command as a universal mandate necessary for salvation.

Jesus isn't calling his followers to sell everything and give to the poor simply as a means of wealth distribution or as the "right thing to do."

> *"But when you give to the needy, do not let your left hand know what your right hand is doing, so that your giving may be in secret. Then your Father, who sees what is done in secret, will reward you." (Mt 6:3)*

Jesus instinctively knew that we could see giving it all away as another means of pride. Poverty could become a way of saying, "Look at how good I am! I have given everything away!"

The act of giving away is like an undressing of the false self. He's calling us to abandon the things that produce a false validation. When we learn to let go, we are removing the obstacles that keep us from seeing our true identity. We're discovering what produces life. To lose our possessions is to find the true self. Once we are undressed, we can begin to be stewards of those things we are called to rule over.

We feel this tension in stuff when we see people hoard. The accumulation of stuff, especially at the expense of the poor around that person, reveals the underlying need for validation. We crave luxury not for the functional value of the thing, but for the story is presents the world. A car is functionally a car. But a Ferrari presents a very different story than a Honda.

The lie of stuff is that it can actually produce validation. Yet those who have, rarely have enough. The acquisition of more reveals the insatiable nature of having. It doesn't work. Once we accumulate, we have to manage it, store it, dust it, retrieve it, and even build storehouses for it. Our attic, basements and garages become jammed because we refuse to let go. To be released from the oppressive weight of our stuff is to be liberated from the endless striving for, acquisition of, and management of it.

Jesus offered a provocative alternative to hoarding. He suggested seeing the moment someone asks as the moment to liberate ourselves.

> *"Give to the one who asks you, and do not turn away from the one who wants to borrow from you." (Mt 5:42)*

The tension we feel in these moments is because we find our security in having. Yet it is the holding onto our stuff that keeps us from seeing our true humanity. Jesus calls us to transcend and rule over our stuff. To transcend our stuff is to begin to see and even validate the objective standard in the kingdom.

This is the real risk of giving. To give is to embrace an identity that is not limited by our possessions. It is to live a life that is undefined by stuff. The act of giving to the poor, or to the one who asks, is then a means of validating the dignity of the "other" because it is true in our lives. It is reminding the world that there is no second-class citizen. Everyone has value. To give is to validate the objective standard. And to validate the standard is to experience it in our own lives.

Once we are released from our material things, we can begin to enjoy them and steward them. Stuff no longer holds sway over us because the power we granted it to validate has been removed. We can begin to enjoy the created order using it for purposes that give life.

~~

The Tribe

Embedded within culture are the naturally-occurring relationships of everyday life. We live in relationship and derive a tremendous amount of validation from having friends, relationships, and loved ones, especially with the famous. Jesus continuously addresses the need for validation in relationships but once again turns it upside down.

The allure of validation in relationships is that we are somebody because we are separated by only a degree from somebody special, are friends with somebody famous, or are related to somebody accomplished. The connection we draw is that we must be somebody because we are close to that person. If that person likes us we must be someone special.

The tribe is a central part of this process. People draw validation from being part of a special group of people willing to band together for a purpose. As long as we are part of that tribe, we are special. Israel feels this. God has chosen them for something special. They win battles. They conquer lands. They must be special. Right? Embedded in the tribal concept is the elder, or someone in authority. These are the greatest. They are the ones with the power and control. To be an elder is to gain validation through identity in the tribe.

The followers of Jesus are not immune to this idea. Their initial perception is that Jesus is probably Moses. He will lead the nation of Israel out of captivity. This is what happened before, right? Their natural bent is to jockey for who will sit at his right hand and in positions of power.

> *At that time the disciples came to Jesus and asked, "Who is the greatest in the kingdom of heaven?" (Mt 18:1)*

Jesus throws them for a loop by completely dismissing that idea.

> *He called a little child and had him stand among them. And he said: "I tell you the truth, unless you change and become like little children, you will never enter the kingdom of heaven. (Mt 18:2-3)*

By calling out the child, Jesus is confronting their system of validation. The child isn't jockeying for position. The child isn't yet caught up in the way of the world. This upside-down approach is founded in addressing the root problem that creates the search. It looks backwards because they can't see the problem. They fail to see how costly it really is.

Managing the validation we receive through relationships requires an amazing amount of effort. Relationships always favored the wealthy because they had the capacity to essentially buy the favor of the other through gifts that created obligation. Someone would throw a lavish party and invite those around them. Or the person would provide a gift of tribute or favor to the other, and in the process would expect a favor in return at some point.

Once again Jesus spins this idea on its ear.

> *Then Jesus said to his host, "When you give a luncheon or dinner, do not invite your friends, your brothers or relatives, or your rich neighbors; if you do, they may invite you back and so you will be repaid. But when you*

give a banquet, invite the poor, the crippled, the lame, the blind, and you will be blessed. Although they cannot repay you, you will be repaid at the resurrection of the righteous." (Lk 14:12-14)

"But when you give to the needy, do not let your left hand know what your right hand is doing." (Mt 6:3)

By addressing the obligation or knowledge of the gift, Jesus is fundamentally taking away the mechanisms inherent in their search for validation. He's confronting their need to seek it out in the other. For those attached to the idea of relationships, this feels like death.

Relationships as a form of validation are extremely common. The original distinction of "Elohim" suggests God is already in relationship. We feel the need to connect with the "other" because we understand the self through relationships. Everyone intrinsically reflects the God imagination in some way. As much as this need for connection is intrinsically true, it becomes distorted when we grant the other the capacity to actually validate us. When we give someone the authority to validate us, we grant the person tremendous power over us. We essentially make them an idol. When those relationships take advantage of us, it directly conflicts with the need for validation, so we get frustrated and lonely.

The Way of Jesus is primarily the practice of discovering the image of God in the "other," which reflects God back to the person. To see the dignity in the other is to love. Instead of following in the way of the world, which seeks to get something, love gives something first and as a result, gets back what it really needs.

To foster this practice, Jesus creates a model for spiritual formation to which his followers are already accustomed: the tribe. He gathers a group of twelve people willing to create an intentional Way of life together rooted in love. This love is not subjective or based upon human opinion. It is based on an objective reality established by God.

This Jesus model becomes the context for addressing the root problem by centering our validation in God's love. Jesus understood we need people around us. We need connection. We need a space to wrestle through the evidence of our own judgments and guilt, and reconcile them against God's love. We need to walk together, deal with life together and step into each other's pain and suffering. We need a group of people deeply committed to restoration as a way of life, to be real with each other, and sit in the midst of our brokenness as we wrestle with the reality of our dignity.

The intrinsic value of the relationship is not political but instead, holistic. It is based on engaging a new way of life together, one that reminds each person of his or her dignity, identity, and purpose.

The value of these relationships is in reminding each other of what is already true, in reflecting God's love to each other, even when it hurts. We sit in the tension of the "other" and are reminded that God's standard of "good" is not reserved for a select few. It includes everyone. The tension of the other is addressed as we wrestle with our own struggles, but now we have a space to work them out.

The deep profundity and validity of the Jesus Model is found in the restoration of Peter. Unlike Judas who kills himself, Peter returns from his act of betrayal to face judgment. He returns to deal with the disgrace. But instead of shame, he returns to discover that his act does not define him. He returns to discover a profound level of grace that transforms his reality of what is true. He returns to discover his own dignity, which is established by Jesus.

The Jesus model also calls each person to practice transcending the validation that could come from being part of the tribe. Missional means being sent to reveal the Way for the other.

> *"Therefore go and make disciples of all nations, baptizing them in the name of the Father and of the Son and of the Holy Spirit." (Mt 28:19)*

Jesus gives his followers three years to engage life together, but then he calls them to go out and lead others in the way. He calls them to consistently transcend the temptation of finding their identity in being part of the tribe. He doesn't establish the parameter of "just Israel." He transcends their traditional thought process and includes the whole world.

~~

The Law Of Love

The dominant structure for addressing human interaction is the law. Even in captivity, keeping the law is still deeply entrenched in Jewish culture. But the problem with the law is that it can only reveal where we are breaking ourselves. If we follow it, it will produce life – but time inevitably reveals we can't. Jesus addresses this problem by completely reframing the law. He reduces it to the simple law of love.

The call to love is not new. It is deeply embedded within the original law. It has no subjective limit on identity, race, creed, tribe, or color. It calls people to love even those who we consider strangers.

> "The alien living with you must be treated as one of your native-born. Love him as yourself, for you were aliens in Egypt. I am the LORD your God." (Lev 19:34)

So when Jesus arrives on the scene, the natural question is what he will do with the law.

> "Do not think that I have come to abolish the Law or the Prophets; I have not come to abolish them but to fulfill them." (Mt 5:17)

The original purpose of the law is to reveal life, and with that came the possibility of completely fulfilling it. The law is the test of purity. This provocative possibility begins to establish not just Jesus' authority but also his command of life. Jesus just keeps getting it right. His life consistently reveals a remarkably different fruit of self-control.

But instead of just living it out, He transforms their understanding of the law.

> Hearing that Jesus had silenced the Sadducees, the Pharisees got together. One of them, an expert in the law, tested him with this question: "Teacher,

which is the greatest commandment in the Law?" (Mt 22:34-36)

The question reveals the subjective nature of their thinking. Much of the cultural law and even the Jewish law are based on do's and don'ts. It's a list actions people have to perform and avoid in order to fulfill the law. But their question also gives Jesus an opportunity to stump them.

Jesus replied: "'Love the Lord your God with all your heart and with all your soul and with all your mind.' This is the first and greatest commandment. And the second is like it: 'Love your neighbor as yourself.' All the Law and the Prophets hang on these two commandments." (Mt 22:37-40)

What Jesus does here is mind-blowing. Jesus reduces an entire Way of life down to two commands. The value of the Way in the Kingdom of God is not in its complexity but in its irreducible, objective simplicity. To reduce a complex set of rituals and laws down to two statements based entirely on love, frames it in such a way that is so simple anyone can do it. It strips away the need for experts of the law.

Love works every time because it directly addresses the root problem. To love is to assume value. It is to assume good. To love God calls us to constantly challenge our assumptions about God, so we can hear for the first time. The value of loving God is to discover the truth about God's response. Once we do, we can begin to engage the God imagination. We can draw close to what is true.

Jesus frames loving others against the standard of the self because the way to treat the other is a direct reflection of how we see ourselves. If we don't love others, it reveals we don't love ourselves. The self was the one relationship that we had to manage. It was the first relationship of judgment in the Garden.

Instead of focusing on what we're not supposed to do, Jesus frames the commands in an active manner. The more common rule in Mesopotamian culture is, *"Don't do unto others what you would not have them do unto you."* It is in essence passive. The call to love is proactive. Jesus is calling people to actively begin with love.

"Do to others as you would have them do to you." (Lk 6:31)

The call to love is not a condition for attaining God's perspective. We don't love because we have to. To make the rule of love the right thing to do in order to attain God's love renders it back to religion. We love because we get to. The act of love is discovering what is already true. To discover is to realize what is already true.

The rule of love is so simple that even a child could do it. It begins with the idea that each and every person has value as a human being created in the image of God. We don't have to consider every nook and cranny of the circumstances. We just have to begin with the idea that the "other" is good.

The simplicity of it tempts us to believe it is easy. Love is only possible when we address the root problem that covers the God imagination. Love is a fruit of the Spirit residing within us. For this reason, the rule of love doesn't strip away the need for community. It reveals it. To live the Way, to love irreducibly happens in community. It is fostered in community. To love the other is to love the self. It's only possible when we love the self. It is to discover the evidence of good in the most needed way.

To help, Jesus reframes the Way as something we are entirely unprepared to do.

In reply Jesus declared, "I tell you the truth, no one can see the kingdom of God unless he is born again." (Jn 3:3)

The image Jesus uses is a baby. A baby exists in a state of total dependence and trust. But there is no condemnation because there is no expectation. There is only grace.

Jesus understands that the law of love is simple but not easy. In fact, it's hard. As adults, it's hard in the beginning because our bodies are bent the other way. We're referencing deeply embedded captivating stories, old wounds, and false identities. It takes slow, progressive development with the support of community. As adults we think we have to know it all before we can begin. Babies don't have a story. They fail long before they ever learn how to do anything. But somehow, magically, a baby learns.

The rule of love does not have boundaries or exception. Jesus transforms the way people see their neighbor by giving them what could be considered a worst-case scenario, the Samaritan. Samaritans were half-breeds between Babylon and the Jews. Both groups reviled them for their racial impurity. They were the true exception.

Jesus stretches their understanding of limitations and essentially takes away the exception.

> *"You have heard that it was said, 'Love your neighbor and hate your enemy.' But I tell you: Love your enemies and pray for those who persecute you, that you may be sons of your Father in heaven." (Mt 5:43-45)*

Jesus extends the rule of love even to the enemy. The brilliance of this moment cannot be understated. By extending the rule Jesus is creating a structure where we can't disqualify ourselves. The lie searches for the exception to the rule because it wants to make us the exception. With love there is no exception.

If we're honest, the problem is not really even the other person we think of as enemy. The true enemy then is our perception of our own self. Where do we go to hide from our own destructive tendencies? Where do we go when we're our own worst enemy? When our bodies produce destructive fruit it is the self that we hide from. So when Jesus says, *"Love your enemies,"* he's really talking about the projected self, the perception that we are the problem. It's a holistic call to embrace reconciliation within.

Loving the enemy is then a brilliant answer to the original question in the Garden. How do you kill the enemy within? With love. The only way to remove the enemy, which is the false self, is to see it as God sees it.

> *"For whoever wants to save his life will lose it, but whoever loses his life for me will find it." (Mt 16:25)*

Love removes the covering to reveal what is already underneath. It strips away the false identity, uncovering the God imagination within. We're not attempting to kill the true self. We're attempting to kill the false reality that we've created, the one we create from our own judgments. When we do, we find the true self.

In order for Jesus to prove our love, He has to take the idea all the way. He has to prove there really is no exception. His own life on the cross becomes an example of how far love will go.

> *"Greater love has no one than this, that he lay down his life for his friends."* *(Jn 15:13)*

And we need this evidence, don't we? We need to know if there is an exception to the rule of love. We need to know that no matter what we do, God doesn't stop loving us. We, then are called to the same standard.

~~

Religulous

The story keeps coming back to religion, doesn't it? Humanity needs some kind of satisfaction. If the story has revealed anything it is the inevitable reality that we need some kind of release from our guilt. Religion reveals a dark tension in the story. Humanity's final method of redemption is an inherently violent means of restoration. It's bloody, requiring endless sacrifices to appease the consciences of humanity for each transgression. Something must die in order for something to live. The system just doesn't work.

Jesus presents a provocative alternative to the religious system. What if there were a single, perfect atonement that would cover every transgression? And not just things we've done, but things we could do. It would once and for all reveal God's true response. In other words, the atonement would release us from the oppressive need for religious justification. It would release us from guilt and shame through true justice.

Instead of worrying about God's response to human transgressions, humanity could begin to focus on the consequences of the actions, which was always the original concern. Morality could give way to consequence. Humanity could begin to see that the original concern was always death: a spiritual death from the covering, and a physical death from decay. It could see the root problem was not an angry God demanding punitive justice, but an angry self, unable to reconcile a false reality.

To get there, humanity has to deal with another provocative reality, the excessively dark nature of the lie. Embedded within humanity is the question of the exception. Is there some act we can perform that will send us over the edge? In other words, is there a limit to God's love and redemption? Much of the journey into captivity is the radical and compulsive exploration of these far reaches. Evil produces captivating and condemning evidence. In our minds there is no way God can love us if we do "that." This "one thing" is impossible for God to forgive.

The atonement presents the radical extreme of this search for the bottom. The act of walking away explores the nature of self-destruction. But what are the limits of it? We can kill ourselves to spite God, but the ego can't enjoy the outcome. We're not around to experience the response. Jesus presents a much darker possibility. What if we could kill the God image, the very Son of God in our midst? Surely then God would refuse the gift of grace? There's nothing else. To kill the God image is the ultimate act of revenge. It's the most profound level of evil human begins can conjure. If this possibility is true, then it is also where we see the true nature of God. Would God truly live up to the rule of love? Would God put it all on the line?

The religious contract is our final demand for satisfaction. We need the atonement. We need a way to appease our own sense of guilt. We demand something so perfect that is will fill our sense of violence with a nauseating stench. The brutality of this act is seen the moment we place our own children in the hands of the crowd. What we would never do, God does for us. The final act of atonement is the father giving up his son at the demands of humanity.

If the cross at Golgotha proves anything it is the ultimate reality of love. The cross is the final destination because it is an appointment with death itself. Death is the original consequence. And it is utterly amazing that God still arrives on the scene.

Chapter 12 – The Evidence Of God's Love

"Do your worst." - Edmond

An Appointment With Death

Imagine growing up with the knowledge that your life would have a profound impact on the world. In fact, you are the savior of the world. Your most courageous act would become the evidence that would redeem all of humanity. Your words would be quoted, and your actions documented for everyone to hear and follow. Your existence would symbolize the answer to the most profound question in all of humanity: Does God really love us?

But then imagine knowing ahead of time that in order to answer this question your life would end up on two intersecting pieces of wood. Imagine knowing that the only way to reveal that love would be to allow your life to end in a torturous, horrifying death. Would you still want to lead that life?

This is the question for Jesus. The missional path is towards pain and suffering. It means facing our fears head on; not so we can enjoy them or find masochistic pleasure in them, but so we can face them, address them head on and overcome them. The point of the cross is not to die, but to prove that death is not the end.

For three years, Jesus spends much of his time revealing what the Kingdom of God looks like to the people. It is restorative and whole. It calls people to repentance, to the rule of love, to true justice, and a Way of living that is unlike that of the world. But as the story enters the final week of Jesus' life, everything slows down to focus on this one moment. Where the first three years have revealed Jesus' command of life, the final week will reveal his command over death.

The central consequence of the root problem is death. Humanity has lost sight of its own dignity, identity and purpose. It has created a covering that hides what is true, and in the process can no longer see the God imagination within. To uncover it is to subject ourselves to the possibility of God's response. Death prevails over humanity for ages, both spiritually and physically. And where most people would run from death, Jesus runs straight to it. Instead of fearing death, he makes it a central part of the restoration process.

> *Then he called the crowd to him along with his disciples and said: "If anyone would come after me, he must deny himself and take up his cross and follow me. For whoever wants to save his life will lose it, but whoever loses his life for me and for the gospel will save it." (Mk 8:34-35)*

Jesus alludes to his own death several times.

> *"We are going up to Jerusalem," he said, "and the Son of Man will be betrayed to the chief priests and teachers of the law. They will condemn him to death and will hand him over to the Gentiles, who will mock him and spit on him, flog him and kill him. Three days later he will rise." (Mk 10:33-34)*

> *Now as Jesus was going up to Jerusalem, he took the twelve disciples aside and said to them, "We are going up to Jerusalem, and the Son of Man will be betrayed to the chief priests and the teachers of the law. They will condemn him to death and will turn him over to the Gentiles to be mocked and flogged and crucified. On the third day he will be raised to life!" (Mt 20:17-19)*

Jesus understands that in order to solve the problem of death, he has to face it. Isn't this way we solve problems anyway, by facing them head-on? The mature path is to address problems rather than to run from them.

Jesus is not a sadist here. He's not inviting us to die simply for the sake of dying. He's inviting us to die for the sake of our own redemption. He's calling us to let go of the coverings and false identities so we can discover the true self, which is hidden underneath.

We can so easily miss this. We often think the process of dying is only dying, as if nothing is produced by it. But it's not. To voluntarily take on death is to discover the freedom from it. What is dying is not the soul but the ego; the broken self that demands to be heard and nourished, pampered and propped up. The ego doesn't want to die. It wants nothing more than to keep us locked in oppression and immaturity. It wants us to do its bidding. And it will do everything it can to convince us not to let it die, because the ego is always willing to settle for less. It's always looking to hold onto the old for survival.

Dying, in a practical sense, becomes our redemption process. It's a process of trading in the lie to discover the truth. To die is the doorway to finding true life. We're trading in the old so we can discover the new. And when we practice this dying process in our own lives, it usually means giving up what we've created so we can discover what is infinitely better–namely, life. But if we don't let go, if we don't participate, we miss what it means truly live.

Jesus is filled with the God imagination, and it would seem counterintuitive to face and even embrace death. But love is fully realized in the act of dying for the other.

> *Greater love has no one than this, that he lay down his life for his friends.*
> *(Jn 15:13)*

Jesus is taking his own words and making them real. He's embodying the ethic of the kingdom of God. He's revealing that the fullest expression of the God imagination is to see the other as so valuable that we would give up what is most precious to us: life.

The final part of our story takes place in Jerusalem during the week of Passover. Jesus announces his arrival with an almost humorous symbol. He enters Jerusalem on a donkey. Where empire is built on pride and might, the Kingdom of God is built on humility.

> *"Say to the Daughter of Zion, 'See, your king comes to you, gentle and*
> *riding on a donkey, on a colt, the foal of a donkey.'" (Mt 21:5)*

For his followers, entering Jerusalem is about leading the people out of captivity. A king has arrived to rescue the people. They assume he must be ready to build another empire. Israel must be restored. But Jesus' idea of restoration is something entirely different. Jesus is going to completely reinvent the idea. Instead of leading the people out of a physical captivity, he's going to give them a way to restore the world in which they already live.

~~

The Withering Fig

The next morning Jesus presents what first appears to be a rather curious object lesson. Jesus searches for food and seems to curse a fig tree.

> *Early in the morning, as he was on his way back to the city, he was hungry. Seeing a fig tree by the road, he went up to it but found nothing on it except leaves. Then he said to it, "May you never bear fruit again!" Immediately the tree withered. (Mt 21:18-19)*

At first glance the event seems entirely random. There is no set-up to the event. Figs don't ever ripen at that time of the year, so expecting the tree to produce fruit is ridiculous.

It's random unless we connect it to the root problem. The fig leaves represent the original means of covering in the Garden. Jesus is calling out the original object that helps produce death. He's calling out the reality that the covering will never work.

> *So they sewed fig leaves together and made coverings for themselves. (Gen 3:7)*

By calling out the fig leaves Jesus creates an object lesson for his followers.

> *When the disciples saw this, they were amazed. "How did the fig tree wither so quickly?" they asked.*
>
> *Jesus replied, "I tell you the truth, if you have faith and do not doubt, not only can you do what was done to the fig tree, but also you can say to*

this mountain, 'Go, throw yourself into the sea,' and it will be done. If you
believe, you will receive whatever you ask for in prayer." (Mt 21:20-22)

Although they probably don't realize it, Jesus is inviting his followers to take command over their own captivity, to participate with Jesus in addressing the original covering that hides their true identity. To address the original obstacle is to uncover what is true.

If they do, they will be able to move mountains. The statement is likely figurative because the obstacle blinding them feels like an unmovable object. It is a mountain of unreasonable proportions. But the moment we participate with God in the process, we can easily cast it aside as though it is nothing. All that needs to change is our perspective.

The idea of a fig tree is not new. They've heard it before. Jesus uses it earlier in a parable to the disciples.

Then he told this parable: "A man had a fig tree, planted in his vineyard,
and he went to look for fruit on it, but did not find any. So he said to the
man who took care of the vineyard, 'For three years now I've been coming
to look for fruit on this fig tree and haven't found any. Cut it down! Why
should it use up the soil?'

"'Sir,' the man replied, 'leave it alone for one more year, and I'll dig
around it and fertilize it. If it bears fruit next year, fine! If not, then cut it
down.'" (Lk 13:6-9)

The brilliance of this parable is only obvious if we connect it to the covering. Jesus calls out humanity's constant search for the covering to work. We buy into the idea that is will actually work. We wait and wait and wait for it to produce the fruit. It's even planted in the vineyard, which is a symbol for the kingdom. We partner with each other to just give it one more shot. We wait just a little bit longer. But no matter how long we wait it just doesn't work. Its failure to produce fruit reveals that this is a false reality.

So Jesus invites the people to do the obvious. He says, "Cut it down!" This idea would be obvious to an agricultural people. It would seem ridiculous to maintain something that produced no fruit for three years. But this is what we do, isn't it?

~~

The End Of Religion

The path to Jerusalem means Jesus will die...but for the sake of something. So it becomes important to communicate the specific purpose to his followers. Jesus begins to tangibly connect his own life to the religious system and its end.

> On reaching Jerusalem, Jesus entered the temple area and began driving out those who were buying and selling there. He overturned the tables of the money changers and the benches of those selling doves, and would not allow anyone to carry merchandise through the temple courts. And as he taught them, he said, "Is it not written:
>
> 'My house will be called a house of prayer for all nations'? But you have made it 'a den of robbers.'" (Mk 11:15-17)

It's very easy to assume Jesus is getting mad because they're selling stuff. But what if it is deeper than that? Religion is in essence a transaction. They are just making it easy for people to do what is already in place. What if Jesus is getting mad because this is the moment they need to be reminded of the original purpose? They need to remember what all this is originally for, the practice of atonement. Jesus even uses the words of the prophets to remind them. His "house of prayer" comment calls them back.

> "These I will bring to my holy mountain and give them joy in my house of prayer. Their burnt offerings and sacrifices will be accepted on my altar; for my house will be called a house of prayer for all nations." (Isa 56:7)

Jesus draws their attention to the idea of acceptance. The purpose of the atonement was to create acceptance. And they needed it.

It is highly likely that the people around him know what Jesus is referencing. They know the prophets. They know the Scripture. Jesus understands that they need to remember the original purpose of the temple. And by calling out the temple he could begin the process of connecting the dots for them.

What is telling, is the response of those in charge of the temple. Instead of agreeing with Jesus, they plot to kill him.

The chief priests and the teachers of the law heard this and began looking for a way to kill him, for they feared him, because the whole crowd was amazed at his teaching. (Mk 11:18)

The next day, Jesus returns to the temple and blatantly implies the end of the religious process.

As he was leaving the temple, one of his disciples said to him, "Look, Teacher! What massive stones! What magnificent buildings!"

"Do you see all these great buildings?" replied Jesus. "Not one stone here will be left on another; every one will be thrown down." (Mk 13:1-2)

The disciples are marveling at the grandeur of the temple, which represents the religious system. They're captured by its magnificence. And Jesus throws them for a complete loop. "(It) will be thrown down." It is highly likely that anyone hearing this would be shocked. The idea of ending one of the central systems within the Jewish world would be unfathomable. How could Jesus do such a thing? The very idea would almost be too much to comprehend.

Jesus is revealing one of the central purposes of his mission. He is subtly alluding to the end of religion as a form of practice for atonement. God uses a means to speak to the people in order to remove it altogether. Where the human system is violent and endlessly bloody, God's response is restorative. It will put an end to the violence once and for all.

Jesus is also likely alluding to the actual destruction of the temple in 70 AD by the Roman armies. The event marks the end of the human system of religious sacrificial atonement and begins to usher in a new era away from sacrifice.

~~

Communion

Jesus takes the symbolism even further by drawing out a direct connection to his death. But he does it in a way that serves multiple purposes. Jesus uses the idea of the meal as a celebration of victory over death.

> *When the hour came, Jesus and his apostles reclined at the table. And he said to them, "I have eagerly desired to eat this Passover with you before I suffer. For I tell you, I will not eat it again until it finds fulfillment in the kingdom of God."*
>
> *After taking the cup, he gave thanks and said, "Take this and divide it among you. For I tell you I will not drink again of the fruit of the vine until the kingdom of God comes."*
>
> *And he took bread, gave thanks and broke it, and gave it to them, saying, "This is my body given for you; do this in remembrance of me."*
>
> *In the same way, after the supper he took the cup, saying, "This cup is the new covenant in my blood, which is poured out for you. (Lk 22:14-20)*

The symbolism of what Jesus is doing cannot be overstated. The bread and the wine are part of the Hebrew story. His listeners would have known the connection.

> *Then Melchizedek king of Salem brought out bread and wine. He was priest of God Most High, and he blessed Abram, saying, "Blessed be Abram by God Most High, Creator of heaven and earth.*
>
> *And blessed be God Most High, who delivered your enemies into your hand." (Gen 14:18-20)*

Jesus is drawing a direct connection between the act of dying and victory. The central message of the meal is not pacification of an angry God, but victory over the enemy. He's informing them of the reality that is already in hand.

When we read the stories of communion we often think this is a moment of remembrance for what Jesus did for us. And it is. The communion is first a tangible reminder of what Jesus did on the cross. We need the evidence. It is also a reminder of our atonement, that nothing separates us from our Creator, our Father, and the one who loves. To participate in communion is a ritual of remembering what is true, designed to remind us of how far God will go to reveal love to us.

Communion invites us into the deep process of continually experiencing the love of God and release from guilt. It offers us a way to deal with our brokenness in a holistic way. To engage communion is to invite true justice into our lies. It is to come to a state of repentance, or honesty, about our own brokenness. But it is also an embrace of the present reality of grace. It's a reminder that what we do does not separate us from the love of God. It does not change our dignity or who we are as children of God, no matter what we've done.

But what if it still goes farther than that? Notice how he says, "DO this in remembrance of me." He's not just calling us to eat. He's calling us to participate, to offer ourselves as a sacrifice for others. Jesus is reminding his followers they are priests. A priest is someone who enters into pain and suffering in order to redeem it. To "do this" is to break ourselves for the sake of others, to be love for people around us and to participate in revealing the kingdom.

Love, embodied in the act of sacrifice, is one of the clearest signs of the kingdom. It is the fruit that is unlike any other. While the rest of the world could only produce death, it is those who actively sacrifice that produce life. The Apostle Paul reiterates this idea in his letter to Romans.

> *Therefore, I urge you, brothers, in view of God's mercy, to offer your bodies as living sacrifices, holy and pleasing to God—this is your spiritual act of worship. (Rom 12:1)*

Communion is then a reminder of our participation with Jesus in the act of sacrifice for the sake of love. The very act of sacrificing ourselves flies in the face of religion, which seeks out an alternative option. Jesus instead calls us to face death head-on and be the sacrifice.

The act of suffering works directly to address the root problem. When we step into someone's pain and suffering and offer ourselves as a sacrifice, we reveal the evidence of someone's worth. No one dies for another unless there is a good reason. When we suffer for someone, even to the point of death, we reveal the evidence of God's kingdom in our midst.

~~

Reconstitution

Of all the places Jesus could have gone in his final moments of freedom before death, he chooses a Garden. It's so obvious that Jesus is drawing our attention back to the scene of the crime that we almost miss the significance. This is where the problem started. It began in a Garden. And it is here that Jesus will experience one of his deepest moments of wrestling.

> *They went to a place called Gethsemane, and Jesus said to his disciples,*
> *"Sit here while I pray." He took Peter, James and John along with him, and*
> *he began to be deeply distressed and troubled. "My soul is overwhelmed*
> *with sorrow to the point of death," he said to them. "Stay here and keep*
> *watch." (Mk 14:32-34)*

We cannot ignore the reality of Jesus' experience. Think about it. He's in a Garden. He is being overwhelmed to the point of death. What is he wrestling with? In essence, Jesus is being asked to voluntarily take on death. In order for Jesus to reveal the path out of death, he has to step into it. He has to become sin. And that means taking on the illusion of being separated from the Father.

It is here we see the deepest aspects of Jesus' own humanity. We get to see trust worked out in its deepest form.

> *And being in anguish, he prayed more earnestly, and his sweat was like*
> *drops of blood falling to the ground. (Lk 22:44)*

Jesus isn't just sweating drops "like" blood. This is blood. There's actually a name for this. It's called, "hematidrosis." Extreme levels of stress make the blood packets around the glands burst and exit out the pores. Jesus, considering the weight of what is happening, is excruciatingly overwhelmed.

In order to understand the stress, we have to understand the nature of God's will here. Jesus is wrestling with his own reality. Jesus has to consider what it means to embrace death. He has to ask the question, "God, what are you doing to me?" He has to consider the goodness of the plan and even his own perception of God. Jesus has never died before. He's never taken on death before. He's never experienced separation from the Father before. Everything in His life stems from this one relationship, his life, his ability to love, and his mission. And now his Father is calling him to step into the very heart of darkness. The whole idea is either stunningly stupid, or insanely brilliant.

It calls into question everything. Is God really good? Then why would God call someone to die? Is Jesus even good? How can he be good and end up having to die? Nothing makes sense. The moment is now here and He must choose which path he will follow. To stay in the moment is to stay grounded in the idea that God is good, even when it doesn't make sense. In many ways, it is the Garden all over again. Jesus is being asked the same question of the Tree in light of absolutely brutal evidence.

In returning to the scene of the crime, the story suggests the biological idea of reconstitution. Jesus is embodying the human conflict. In order to change reality, we have to dig it up and wrestle with the facts and emotions of the story again. We have to look at everything with fresh eyes and see it from God's perspective. And when we do, we embrace the means to change it.

> *Going a little farther, he fell to the ground and prayed that if possible the hour might pass from him. "Abba, Father," he said, "everything is possible for you. Take this cup from me. Yet not what I will, but what you will."* (Mk 14:35-36)

If there is a moment Jesus stretches out his arms and gives himself up to death, this is it. This is the moment Jesus surrenders to the idea of taking on death directly. He actively chooses to trust in God's redemptive process even though it produces a staggering amount of fear.

It is here that we see unfolding the original possibility in the Garden. The original statement, "The man has now become like one of us, knowing good and evil" is being replayed. If Jesus is God incarnate, he's revealing the experience of evil does not fundamentally make someone evil. But in order to prove that is true, Jesus must live into it. He must encounter it, in order to overcome it.

Jesus is giving us perhaps the most unorthodox idea ever presented. We often think that the way to overcome evil and death is to refuse it, to deny its power in our life and even pretend it's not true. Our resistance to evil and death actually fuels its power over us. To deny its existence is much the same as covering it. Our primary concern is its capacity to fundamentally change us. We assume that if we experience it, it will make us evil. We cover what is true, pretending to hide it, and in doing so, partner in our own demise.

What Jesus is revealing is that the way to overcome evil and death is to surrender to the presence of it. By surrendering to the presence of evil and death, we're destroying its hold over us. We're calling it out and addressing it for what it really is. We're being honest that it exists in our lives. And it is only then that we can overcome it. It is only by surrendering to the reality of evil that we discover we are not changed by it. It is only by surrendering to death that we can discover that it is not our end.

In the act of surrender, Jesus is revealing the brilliance of God's plan. The pathway towards restoration is not away from evil and death but through evil and death. It is no coincidence then that Jesus is arrested IN the Garden. The process of captivity is literally played out. The process of death continues right where it started.

~~

Perfection

The concept of atonement through sacrificial means is essentially a transactional agreement. Humanity wants blood in order to feel justified for its guilt. A life is given in place of the transgression, and life is represented in the blood. The blood creates a covering for the guilt.

For the life of a creature is in the blood, and I have given it to you to
make atonement for yourselves on the altar; it is the blood that makes
atonement for one's life. (Lev 17:11)

Within the atonement construct is a unique problem. How perfect does the
sacrifice have to be? If one offers a sacrifice but it contains even the tiniest
of flaws, is it really good enough? In other words, even the sacrifice has a
potential exception clause. What humanity needs is something so perfect that
we can't find the exception.

The original atonement process defined this. It included detailed instructions
on finding offerings that were free of defect. Humanity needs something
valuable, something whole. It had to have exceptional value in order to feel
justified.

He is to bring to the priest as a guilt offering a ram from the flock, one
without defect and of the proper value. (Lev 5:18)

The final hours of Jesus' life are essentially a scrutiny process over this one
matter. Is Jesus without flaw? Is Jesus really the perfect atonement? Over the
next twelve hours, Jesus experiences a series of examinations that are deeply
purposeful. One of the most important responsibilities of Israel is about to be
realized.

Then the detachment of soldiers with its commander and the Jewish
officials arrested Jesus. They bound him and brought him first to Annas,
who was the father-in-law of Caiaphas, the high priest that year.
Caiaphas was the one who had advised the Jews that it would be good if
one man died for the people. (Jn 18:12-14)

Meanwhile, the high priest questioned Jesus about his disciples and his
teaching.

"I have spoken openly to the world," Jesus replied. "I always taught in
synagogues or at the temple, where all the Jews come together. I said
nothing in secret. Why question me? Ask those who heard me. Surely they
know what I said."

When Jesus said this, one of the officials nearby struck him in the face. "Is this the way you answer the high priest?" he demanded.

"If I said something wrong," Jesus replied, "testify as to what is wrong. But if I spoke the truth, why did you strike me?"

Then Annas sent him, still bound, to Caiaphas the high priest. (Jn 18:19-24)

One of the central roles of the priest is to look over the offering and to declare it satisfactory. In Jesus' case it's not just a priest but the high priest.

Those who had arrested Jesus took him to Caiaphas, the high priest, where the teachers of the law and the elders had assembled. But Peter followed him at a distance, right up to the courtyard of the high priest. He entered and sat down with the guards to see the outcome.

The chief priests and the whole Sanhedrin were looking for false evidence against Jesus so that they could put him to death. But they did not find any, though many false witnesses came forward. (Mt 26:57-60)

In normal situations an assembly is not required. But in Jesus' case, because of the Passover, the entire Sanhedrin is present. The Sanhedrin was an assembly of 71 priestly "judges" which acted like a Supreme Court. They were responsible for the most important decisions in the Jewish culture. In other words, every important decision-maker in the Jewish world is present to make a judgment. There is no exception. Nobody can say, "But I wasn't there to find that one thing." They can't even find false information about Him. And their conclusion is that Jesus is blameless.

"What do you think?"

"He is worthy of death," they answered. (Mt 26:66)

God is using the religious system to once and for all end the religious system. It's an absolutely brilliant move on God's part. The priests are essentially fulfilling their original role, which is to find a blameless offering and present it as sacrifice. But the sacrifice is for humanity, which is represented in the empire.

It is here that we see the role of the priests truly played out. The priests cannot execute people without permission from the empire. They need the approval of humanity. So Jesus begins the second round of scrutiny. He's sent before Pilate.

> *So Pilate came out to them and asked, "What charges are you bringing against this man?"*
>
> *"If he were not a criminal," they replied, "we would not have handed him over to you."*
>
> *Pilate said, "Take him yourselves and judge him by your own law."*
>
> *"But we have no right to execute anyone," the Jews objected. (Jn 18:29-31)*

Pilate questions Jesus but finds no basis for guilt.

> *"What is truth?" Pilate asked. With this he went out again to the Jews and said, "I find no basis for a charge against him." (Jn 18:38)*

The priests have delivered the perfect sacrifice. They have fulfilled their role. They have delivered the atonement to humanity. The representative of the empire sits in judgment and also agrees. Both parties have agreed. Humanity has found its perfect sacrifice. Pilate even announces it to the people.

> *"Here is your king," Pilate said to the Jews. (Jn 19:14)*

Israel then reveals the reality of what it means to be chosen. They too are part of the empire.

> *"We have no king but Caesar," the chief priests answered. (Jn 19:15)*

In this moment Israel is declaring reality. There is no separation between Israel and the empire. There is only one humanity. And much as this seems like a betrayal, it is actually an important and restorative distinction. By including themselves in the empire, they are embracing the atonement.

~~

The Exchange

Humanity has now found a perfect sacrifice. But the story reveals two final symbolic moments that complete the transaction. It could be called the exchange of the innocent for the guilty. The first is the exchange.

> Now it was the custom at the Feast to release a prisoner whom the people requested. (Mk 15:6)

During Passover, it is the custom of the governor to set a guilty person free. Pilate offers Jesus. A guilty man named Barrabas is brought before the people.

> But the chief priests and the elders persuaded the crowd to ask for Barabbas and to have Jesus executed.
>
> "Which of the two do you want me to release to you?" asked the governor. "Barabbas," they answered.
>
> "What shall I do, then, with Jesus who is called Christ?" Pilate asked. They all answered, "Crucify him!"
>
> "Why? What crime has he committed?" asked Pilate. But they shouted all the louder, "Crucify him!" (Mt 27:20-23)

The name Barrabas, or bar-abba, means "son of the father". It couldn't get any more symbolic of the original Adam. Barrabas' crime is essentially participation in a revolt of the people. He represents the human construct of the inward striving of humanity to solve the problem through might. This period of striving is over. The people are being set free.

> When Pilate saw that he was getting nowhere, but that instead an uproar was starting, he took water and washed his hands in front of the crowd. "I am innocent of this man's blood," he said. "It is your responsibility!" (Mt 27:24)

To argue in any way that the death of Jesus is the responsibility of Israel is irresponsible. If anything, Pilate's denial of responsibility is an emphasis on the true cowardice of the empire. This is the moment humanity needs but it can't do it by itself. It needs help. If Israel does anything, it is courageously performing what it has been called to do. It has been chosen to perform what is arguably one of the most important acts in the human story, the act of atonement. The empire approves the process.

This second symbolic act is in the response of the people to what could be considered the final judgment.

> All the people answered, "Let his blood be on us and on our children!"
> (Mt 27:25)

The priests are acting for humanity, but the atonement is for all the people. The blood is a final inclusive covering, even to the children.

~~

Becoming Sin

The final hours of Jesus' life can literally be described as a walk through hell on earth. Over the course of approximately fifteen hours, Jesus experiences rejection after rejection, even from his closest followers. He's betrayed, arrested, falsely accused, spit on, punched, condemned, whipped, mocked, crowned, and eventually crucified. Death has arrived.

The agony in the Garden begins a series of rejections. The evidence of death begins to mount. First, the disciples fall asleep on Jesus at his most critical hour.

> Then he returned to his disciples and found them sleeping. "Simon," he
> said to Peter, "are you asleep? Could you not keep watch for one hour?"
> (Mk 14:37)

Second, Judas, who many scholars consider to be the one trusted with the money, betrays Jesus to the Sanhedrin. The event is made all the more painful with a symbolic kiss.

> Now the betrayer had arranged a signal with them: "The one I kiss is the
> man; arrest him and lead him away under guard." Going at once to Jesus,

Judas said, "Rabbi!" and kissed him. (Mk 14:44-45)

Jesus is arrested and his followers immediately flee.

Then everyone deserted him and fled. (Mk 14:50)

Peter, arguably his most passionate follower, betrays him not once but three times, right in front of him.

Peter replied, "Man, I don't know what you're talking about!" Just as he was speaking, the rooster crowed. The Lord turned and looked straight at Peter. Then Peter remembered the word the Lord had spoken to him: "Before the rooster crows today, you will disown me three times." And he went outside and wept bitterly. (Lk 22:60-62)

The Sanhedrin scrutinizes Jesus all night, accusing him of blasphemy and even hitting him.

Then the high priest tore his clothes and said, "He has spoken blasphemy! Why do we need any more witnesses? Look, now you have heard the blasphemy. What do you think?"
"He is worthy of death," they answered.

Then they spit in his face and struck him with their fists. Others slapped him and said, "Prophesy to us, Christ. Who hit you?" (Mt 26:65-68)

Pilate scrutinizes Jesus all morning, sentences him to death, and has him beaten and scourged, all before hanging him on one of the most punishing torture devices ever invented.

Then Pilate took Jesus and had him flogged. The soldiers twisted together a crown of thorns and put it on his head. They clothed him in a purple robe and went up to him again and again, saying, "Hail, king of the Jews!" And they struck him in the face. (Jn 19:1-3)

When they came to the place called the Skull, there they crucified him, along with the criminals—one on his right, the other on his left. (Lk 23:33)

Virtually everyone mocks him.

> *Those who passed by hurled insults at him, shaking their heads and
> saying, "You who are going to destroy the temple and build it in three
> days, save yourself! Come down from the cross, if you are the Son of
> God!"*

> *In the same way the chief priests, the teachers of the law and the elders
> mocked him. "He saved others," they said, "but he can't save himself! He's
> the King of Israel! Let him come down now from the cross, and we will
> believe in him." (Mt 27:39-42)*

His world is crashing down around him. He's now hanging on the cross between
two thieves, beaten and humiliated beyond recognition. The original fear in the
Garden has come true.

> *From the sixth hour until the ninth hour darkness came over all the land.
> About the ninth hour Jesus cried out in a loud voice, "Eloi, Eloi, lama
> sabachthani?"—which means, "My God, my God, why have you forsaken
> me?" (Mt 27:45-46)*

In this brief moment, we see Jesus taking on the first reality of death, which is
a perceptual separation. In order to fully represent the human experience, he
has to fully become the human experience. This act is a voluntary taking on of
the world's sin. He's not choosing to sin. To understand what is going on it is
helpful to turn to the words of the Apostle Paul.

> *God made him who had no sin to be sin for us, so that in him we might
> become the righteousness of God. (2 Cor 5:21)*

> *Christ redeemed us from the curse of the law by becoming a curse for us,
> for it is written: "Cursed is everyone who is hung on a tree." (Gal 3:13)*

Jesus is literally becoming sin. The act of becoming sin is not a traditional
sense of sin, which is breaking the will of God through an action. Jesus is not
choosing to break the will of God because this is the will of God. To break the
will of God would ruin the point of the sacrifice. Jesus enters the one place God

doesn't appear to exist: the space of death. Jesus is entering into the one space where humanity thinks God cannot be found. The only way to redeem it, to prove God is there, is to enter into it. Jesus is taking on the perceptual reality of separation from God for the sake of the world around him.

Becoming sin is a process of experiencing perceptual separation from God. There is no actual separation happening. This perceptual understanding of sin goes back to both Adam and Cain, who saw God as forsaking them. From this perspective Jesus is taking on the fullest human experience.

It is here that we also run into a strange paradox with our traditional stories. If the root problem were humanity's captivity to Satan, we would expect the story to provide at least some detail that Jesus' death is making a payment. But the story points to no transaction or payment of any kind to Satan. Satan is not even mentioned as being involved in anything other than Judas' deception. It offers no detail or even allusion to Satan being tricked by the death of Jesus.

If the root problem were God's need to satisfy a punitive sense of justice and anger, it creates a debt that can only be satisfied by innocent exchange. For our sake we can imagine the debt as a dead weight or something like a rock. By becoming sin FOR the world, Jesus is taking the rock. But in taking the rock, what does he do with it? Where does he put it? He's stuck with it because release would require atonement for Jesus. How can Jesus now be saved if he's got the rock?

But if the problem is located in humanity, what Jesus is doing on the cross is both a payment to humanity and satisfaction for justice. Overcoming death becomes entirely possible because we now have the overwhelming evidence of God's love. Change comes from dealing with and letting go of the original judgment of evil taking place in the mind. Salvation is then recognizing there is no rock. There is no chasm. There is no separation.

It is important to remember that if Jesus is the best representation of humanity, the purpose is not for him to become sin permanently. The purpose is to reveal it is possible to overcome sin. The purpose is to reveal that there is no chasm and that we can find our way back to God.

One of the primary questions in the Garden of Eden is, "What is God's response to our human transgression?" The cross is it. When all is said and done, God's final response is to allow humanity to pour its anger onto the God image, the whole child of God, and kill him. This releases the anger so we don't have to take it out on ourselves. The response is counterintuitive because we would never think of it during a state of captivity. We would never think that God would be big enough to actually handle our anger, or to overcome the problem. But once released from captivity, God's response makes obvious sense. God is the only one who can truly handle our anger. So God allows us to pour it out back onto the God image.

The power of love puts evil on display. In refusing to strike back, Jesus is allowing evil to be exposed for what it is. It's violent and brutal, horrific and repulsive. Every negative feeling we can imagine about the cross is true. The image of Jesus on the cross exposes the root problem, bringing it out into full view. Humanity, fully represented as empire, is confronted with the presence of evil's true nature.

And it is here, at this moment, where humanity is at its worst, that we redeem the image of God. This is God's true nature. When humanity is at its worst, God still doesn't change. Love is still true. Every image of God we create or construct must now go through the cross. It becomes a clarifying reality of God's love, a suffering Christ willing to go all the way, willing to prove that there is nothing we can do to separate humanity from God's love.

We can't ignore the historical reality of our traditional theories. They exist and flourish, even in the face of contradictory and paradoxical evidence. But the story clearly reveals a different picture. We just have to look for it. So the question is, why do they persist?

If these traditional theories offer anything, it is an expected response from the ego. The ego wants, and even needs, this to be God reigning down anger onto humanity. It needs an angry God to enact revenge. It feeds off of suffering and oppression. But the story undoubtedly portrays it as humanity's anger. This is not God satisfying God's own sense of anger. It is God satisfying the sense of anger that we have projected onto God.

~~

Overcoming Death

As much as death is perceptual, it is also physical. The shadow of death looms over humanity as the final end. What happens after we die? Is this life it? So in order to reveal the way through death, Jesus must deal with the second definition of it and overcome it as well.

> *Jesus called out with a loud voice, "Father, into your hands I commit my spirit." When he had said this, he breathed his last. (Lk 23:46)*

Jesus' final words suggest that at some point he has crossed the chasm back to God. He's completed the circle revealing the pathway through the first death is possible. The perception of separation is not the end reality. Evil does not truly separate humanity from God.

At the moment of Jesus' death several deeply symbolic events happen. God deals with the root problem in a very creative way. The first event happens inside the Tabernacle.

> *At that moment the curtain of the temple was torn in two from top to bottom. The earth shook and the rocks split. The tombs broke open and the bodies of many holy people who had died were raised to life. They came out of the tombs, and after Jesus' resurrection they went into the holy city and appeared to many people. (Mt 27:51-53)*

God rips the curtain from top to bottom. God literally tears it away. If we assume the curtain is to keep people away from God and to hide God in, it reinforces our traditional theories of God's anger. But if we see the curtain as a symbol of our covering, this is the moment when the evidence of God's love literally tears the covering away. God can now tear away the division because the human contract has been fulfilled. There is nothing left to prove. The event is so dramatic, so affecting, that the earth itself can't help but respond. Death gives up its grip and many are literally brought back to life.

The second event is the voice of the empire. What is the judgment in the face of overwhelming evidence? How does humanity really judge now that evil has been exposed? The story offers us a unique response in the form of the centurion, a symbol of might.

The centurion, seeing what had happened, praised God and said, "Surely this was a righteous man." (Lk 23:47)

Even empire cannot help but see the truth. With the covering removed, reality is obvious. Even when Jesus goes through evil and death, he is not transformed by it. He is not changed by it. He remains good.

The moment Jesus breathes his last breath is when Jesus gives himself up to the second definition of death, which is physical. He physically dies. The story is careful to provide physical evidence of his death.

Instead, one of the soldiers pierced Jesus' side with a spear, bringing a sudden flow of blood and water. (Jn 19:34)

The common method of ending a crucifixion is called, "crurifracture". Soldiers would break the bones of the person's legs, preventing him from pushing himself upward, and relieving the stress on the lungs and heart. When the legs are broken the person experiences rapid suffocation. If Jesus died of suffocation, it would be easy to suggest that maybe he really didn't die. We need to know Jesus actually dies.

So instead of breaking Jesus' legs, the guards pierce his side. The evidence of blood and water reveal the guard has pierced his heart. The water comes from the sac surrounding his heart and the blood from the heart, suggesting Jesus died from heart failure due to shock and constriction of the heart by fluid in the pericardium.

But the symbolism of blood and water suggests something deeper than that. In the tabernacle, there are two stations once the priest has entered the surrounding wall: the altar and the laver. The altar is for the blood offering. The laver is for water cleansing. This final moment of Jesus' death gives us evidence of the final atonement happening directly on the cross.

~~

Resurrection

From the moment of Jesus' physical death to the moment of his resurrection, time must have seemed to stand still. God's response is so counterintuitive that it dumbfounds the crowd. The world has crashed down onto everyone who has followed Jesus. Everything their previous story suggested about rescue didn't happen. The followers are so awestruck they immediately go back to their previous lives, bewildered by the whole experience. The mood must have been extremely depressing.

And then Sunday comes.

> On the first day of the week, very early in the morning, the women took the spices they had prepared and went to the tomb. They found the stone rolled away from the tomb, but when they entered, they did not find the body of the Lord Jesus. (Lk 24:1-3)

The tomb is empty. Jesus is not there. This is literally one of the most earth-shattering moments in the story. The central problem of death has been defeated in its entirety. Jesus has come back to life, revealing that death is not the end.

In the act of dying, Jesus addresses the fundamental problem of the physical corruption of the body. To get a deeper picture here, we turn to the words of the Apostle Paul.

> But our citizenship is in heaven. And we eagerly await a Savior from there, the Lord Jesus Christ, who, by the power that enables him to bring everything under his control, will transform our lowly bodies so that they will be like his glorious body. (Phil 3:20-21)

Jesus' body is literally transformed into something glorious. Death is a necessary part of the process because we need new bodies. Death is redemptive because we need a way out of our corrupted structures. What exactly happens is not entirely clear. But once again the point is not simply to die. The point is always to reveal the way through death.

The problem is that this idea is so revolutionary, so completely out of synch with humanity, that it is hard to believe. Even the followers of Jesus struggle to comprehend it.

> *While they were still talking about this, Jesus himself stood among them and said to them, "Peace be with you."*
>
> *They were startled and frightened, thinking they saw a ghost. He said to them, "Why are you troubled, and why do doubts rise in your minds? Look at my hands and my feet. It is I myself! Touch me and see; a ghost does not have flesh and bones, as you see I have." (Lk 24-36-39)*

Jesus takes the idea even further, just to let them know he's real. So he eats something in front of them.

> *When he had said this, he showed them his hands and feet. And while they still did not believe it because of joy and amazement, he asked them, "Do you have anything here to eat?" They gave him a piece of broiled fish, and he took it and ate it in their presence. (Lk 24-40-42)*

Those who would follow after Jesus wrestled deeply with this issue and come to the same conclusion. Jesus conquers the problem of death and its companion, captivity.

> *The last enemy to be destroyed is death. (1 Cor 15:26)*
>
> *Since the children have flesh and blood, he too shared in their humanity so that by his death he might destroy him who holds the power of death— that is, the devil— and free those who all their lives were held in slavery by their fear of death. (Heb 2:14-15)*
>
> *But it has now been revealed through the appearing of our Savior, Christ Jesus, who has destroyed death and has brought life and immortality to*

light through the gospel. (2 Tim 1:10)

The words of Paul even provide us with a glorious muse on the thrill of the victory. He seems to revel in the glorious reality of victory in his letter to the Corinthians.

"Where, O death, is your victory? Where, O death, is your sting?" (1 Cor 15:55)

He also revels in the notion that the captives have been set free.

You have been set free from sin and have become slaves to righteousness. (Rom 6:18)

That the creation itself will be liberated from its bondage to decay and brought into the glorious freedom of the children of God. (Rom 8:21)

It is for freedom that Christ has set us free. Stand firm, then, and do not let yourselves be burdened again by a yoke of slavery. (Gal 5:1)

Because anyone who has died has been freed from sin. (Rom 6:7)

Jesus' final moment on earth begins to complete the circle. Jesus is drawn up towards God, a symbolic act for the people, who think God is "up there."

When he had led them out to the vicinity of Bethany, he lifted up his hands and blessed them. While he was blessing them, he left them and was taken up into heaven. (Lk 24:50-51)

After the Lord Jesus had spoken to them, he was taken up into heaven and he sat at the right hand of God. (Mk 16:19)

The final image of Jesus in the story is one of intimacy and restored relationship. Jesus sits at the right hand of God, which is a sign of honor and rule. There is no separation. There is no shame or guilt. Reconciliation is complete because the God imagination is fully realized.

Chapter 13 – Overcoming

"These streets will make you feel brand new, the lights will inspire you..." -
Alicia Keys

The Promise

The resurrection ushers in a new reality that continues to be shaped more by discovery than by the forcefulness of the religious approach. What does it mean to have full freedom to engage life, to sit with God and know love? Life has prevailed over death. The covering that captivates humanity has been torn apart. God's Kingdom is re-established on the invitational command of justice as opposed to the religious demand of the law and sacrifice.

Immediately following the resurrection, Jesus spends 40 days with the people. But other than a few brief moments of interaction with the disciples to reveal that it is true, the story gives us very little detail of these 40 days. The story spends almost no time trying to convince us of what it all means. The story doesn't invade our lives, demanding that we accept it as true. It simply offers the evidence as true. It allows us to wrestle with the reality and nature of the cross.

Where does that leave us? With the undeniable evidence of the cross and the resurrection, humanity is now free to fully realize the God imagination. The evidence does suggest humanity is good. The cross suggests God's love and grace are true. But just because the evidence is present and true doesn't mean it's fully realized. Humanity needs to discover the animating presence of God transforming them from the inside.

Just before Jesus leaves, he makes a promise to the followers. God is about to release the God imagination in the people freely.

> *"I am going to send you what my Father has promised; but stay in the city until you have been clothed with power from on high." (Lk 24:49)*

> *Again Jesus said, "Peace be with you! As the Father has sent me, I am sending you." And with that he breathed on them and said, "Receive the Holy Spirit." (Jn 20:21-22)*

The word for Spirit here is "pneuma", which literally means the breath or wind. What the Spirit does is intriguing. The Spirit functionally imparts life or animation to the person. Some people call it charisma. It's the life-giving power that produces effective action in our own experience. This includes wisdom, love, joy, peace, patience, and kindness. It is the Spirit that produces these fruits in our life.

Once again Jesus goes back to the original form of God, the breath of life. He breathes on them the God imagination. This filling of the Spirit could be likened to an illumination of God's perspective. In order to engage the God imagination we must receive it into our lives.

The word, "receive" means "to lay claim, or to take with the hand." The assumption is that it is already there. The act of receiving is much like the act of baptism. It is for humanity. It is an internal acknowledgement of what is already in humanity. It is an awakening of the reality of the breath of God within each human being. To receive is to internally awaken the reality of God's presence that is already in our lives. Receiving is only possible with God's reality, if we have overcome the judgments that separate us from God.

Jesus describes this tension as a "waiting." Once again, God will not invade or evade our lives.

> *"Here I am! I stand at the door and knock. If anyone hears my voice and opens the door, I will come in and eat with him, and he with me." (Rev 3:20)*

This receiving is our permission process for God to inform and transform our lives, to work in the dark recesses of our life and restore our broken perceptions.

For ten days, the people wait and then without notice, God releases the Spirit onto the people. The story presents the initial experience as uncontrollable, fierce, and even violent. In other words, the process of receiving the Spirit cannot be controlled.

> *Suddenly a sound like the blowing of a violent wind came from heaven and filled the whole house where they were sitting. They saw what seemed to be tongues of fire that separated and came to rest on each of them. All of them were filled with the Holy Spirit and began to speak in other tongues as the Spirit enabled them. (Acts 2:2-4)*

The Spirit literally illuminates the people's imagination, filling them with prophecy, visions, dreams, wonders, and knowledge. This process can be likened to an inspired, perceptual awakening. God awakens the people's minds, filling them with awareness of what is already true. The knowledge is not created or manufactured. It is received.

This illumination of the imagination produces strange evidence. The people can suddenly speak in other languages. This strange evidence suggests a sense of unity with the "other," an ability to communicate and relate with those around us. Instead of disconnection, the Spirit gives us connection at the most fundamental level: language.

And while the crowd initially writes it off to drunkenness, Peter quotes the Prophet Joel, reshaping their understanding of what is happening.

> *"In the last days, God says, I will pour out my Spirit on all people. Your sons and daughters will prophesy, your young men will see visions, your old men will dream dreams.*
>
> *Even on my servants, both men and women, I will pour out my Spirit in those days, and they will prophesy. I will show wonders in the heaven above and signs on the earth below, blood and fire and billows of smoke. The sun will be turned to darkness and the moon to blood before the coming of the*

great and glorious day of the Lord. And everyone who calls on the name of
the Lord will be saved." (Acts 2:17-21)

The Spirit is poured out on "all people." There is no exception. Peter then reconnects what is happening back to its original purpose, which is a transformation of the mind. People will see visions, which is an illumination of the imagination. Their capacity to "realize" or see reality will be fundamentally altered.

He invites them to publicly acknowledge what is true.

> *Peter replied, "Repent and be baptized, every one of you, in the name of*
> *Jesus Christ for the forgiveness of your sins. And you will receive the gift of*
> *the Holy Spirit. The promise is for you and your children and for all who*
> *are far off—for all whom the Lord our God will call." (Acts 2:38-39)*

The Spirit illuminates our understanding of reconciliation and justice from within. No longer do we need a violent and bloody religious construct. God will fill our imaginations with the very knowledge of God.

Early in His ministry, Jesus spoke of the coming of the Spirit in our lives, who would teach us and remind us of everything we needed to know.

> *¡All this I have spoken while still with you. But the Counselor, the Holy*
> *Spirit, whom the Father will send in my name, will teach you all things and*
> *will remind you of everything I have said to you." (Jn 14:25-26)*

The word Counselor here is the word *"paraclete"*. It essentially means the one who walks alongside of us. In other words, the Spirit's role is to actively guide us in what it means to live. The Spirit will provide us with the right steps. This is the central role of the Spirit in our lives: to walk alongside of us and give us wisdom. Wisdom is first the answer to the original question. It is to remind us that everything is good at its most fundamental level.

> *"And I will ask the Father, and he will give you another Counselor to be*
> *with you forever— the Spirit of truth." (Jn 14:16-17)*

Where the Garden produced the evidence of guilt, the Spirit would produce evidence of transformation. It would illuminate our imagination with the answer to the most important and pressing question in humanity. Are we good? The Spirit would produce life in the form of fruit.

But the fruit of the Spirit is love, joy, peace, patience, kindness, goodness, faithfulness, gentleness and self-control. (Gal 5:22-23)

The fruit of the Spirit would become the reality of the kingdom of God within us. It would become the evidence reminding us that it is real.

The imparting of the Spirit is God's way of solving the original problem in the Garden, which is the original lack of wisdom. The Spirit imparts wisdom, or the knowledge of God's perspective, into humanity. We don't earn it, create it, or even become good. We receive "good" as God's perspective. God doesn't create conditions for it. It's already there. We just have to discover it.

~~

The Witness

The entire process has been about getting back to wisdom, getting back to God's perspective in the matter. The story now includes the evidence of God's love. Those who receive the message realize the wisdom of God, that the created order is good. Humanity has dignity, identity and purpose. The question is then, "How do you extend that message?" Jesus needs a witness to go out and tell the story.

It is here, after the cross, that we must confront the reality of the story. Just because it is true, doesn't mean it has been completely discovered. Just because the evidence of God's love exists doesn't mean everyone instantly realizes it. Before Jesus leaves, he mobilizes the people to act by sending his followers outward with the Good News.

Again Jesus said, "Peace be with you! As the Father has sent me, I am sending you." (Jn 20:21)

Then Jesus came to them and said, "All authority in heaven and on earth has been given to me. Therefore go and make disciples of all nations,

baptizing them in the name of the Father and of the Son and of the Holy
Spirit, and teaching them to obey everything I have commanded you. And
surely I am with you always, to the very end of the age." (Mt 28:18-20)

This is often called the Great Commission. It is Jesus' invitation to participate in God's mission of reconciliation and restoration. The act of co-missioning is much like the co-mmandment. God invites us into the process of bringing the good news to the world through shared partnership. We are called to be priests — people who step into pain and suffering and bless. God includes us in the process of transforming reality.

Jesus' invitation to "go and make disciples" is surprisingly pragmatic. The more we participate, the higher our retention rate. Research into learning methods reveal that students retain only about 10-20% in what they read or hear, minimal levels at best. (In other words, our traditional models of church produce the lowest level of retention.) During the first three years, Jesus invited His disciples to practice following, which increases learning to 50-75%. But the call to leadership, to now lead others in their own restoration, increases learning to as high as 90%. To model for other is the most effective way to reconstitute learning events.

Memory experts picked up on this, offering a very simple trick to increase effectiveness. To fix information in your brain, simply teach it to someone else around you. This process of teaching solidifies what we truly say we believe by revealing it to the world and subjecting it to scrutiny. And as much as we don't like it, we're actually doing ourselves a favor by doing so. Scrutiny essentially removes the lies and inconsistencies onto which we still hold.

Instead of reverting back to the religious model, Jesus instructs his followers to engage the Jesus model through which he has led them. He understands that the process of discovering the God imagination is both immediate and lifelong. We're constantly discovering what is true over time as we reinforce the evidence in the story. We may realize the reality of God's love, but the process of living into that reality sometimes takes time. It requires dealing with our embedded captivating stories, engaging the God imagination, and allowing it to settle into our lives.

Jesus knows we need an intentional but grace-filled community reminding us of what is true. We need a space to work out our own restoration, to find the God imagination in our own lives and in the "other." We need people in our lives pushing us and challenging with our own coverings. We need people who can live in the midst of our stories but remind us there is nothing we can do to change our dignity, identity and purpose. We need people modeling grace and love as an objective way of life.

Jesus invites humanity into the process of restoring the world around us. Followers of Jesus are people who have answered, and are continuing to answer, the original question. It would be so easy to say, "God, just do it for me." But it doesn't work that way. We don't get to burden-shift and remain spectators in the process. Participation is our responsibility. It's taking hold of what allows us to grow up. It's reversing the root problem that humanity picked up in the Garden.

To engage God's mission for the other, to be a witness, is simply helping people uncover the truth of the original question. It's revealing the reality of God's love into someone's life. It's sitting in the midst of the muck and the mire and reminding someone over and over again that he or she is worth it.

The act of sending releases the disciples from the original community and calls them outward. Jesus is protecting them from the leadership trap of finding their validation from the tribe. Jesus even models this for his own disciples by leaving. He doesn't stick around to do it for them.

As much as we are the messengers, we are not the power behind the message. The temptation of the message is to assume we can control the message, to draw a source of pride from being the one who delivered the message that changed someone's reality.

Now for some time a man named Simon had practiced sorcery in the city and amazed all the people of Samaria. He boasted that he was someone great, and all the people, both high and low, gave him their attention and exclaimed, "This man is the divine power known as the Great Power." (Acts 2:9-10)

Simon's original desire is to be validated. He longs to be known as someone great. When he sees the power of the Spirit he wants to control it.

When Simon saw that the Spirit was given at the laying on of the apostles' hands, he offered them money and said, "Give me also this ability so that everyone on whom I lay my hands may receive the Holy Spirit." (Acts 2:18-19)

This is the temptation of the followers. It's powerful. It changes lives. But it can't be controlled. To control it is to jump back into captivity again.

Jesus even reminds his followers that He will be the one to lead. They are to continuously remain followers.

Nor are you to be called 'teacher,' for you have one Teacher, the Christ. (Mt 23:10)

Jesus is releasing the followers from having to have it all figured out. He's releasing his followers from the leadership trap of finding one's validation in the act of spiritual formation or transformation. Jesus even instructed his followers that He would build the church.

And I tell you that you are Peter, and on this rock I will build my church, and the gates of Hades will not overcome it. (Mt 16:18)

In releasing the followers from performance, Jesus frees them to focus on the act of love, to be the God imagination to the world around them. They don't have to worry about who is in or out, who is aware and who's not, or how big the organization is, because Jesus will take care of this role. It releases them to focus on being love in the moment.

This time around, God doesn't rescue humanity from the empire. We're called to live in the world, but not in the way of the world. Like Jesus, as we begin to live the Way of love, we will encounter intense scrutiny and even opposition. The reality is, the world does not begin from love. It begins from distrust. It will push the follower to the exception, asking if love is really, really true, even in the worst-case scenario.

The act of persecution in many ways calls the follower's bluff. It's asking if he truly believes the other is good, even in the face of the same evil. Will he hold onto the rule of love? Every one of the twelve disciples would have to endure this question in order to be a witness. Eleven of the twelve and countless others would give their lives to prove its truth. Following Jesus then becomes a lifelong process of continually engaging the rule of love, even in the face of pain and suffering.

The principal message is love, or the validation of the other. It is the restoration of relationship with the self, but also with God, the other and the entire created order. The other once again becomes the testing ground for how much we are engaging truth in our own lives. If we cannot love the other, it means we are not fully realizing love for ourselves. This love extends all the way to the poor, the oppressed, and even to the enemy. To transform the world begins with seeing the dignity of the other and then revealing that as true to that person.

~~

Removing The Exception

As the followers of Jesus begin to wrestle with the God imagination, a natural question begins to emerge. How far does the message extend? The answer is: to everyone, because from God's perspective everyone is part of the created order. There is no exception. God's love is true even to those who don't know it yet.

As the followers of Jesus begin to wrestle with the cross and the resurrection, it is inevitable that they will wrestle with the nature of identity. They are the chosen people who reveal the story to the world. And where the responsibility is profound, the story reveals the message goes beyond them.

As the Apostle Peter begins to share the Good News to the people around him, he makes an astonishing statement to the crowd.

(Jesus) must remain in heaven until the time comes for God to restore everything, as he promised long ago through his holy prophets. (Acts 3:20)

For the followers of Jesus, there is no exception to God's mission of restoration. God's intent is to restore everything. Intrinsic to the prophets is this idea that God's mission of restoration extends to the ends of the earth.

All the nations you have made will come and worship before you, O Lord; they will bring glory to your name. (Psa 86:9)

Give thanks to the LORD, for he is good; his love endures forever. (1 Chr 16:34)

"And afterward, I will pour out my Spirit on all people." (Joel 2:28)

The LORD will lay bare his holy arm in the sight of all the nations, and all the ends of the earth will see the salvation of our God. (Isa 52:10)

And the glory of the LORD will be revealed, and all mankind together will see it. For the mouth of the LORD has spoken." (Isa 40:5)

You open your hand and satisfy the desires of every living thing. (Psa 145:16)

"I revealed myself to those who did not ask for me; I was found by those who did not seek me. To a nation that did not call on my name, I said, 'Here am I, here am I.'" (Is 65:1)

The LORD is good to all; he has compassion on all he has made. (Psa 145:9)

All the ends of the earth will remember and turn to the LORD, and all the families of the nations will bow down before him. (Psa 22:27)

O you who hear prayer, to you all men will come. (Psa 65:2)

All the earth bows down to you; they sing praise to you, they sing praise to your name." Selah (Psa 66:4)

For men are not cast off by the Lord forever. Though he brings grief, he will show compassion, so great is his unfailing love. (Lam 3:31-32)

I will not accuse forever, nor will I always be angry, for then the spirit of man would grow faint before me—the breath of man that I have created. (Isa 57:16)

This idea continues with Jesus and to his followers. It's in every Gospel account, every letter Paul writes, and almost every part of the New Testament.

"What do you think? If a man owns a hundred sheep, and one of them wanders away, will he not leave the ninety-nine on the hills and go to look for the one that wandered off? And if he finds it, I tell you the truth, he is happier about that one sheep than about the ninety-nine that did not wander off. In the same way your Father in heaven is not willing that any of these little ones should be lost." (Mt 18:12-14)

But the angel said to them, "Do not be afraid. I bring you good news of great joy that will be for all the people." (Lk 2:10)

The next day John saw Jesus coming toward him and said, "Look, the Lamb of God, who takes away the sin of the world!" (Jn 1:29)

For God so loved the world that he gave his one and only Son, that whoever believes in him shall not perish but have eternal life. For God did not send his Son into the world to condemn the world, but to save the world through him. (Jn 3:16-17)

"But I, when I am lifted up from the earth, will draw all men to myself." (Jn 12:32)

So then as through one transgression [Adam's] there resulted condemnation to all men, even so through one act of righteousness [Christ's] there resulted justification of life to all men. For as through the one man's disobedience the many were made sinners, even so through the obedience of the One, the many will be made righteous. And the Law came in that the transgression might increase; but where sin increased, grace abounded all the more! (Rom 5:18-20)

For the anxious longing of the creation waits eagerly for the revealing of the sons of God. For the creation was subjected to futility, not of its own will, but because of Him who subjected it in hope, that the creation itself also will be set free from its slavery to corruption into the freedom of the glory of the children of God. (Rom 8:19-21)

For God has bound all men over to disobedience so that he may have mercy on them all. (Rom 11:32)

For from him and through him and to him are all things. To him be the glory forever! Amen. (Rom 11:36)

It is written: "'As surely as I live,' says the Lord, 'every knee will bow before me; every tongue will confess to God.'" (Rom 14:11)

For as in Adam all die, so in Christ all will be made alive. (1 Cor 15:22-23)

For Christ's love compels us, because we are convinced that one died for all, and therefore all died. And he died for all, that those who live should no longer live for themselves but for him who died for them and was raised again. (2 Cor 5:14-15)

The Scripture foresaw that God would justify the Gentiles by faith, and announced the gospel in advance to Abraham: "All nations will be blessed through you." (Gal 3:8)

And he made known to us the mystery of his will according to his good pleasure, which he purposed in Christ, to be put into effect when the times will have reached their fulfillment—to bring all things in heaven and on earth together under one head, even Christ. (Eph 1:9-10)

And God placed all things under his feet and appointed him to be head over everything for the church, which is his body, the fullness of him who fills everything in every way. (Eph 1:22-23)

Therefore God exalted him to the highest place and gave him the name that is above every name, that at the name of Jesus every knee should bow, in heaven and on earth and under the earth, and every tongue confess that Jesus Christ is Lord, to the glory of God the Father. (Phil 2:9-11)

For God was pleased to have all his fullness dwell in him, and through him to reconcile to himself all things, whether things on earth or things in heaven, by making peace through his blood, shed on the cross. (Col 1:19-20)

Here there is no Greek or Jew, circumcised or uncircumcised, barbarian, Scythian, slave or free, but Christ is all, and is in all. (Col 3:11)

For there is one God and one mediator between God and men, the man Christ Jesus, who gave himself as a ransom for all men—the testimony given in its proper time. (1 Tim 2:5-6)

For the grace of God that brings salvation has appeared to all men. (Tit 2:11)

In putting everything under him, God left nothing that is not subject to him. Yet at present we do not see everything subject to him. But we see Jesus, who was made a little lower than the angels, now crowned with glory and honor because he suffered death, so that by the grace of God he might taste death for everyone. (Heb 2:8-9)

For this is the reason the gospel was preached even to those who are now dead, so that they might be judged according to men in regard to the body, but live according to God in regard to the spirit. (1 Pet 4:6)

He is the atoning sacrifice for our sins, and not only for ours but also for the sins of the whole world. (1 Jn 2:2)

And we have beheld and bear witness that the Father has sent the Son to be the Savior of the world. (1 Jn 4:14)

Then I heard every creature in heaven and on earth and under the earth and on the sea, and all that is in them, singing: "To him who sits on the throne and to the Lamb be praise and honor and glory and power, forever and ever!" (Rev 5:13)

God is literally working to restore everything. There's no "us and them" in the Kingdom of God. There is only God's creation.   The story does it once again. In removing the exception, Jesus is taking away the exception we can use on ourselves. He's taking away the exception we can use for our enemy, or for our frustrating neighbor. Jesus sees the kingdom of God as entirely inclusive.

The question of a radical inclusivity presents a troubling issue for many scholars. But just as the story consistently points to it, the nature of truth and the call to witness reveals that it is already true. In order for someone to offer good news, it must already be true. To place a condition of acceptance upon grace negates it and makes it a transaction. This removes any temptation to add to grace or make it predicated on our own efforts. Our realization of truth happens locally, not cosmically.

The immediate tension humanity will experience is the desire to revert to the captive state, and to see love as something we earn. Instead, the knowledge of God's perspective, the original wisdom, is presented as a gift. Humanity could not change God's response. It could only receive it. The Apostle Paul would later express the idea this way:

> For it is by grace you have been saved, through faith—and this not from yourselves, it is the gift of God— not by works, so that no one can boast. (Eph 2:8-9)

The gift is a powerful metaphor. The idea of a gift suggests something that is undeserved and given out of pleasure. It just needs to be received. The fun of the gift is typically in the surprise of unveiling. Something is hidden and then discovered.

Grace is the same thing. What Jesus is doing is revealing what has always been true. He's uncovering the gift of God that is present in kairos, in God's sense of time. It is unchanging, and unbelievable. But it can be hidden. To receive the gift is to uncover it again, but the gift must be received in order be realized. It also means the gift must be shared.

Salvation is the moment of realizing the original answer to the tree in the Garden, that all of humanity is good. It is discovering God's response to our transgressions, which is grace. This awakening happens when we discover the truth and become informed of God's perspective by the Spirit. The state of grace applies to each and every human being; this is already true before our awakening. Salvation then becomes the act of realizing it locally in the mind, not an act that fundamentally makes it true in a cosmic sense. Humanity takes part in this process through repentance. But repentance still doesn't make it true. It reveals it as true. In other words, when humanity receives the knowledge of God, it becomes true for that person, but it has always been true from God's perspective. To understand this, it is helpful to look at the original covering.

The original problem is a covering of what is true, much like a blanket over a box. The act of covering hides what is true from a human perspective. We can't see it. But the box is still there underneath the blanket. The cross and the resurrection don't make something true. They discover what is already true. The act of witness is then not to convince someone it becomes true cosmically through our acceptance, but to share that it becomes true for the person when they accept it.

Our acts of love become paramount to this idea because if we say it is true, but live contrary to that idea, we are invalidating the original idea with our life. We are inadvertently living out a false reality, while telling a true story.

The temptation is then to systematize the act of belief and salvation. How do you convince someone that God's love is true? But even within the story there is no magical moment or pattern of salvation. Of the 26 ways people come to belief in Jesus, there is no discernable methodology. The process of belief is often just as slow and painful as it is miraculous and instantaneous. Every one of the followers abandons Jesus at some point. The act of belief is then a process of realization, not something that instantaneously makes something true.

~~

A Grace Full Responsibility

The story continues to come full circle as God deals with the human construct of the law. The law provides a sense of boundaries and a framework for social interaction. But now that death has been defeated, and the Spirit has been released, the purpose of the law is moot. But removing the law as a framework for social interaction creates a profound tension, suggesting the idea of license, or the capacity to do anything one wants. Resolving this tension is paramount to living in the Kingdom of God.

As the followers of Jesus begin to grow and wrestle with the concept of the cross, resurrection and grace, they are confronted with a transition to the rule of love. Love simplifies everything. What do they do with the ritual and even social laws that are deeply important to Israel's history? The earliest tension is over the issue of circumcision. Is this deeply symbolic ritual that once set the people apart actually necessary for grace?

> Some men came down from Judea to Antioch and were teaching the brothers: "Unless you are circumcised, according to the custom taught by Moses, you cannot be saved." (Acts 15:1)

The temptation is to control the process of who is in and who is not. But once we add something to it, it's no longer grace. To add to grace is to take back the burden of earning our relationship with God, which we can't do. So Peter puts an end to this idea.

> The apostles and elders met to consider this question. After much discussion, Peter got up and addressed them: "Brothers, you know that some time ago God made a choice among you that the Gentiles might hear from my lips the message of the gospel and believe. God, who knows the heart, showed that he accepted them by giving the Holy Spirit to them, just as he did to us. He made no distinction between us and them, for he purified their hearts by faith. Now then, why do you try to test God by putting on the necks of the disciples a yoke that neither we nor our fathers have been able to bear? No! We believe it is through the grace of our Lord Jesus that we are saved,

just as they are." (Acts 15:6-11)

Peter is able to do this because God requires him to wrestles with his own limitations of grace. He is granted a dream that begins the long, slow journey of engaging the profound level of grace which God is establishing after Jesus.

> *About noon the following day as they were on their journey and approaching the city, Peter went up on the roof to pray. He became hungry and wanted something to eat, and while the meal was being prepared, he fell into a trance. He saw heaven opened and something like a large sheet being let down to earth by its four corners. It contained all kinds of four-footed animals, as well as reptiles of the earth and birds of the air. Then a voice told him, "Get up, Peter. Kill and eat."*
>
> *"Surely not, Lord!" Peter replied. "I have never eaten anything impure or unclean."*
>
> *The voice spoke to him a second time, "Do not call anything impure that God has made clean."*
>
> *This happened three times, and immediately the sheet was taken back to heaven. (Acts 10:9-16)*

God literally ends the ritual law. Humanity doesn't need it anymore. Everything is clean. Everything is permissible. But to abandon the law is to give up the idea that we can earn our way to God's love. It doesn't mean humanity has to eliminate the idea of rituals. Rituals can hold sacred value as long as they are not requirements.

Grace is God's new playing field. But it's not really new. Grace is the original operating structure of the kingdom. It is the original framework God establishes in the Garden. The only sin humanity has to worry about is the original one, getting the question of the Tree wrong. Everything else is an extension of the root problem.

God returns humanity to an extremely simple and objective system of living, one grounded in the original created order. Everything is good. Everything has value. The only way to fall back into captivity is to once again lose sight of God's perspective. Was God serious about this? How far did it really extend? How far would love really go? There had to be a catch, right? But there wasn't.

As God begins to lift up new leaders in the ecclesia, the Apostle Paul seriously grapples with these ideas. In a series of letters to different churches, he wrestles with many of the questions that arise in life on this side of the cross. And in a letter to the ecclesia in Corinth, he makes the following statement.

> *"Everything is permissible"—but not everything is beneficial. "Everything is permissible"—but not everything is constructive. (1 Cor 10:23)*

Paul, who is arguably one of the most influential followers of Jesus, establishes the radical notion that everything is permissible. It's a mind-blowing reality. Paul is literally unleashing people from their shackles. We read this and shake our heads. Everything inside of us just wants to go out and do something from which we've been held back. And there's a good side to that. To break free is the essence of what it means to come out of oppression. To be released from the law is restoration.

But the tension resides in what it means when other people have the same freedom. We wrestle with what the "other" could now do to us. What would it mean to forgive, and forgive, and forgive some more? But the ability to forgive resides in the God imagination, in the ability to consistently return to the God perspective. When someone does something to us, and it feels invalidating, we're losing that perspective. To forgive is to return to the idea that the act cannot invalidate us. Forgiveness is then as much for us as it is for the other. To forgive is to restore equilibrium and harmony in our own lives.

Paul then returns the conversation back to consequence. God's original concern was always the consequence, not the morality. The primary question is about the cost to relationship, especially to the self. To break oneself is to harm the created order. To consider the cost is to begin with the assumption that we are valuable.

So when Paul condemns specific acts, he's recognizing that they are destructive to the person.

> *Put to death, therefore, whatever belongs to your earthly nature: sexual*
> *immorality, impurity, lust, evil desires and greed, which is idolatry. (Col*
> *3:5)*

Paul calls out idolatry, which brings us back to the root problem. We're still searching for something to validate us. The destructive act reveals we're still getting the question wrong.

He is essentially asking, "Weren't we trying to come out of oppression?" If sin is about breaking ourselves, then shouldn't we be trying to avoid it? Isn't following Jesus about engaging our own restoration and reconciliation with God and others? Isn't it about coming out of death? The other side of the cross represents a new life, one defined by wholeness. Everything is permissible, but not everything is profitable. And we're not avoiding sin to fulfill a law or appease God. We can't. We're avoiding the things that harm us by turning to the things the restore us.

And so with freedom comes the responsibility to grow up, to embrace our own maturity that comes with grace. The real question is: "Does this produce life?" This is our original design. When we rule over the self it naturally produces life. Paul understands that we aren't looking for the freedom to do anything we want. We're looking for the freedom to live courageous, whole lives. The difference is light years apart. To embrace grace is the embrace the responsibility of growing up into what it means to be fully human. To embrace grace means we refuse to live in the excuse of our brokenness.

And so we embrace grace as the defining ethic. There is nothing we can't forgive, nothing we can't overcome, and no transgression of which we can't let go. We return to the idea that no matter what someone does, it does not fundamentally define the person. Grace holds onto good, even in the midst of suffering. This is the embodiment of the kingdom of God. To continue breaking ourselves would be to miss the resurrection Jesus came to give us.

As the story brings us back to the beginning, to the idea of good, life presents us with the opportunity to embrace the God imagination. The simplicity of it is astounding, the value of it is compelling, and the necessity of it is undeniable. But that doesn't make it easy. Embracing the God imagination is arguably the hardest thing we will ever do.

James, the brother of Jesus, provides an astoundingly simple construct for engaging the God imagination. Ask.

> *If any of you lacks wisdom, he should ask God, who gives generously to all without finding fault, and it will be given to him. (Jam 1:5)*

Once we open the door, God is more than willing to fill us with wisdom, or the knowledge of God's love, if we ask. And when we ask, we will be filled with the Spirit. We will be able to see what God sees.

> *"But what about you?" he asked. "Who do you say I am?"*
>
> *Simon Peter answered, "You are the Christ, the Son of the living God."*
>
> *Jesus replied, "Blessed are you, Simon son of Jonah, for this was not revealed to you by man, but by my Father in heaven." (Mt 16:15-17)*

Peter sees because he is open to it. He has made himself available to what God is already doing. And he can see what is already true.

To embrace wisdom is to be filled with life from God's perspective. It is to restore the image of God within us. It is to uncover the shared dignity that establishes us as very good. It is to reveal our original identity that calls us human beginnings, created in the image of God. It is to disclose our true purpose, which is to rule over the created order. It is to discover life eternal.

It is to confront the evidence of brokenness in our lives and realize that it cannot, nor has it ever, defined us. It is to abandon the false and limiting identities, the victim or perpetrator mentalities, the idols, the comparisons, and the religious practices designed to remove the guilt. It is to embrace the freedom that resides in the construct of grace, the courage that resides in the act of loving, and the wholeness that resides in the act of being.

The fullness of life then resides in the act of love. Love is the judgment of good.

It is any act that validates, holds, or restores a person's dignity to wholeness. It is any response that conforms to God's perspective.

> *Let no debt remain outstanding, except the continuing debt to love one another, for he who loves his fellowman has fulfilled the law. (Rom 13:8)*

With love, we didn't need the law to define our social interactions because love is the perfect fulfillment of the law. This was the brilliance of God. The tens of thousands of laws that man had created were all fulfilled in love. To love is to restore our dignity, our identity, and our purpose, and reveal the glory of God.

~~

The Final Judgment

In many ways the story is a grand circle taking us from wholeness to captivity and back to wholeness. But what is the real purpose of the whole process? What is the real meaning of it all? Why spend so much time actually working out our faith? The story leaves one thing undone. How does it all end? The story concludes with an apocalyptic story that suggests final judgment. Much like a bookend it essentially asks only one question. Are we good or evil? The story suggests a provocative possibility that completes the circle.

Sometimes it helps to go back to the prophets to get a glimpse of God's perspective.

> *I make known the end from the beginning, from ancient times, what is still to come. I say: My purpose will stand, and I will do all that I please. (Isa 46:10)*

Isaiah's words suggest the beginning informs the end. What if God is suggesting that the final judgment is still about us making the mature judgment of reality? This is the story presented in the beginning. Most of the story is humanity wrestling with the responsibility of that judgment. If the story begins with God's making a judgment and then allowing us to wrestle with that judgment, what if the end is really about bringing all creation into a mature grasp of that answer? It's still about coming to terms with the God imagination.

God's mission in the story is the restoration of all things. The concept of God restoring everything is so overwhelming it often seems hard to reconcile that against how the story seems to end. At first blush, it seems like God actually does pull a trump card at the end.

Many of our traditions suggest a final momentous judgment of God that ultimately puts things right. Some will go to heaven with God for eternity and some will go to hell, burning in horrific torment for eternity. This is the way it should be, shouldn't it? The final judgment is then seen as a moment when God pulls out the exception card after all. The story even seems to support this idea.

> *Then I saw a great white throne and him who was seated on it. Earth and sky fled from his presence, and there was no place for them. And I saw the dead, great and small, standing before the throne, and books were opened. Another book was opened, which is the book of life. The dead were judged according to what they had done as recorded in the books. The sea gave up the dead that were in it, and death and Hades gave up the dead that were in them, and each person was judged according to what he had done. Then death and Hades were thrown into the lake of fire. The lake of fire is the second death. If anyone's name was not found written in the book of life, he was thrown into the lake of fire. (Rev 20:11-15)*

Jesus' own words also seem to support this idea.

> *When the Son of Man comes in his glory, and all the angels with him, he will sit on his throne in heavenly glory. All the nations will be gathered before him, and he will separate the people one from another as a shepherd separates the sheep from the goats. He will put the sheep on his right and the goats on his left. (Mt 25:31-33)*

Reconciling these elements is critical to suggesting possibilities for how the end of the story.

The story does present a rather intriguing reality that informs our understanding of the final judgment. Jesus declares God is actually not the final judge. Jesus is.

Moreover, the Father judges no one, but has entrusted all judgment to the
Son. (Jn 5:2)

In other words, God places the role of judgment back onto humanity's
representative. We have to ask a rather strange but important question. Why
would Jesus go to such great lengths to prove the reality of one judgment at the
cross and then make a different one at the final judgment? This is the tension
with the end of the story. It seems to suggest God just gives up on the mission
as opposed to bringing everything back into wholeness.

But what if it's once again deeper than that? Jesus is the representation of
humanity. For Jesus to represent reality, he must remain consistent with God's
declarations presented in the story. Everything is good. When Jesus says he
is the judge, what if he's pointing to the reality that judgment resides in us.
God already knows reality. It is humanity that must wrestle with and discover
reality. Everything Jesus did is to show us our humanity and what was true for
us. Why would that suddenly change in the afterlife? Therein lies the problem.
At the moment of final judgment, are we prepared to make a restorative call?

The judgment stories actually present the same construct as the rest of the story.
We just have to be open to it to see it. Jesus begins with a king, which suggests
rule. Jesus separates the two using the human construct of judgment. He uses
their actions instead of God's declarations to judge.

"Then the King will say to those on his right, 'Come, you who are blessed
by my Father; take your inheritance, the kingdom prepared for you since
the creation of the world. For I was hungry and you gave me something to
eat, I was thirsty and you gave me something to drink, I was a stranger and
you invited me in, I needed clothes and you clothed me, I was sick and you
looked after me, I was in prison and you came to visit me.'

"Then the righteous will answer him, 'Lord, when did we see you hungry
and feed you, or thirsty and give you something to drink? When did we see
you a stranger and invite you in, or needing clothes and clothe you? When

did we see you sick or in prison and go to visit you?'

"The King will reply, 'I tell you the truth, whatever you did for one of the least of these brothers of mine, you did for me.'

"Then he will say to those on his left, 'Depart from me, you who are cursed, into the eternal fire prepared for the devil and his angels. For I was hungry and you gave me nothing to eat, I was thirsty and you gave me nothing to drink, I was a stranger and you did not invite me in, I needed clothes and you did not clothe me, I was sick and in prison and you did not look after me.'

"They also will answer, 'Lord, when did we see you hungry or thirsty or a stranger or needing clothes or sick or in prison, and did not help you?'

"He will reply, 'I tell you the truth, whatever you did not do for one of the least of these, you did not do for me.'" (Mt 25:34-45)

The key distinction between the two categories lies in how each sees both the self and the evidence. The first group sees themselves as righteous. They see themselves as already blessed, but they aren't relying on the evidence. The state of judgment isn't coming from the king. It's a present reality that already exists in the person. They're not using action to justify themselves. They have in essence come into another reality. Their lives reveal the God imagination as a way of life.

The second group is asked to depart. The story doesn't actually present a judgment but a request to leave. Why? The next line provides the answer. "You who are cursed." They have entered the king's presence already having judged themselves. The king is simply giving this group what it already believes is true. He uses the same evidence but this group defends itself asking, "When did…we NOT help you?" They are still using the human construct to justify themselves. They haven't let go of the lie.

The final judgment suggests that God still doesn't invade our lives. But if we're not prepared to make that judgment, we may not get it right. It's important to clarify that the king doesn't use declared belief as a dividing construct. He doesn't ask the person what many would consider the dividing line, a profession of faith. The king uses tangible evidence that is still undeniable. It acts like a mirror to the embedded judgments each category already holds.

The consequence of that judgment is largely the same as the story.

> *"Then they will go away to eternal punishment, but the righteous to eternal life." (Mt 25:46)*

The story then presents the consequence as the idea of eternal punishment and eternal life. The word for eternal is "aiōnios". Some scholars wrestle with the definition of the word, suggesting the idea of aionios actually means an eternal state that is unchanging. Others suggest that the word is better translated as "an age," which suggests a period of time.

What if they're both right? When humanity makes a judgment it is declaring a sense of reality. What is true is in essence eternal. From the perspective of humanity the feeling of punishment is then felt as unchanging. It has no end. But from God's perspective, the idea of age recognizes that truth doesn't change, but our perspective can. This state is arguably the truest definition of hell we could imagine. Life outside of God's perspective is a state of hell. It doesn't look like heaven in any sense because it is untrue.

The reason some scholars hesitate to call it an eternal state is that the idea of punishment from God's perspective is always corrective in nature. It's designed to restore humanity, not eliminate it. The principal means of punishment is the concept of fire.

> *The Son of Man will send out his angels, and they will weed out of his kingdom everything that causes sin and all who do evil. They will throw them into the fiery furnace, where there will be weeping and gnashing of teeth. (Mt 13:41-42)*

> *But the cowardly, the unbelieving, the vile, the murderers, the sexually immoral, those who practice magic arts, the idolaters and all liars—their place will be in the fiery lake of burning sulfur. This is the second death. (Rev 21:8)*

His winnowing fork is in his hand, and he will clear his threshing floor, gathering his wheat into the barn and burning up the chaff with unquenchable fire. (Mt 3:12)

The principal purpose of fire is to burn away impurities, not to eliminate or to torture. The purpose of the fire is then to burn away the chaff, or the lie, not the person.

To the Israelites the glory of the LORD looked like a consuming fire on top of the mountain. (Ex 24:17)

For the LORD your God is a consuming fire, a jealous God. (Deut 4:24)

From the perspective of judgment, the consuming fire is seen as terrifying.

The sinners in Zion are terrified; trembling grips the godless: "Who of us can dwell with the consuming fire? Who of us can dwell with everlasting burning?" (Isa 33:14)

The second consideration is the fire comes from heaven.

But fire came down from heaven and devoured them. (Rev 20:9)

The state of fire, or hell, is then arguably the presence of God as opposed to the absence of it. From their perspective the presence of God will consistently be perceived as judgment, instead of grace. It will be punishing because they won't be able to hide from the truth.

The final images God provides in the story offer a vision of a new heaven and earth. Life includes several important distinctions that seem to complete the circle and bring us back to the beginning. The first distinction is the idea of a new beginning.

Then I saw a new heaven and a new earth, for the first heaven and the first earth had passed away. (Rev 21:1a)

God seems to provide a deep sense of restoration that encompasses everything, which includes the end of death.

And I heard a loud voice from the throne saying, "Now the dwelling of God is with men, and he will live with them. They will be his people, and God himself will be with them and be their God. He will wipe every tear from their eyes. There will be no more death or mourning or crying or pain, for the old order of things has passed away."

He who was seated on the throne said, "I am making everything new!" Then he said, "Write this down, for these words are trustworthy and true." (Rev 21:1-5)

Within this new reality is the Tree of Life. Humanity can eat of it freely because there is no curse.

Then the angel showed me the river of the water of life, as clear as crystal, flowing from the throne of God and of the Lamb down the middle of the great street of the city. On each side of the river stood the tree of life, bearing twelve crops of fruit, yielding its fruit every month. And the leaves of the tree are for the healing of the nations. No longer will there be any curse. The throne of God and of the Lamb will be in the city, and his servants will serve him. (Rev 22:1-3)

The story then suggests gates of heaven will remain open, but not everyone will enter in.

On no day will its gates ever be shut, for there will be no night there. The glory and honor of the nations will be brought into it. Nothing impure will ever enter it, nor will anyone who does what is shameful or deceitful, but only those whose names are written in the Lamb's book of life. (Rev 21:25-27)

The final mystery is how God creates a new beginning, which removes the problem of death and the curse, yet at the same time suggests there are still people outside the gates. It doesn't exclude the possibility of someone entering into this new reality. The gates are open. But it is also possible that those on the outside have imprisoned themselves. To enter in would mean letting go of the old reality.

~~

The Final Question

Humanity has wrestled with the only question that really matters. The story leaves us with a mystery, wondering who will enter this new reality. In essence, it leaves us right back where we started, with a question of judgment. Are we good or evil? The story does reveal who gets in.

> *He said to me: "It is done. I am the Alpha and the Omega, the Beginning and the End. To him who is thirsty I will give to drink without cost from the spring of the water of life. He who overcomes will inherit all this, and I will be his God and he will be my son. (Rev 21:6-7)*

The final reality is reserved for the one who thirsts and for the one who overcomes. This provocative ending invites us into the beginning. It invites us to wrestle with the question and to resolve it. Participation is required in order to do so.

It's rather provocative of God not to solve the puzzle for us. But isn't that the point, to help us engage the question rather than solve it for us? To follow in the footsteps of Jesus is to discover the answer. Are you the one who overcomes?

Made in the USA
Lexington, KY
20 February 2011